FLIPPED

FLIPPED

How Georgia Turned
Purple and Broke
the Monopoly on
Republican Power

GREG BLUESTEIN

VIKING

VIKING
An imprint of Penguin Random House LLC
penguinrandomhouse.com

LIBRARY OF CONGRESS CATALOGING-IN-PUBLICATION DATA
Names: Bluestein, Greg, author.
Title: Flipped : how Georgia turned purple and broke
the monopoly on Republican power / Greg Bluestein.
Description: [New York] : Viking, [2022] | Includes index.
Identifiers: LCCN 2021045125 (print) | LCCN 2021045126 (ebook) |
ISBN 9780593489154 (hardcover) | ISBN 9780593489161 (ebook)
Subjects: LCSH: United States. Congress. Senate—Elections—2020. |
Elections—Georgia—History—21st century. |
Presidents—United States—Election—2020. | Political participation—Georgia. |
Political parties—Georgia. | Georgia—Politics and government—1951
Classification: LCC JK4393 2020 B58 2022 (print) | LCC JK4393 2020 (ebook) |
DDC 324.973—dc23/eng/20211206
LC record available at https://lccn.loc.gov/2021045125
LC ebook record available at https://lccn.loc.gov/2021045126

Printed in the United States of America
1 3 5 7 9 10 8 6 4 2

Book design by Daniel Lagin

To Sheryl, who hung the moon
Nicole, who shoots for the stars
Brooke, who wants to heal the world
and Charlie, who keeps us all grounded

CONTENTS

PART 3: A BATTLE FOR THE SENATE

FLIPPED

PROLOGUE

When Georgia Republicans need a go-to venue for a big celebration, there is no shortage of options around Atlanta: well-appointed conference rooms in lakeside resorts, elaborate ballrooms, the artificial turf of the College Football Hall of Fame in the heart of downtown. But none looms larger than the InterContinental Buckhead in Atlanta's ritziest neighborhood. Towering over luxury malls and boutiques along the city's iconic Peachtree Road, the hotel was the site of the Republican "victory party" on election night 2020, where hundreds of members of the Georgia GOP sipped overpriced beers and watched returns on oversized screens while in the grip of a pandemic.

The crowd had reason to be optimistic. Republicans had shut out Democrats in every presidential election in Georgia since 1996 and hadn't lost a statewide seat since 2006. The Georgia GOP was so dominant that for much of the decade Democrats struggled to recruit even fringe candidates for some top-tier races or, worse, didn't bother running anyone at all while Republicans built commanding majorities in the state legislature and maintained control of every statewide office. Stacey Abrams might have caught some off guard in 2018 when the Democrat lost the governor's race to Brian Kemp by fewer than fifty-five thousand votes. But Republicans weren't taking the threat lightly this time. Even President Donald Trump had reluctantly visited the state as part of his whirlwind final campaign tour on November 1, urging Georgians at a windswept rural airport to defend his administration as he promised a "great red wave" would swamp Joe Biden and his Democratic supporters across the country.

Rows of mask-wearing reporters lined the walls of the InterContinental's banquet hall, while grizzled activists mingled with college interns as Fox News commentators reported the early returns from a booming speaker system: one Republican state after another had gone Trump's way, as strongholds like Alabama, South Carolina, and then, especially sweet, the contested swing state of Florida each turned a bright shade of red.

In the back of the room, a nervous Brandon Phillips paced between the partygoers. A savvy Republican strategist who had led the president's Georgia operation for about a year during the 2016 cycle, Phillips was as comfortable hunting for wild hogs or spearfishing in shark-infested Gulf Coast waters as he was designing a campaign field strategy. His social media accounts brimmed with photos of his political exploits, none more proudly displayed than the black-and-white picture of him striding down a convention hall corridor with Trump, both grinning from ear to ear with matching thumbsups. Since Trump's 2016 victory, Phillips had honed a reputation as a sharp-elbowed brawler with a specialty of helping local candidates try to channel the president's appeal.

But there was no trace of that easy smile on Phillips's face on this night as he scanned the room of tipsy revelers in search of others who shared his trepidation. Cody Hall, a young aide to Governor Brian Kemp, was also milling about the crowd with unspoken anxiety. "They don't even know why they shouldn't be celebrating yet," Hall said, glancing back and forth from an election analysis on his weathered smartphone to the joyful throng in front of him.

Trump was winning the states he was expected to win. But he was falling behind in Arizona. And his numbers in Georgia weren't much better. Late that night, as the celebration continued around him, Phillips peered into his phone and groaned. The *New York Times* needle, the tracking tool designed to predict which candidate was on track to win an election, had suddenly swung decisively toward Biden in Georgia when vote totals from heavily

Democratic DeKalb County had started to come in. One nervous operative sequestered himself in an empty conference suite just outside the ballroom and dialed up an election expert. "Are there really enough votes left to swing this thing?" he asked.

On the second floor of the hotel, Republican senator David Perdue's strategists were hunkered down in a war room, poring over numbers that would determine whether the incumbent would win a second term—or be forced by Georgia's peculiar state law into a runoff against his Democratic opponent, the investigative filmmaker Jon Ossoff. Perdue had won office six years earlier with a carefully cultivated outsider image that belied his family's deep roots in Georgia politics. Every so often, he'd unpack the iconic jean jacket that had made him a star to Georgia's right, wrap it around his broad shoulders, and take it for a spin on the trail. But the truth was, the former Fortune 500 chief executive was just as comfortable in a finely tailored suit as he was in the worn denim of his campaign ads.

Earlier in the night, exhausted aides and strategists in the war room had been bombarded with congratulations on a hard-fought victory. *Unbelievable job! It's over!* But Perdue's most senior loyalists tamped down the premature celebration. There were still hundreds of thousands of votes to be tallied, and many would be coming from areas where Democrats dominated. One aide bolted upstairs to Perdue's suite, where the senator was preparing for a victory speech, to deliver the news. "Ignore what you're hearing," he told the Republican. "This is going to be very, very close." Perdue sat in stony silence with his wife, Bonnie, for a few heartbeats, but he wasn't surprised. "How much longer will it take?" he asked.

In fact, Perdue was painfully aware of troubling data for his campaign and those of other Republicans in Georgia. And he had sounded the alarm early and often, pleading for Trump and national Republicans to send his campaign more resources in the face of an epic election cycle shaped by a pandemic and nationwide movement for social justice.

What made the situation more frustrating for Perdue was that his opponent was not another veteran of Georgia's hallowed corporate community but a political newcomer about the same age as his two sons. To him, Ossoff, a thirty-three-year-old former congressional aide, was little more than a privileged wannabe whose greatest gift was the silver tongue he used to convince liberals to dig into their wallets for campaign donations. On the campaign trail, Perdue couldn't hide his disdain: Ossoff was a "trust fund socialist who lives off his family's money-making documentary movies that no one's ever watched," Perdue vented at one stop. Behind closed doors, Perdue wasn't any kinder in his assessment of the matchup: he was a former Fortune 500 CEO in the fight of his political life against a "little shit" who, he claimed, had never created a job.

On the road, Perdue drew decent-sized crowds, but his young opponent knew how to strike him where it hurt the most. A debate held about a week before the election left Perdue bloodied and seething after Ossoff dismantled him, calling him a "crook" during a scathing minute-long monologue that was watched more than 15 million times on social media. How could I respect a man like that? Perdue asked his closest friends.

In the final sprint, Perdue's team tried to re-create some of the magic of his runaway victory six years earlier: a luxury campaign bus stocked with his favorite Chick-fil-A chicken biscuits and wrapped with Perdue's slogan, branding him "The Original Outsider" in red, white, and blue glory; the reassuring presence of his wife, a serene grandmother who never envisioned her golden years spent on the campaign trail; a pre–Election Day fly-around tour that ended at the same suburban Atlanta airport where his first cousin, Sonny Perdue, had launched his successful bid for governor almost two decades earlier. Anything to give him a sense of momentum going into the final stretch.

This was never going to be the clean victory Perdue had enjoyed in 2014. But as the returns came in, the senator's senior advisers quietly reckoned that it wasn't going to be any sort of victory at all. The results pointed to a nine-week overtime bout that Republicans dreaded. With the nation's attention turned to the race, anything could happen during the runoff. And if Perdue's seat was in question, then surely Trump's fate was also in doubt. Instead of delivering a finely tuned victory speech, Perdue stayed in his upstairs suite with his wife, leaving it to sullen deputies to deliver the unhappy news that the senator wouldn't be joining the party.

Elsewhere around Georgia, other Republican celebrations shared the same deflated ending. At Congressman Doug Collins's gathering near his North Georgia hometown of Gainesville, the music abruptly stopped as fidgety supporters zeroed in on a TV projector with returns showing Trump struggling—and Collins falling further behind Senator Kelly Loeffler, the Republican he'd challenged for her seat. Loeffler's bash at the venerable Buckhead Ballroom at the Grand Hyatt offered an unsettling tangle of emotions: jubilation over her victory against Collins and a grim acknowledgment of the lengthy runoff campaign ahead against Reverend Raphael Warnock, the Democratic pastor of Atlanta's storied Ebenezer Baptist Church.

Democrats had a tantalizing sense that they were on the cusp of an accomplishment many, even the most loyal of the optimists, privately thought was impossible. As Warnock put it that night, "Something special and transformational is happening right here." Stacey Abrams, whose work over the past decade set the foundation for her party's success, went to bed that evening convinced that Georgia Democrats would finally snap their long presidential losing streak. The biggest question she asked herself before drifting to sleep was whether the party would be able to hold on to the victory against a Republican onslaught challenging the results that was just revving up.

Back at the InterContinental, a hush descended on Perdue's war room as more results came streaming in. In June, the campaign's smartest minds had hashed out a "vote goal" of 2,482,000 ballots to win without a runoff. The senator was on track to fall about 20,000 votes shy of the target. Even the most junior operative could see that the math spelled trouble for Republicans, who were now at risk of losing both the White House and the Senate.

"It's going to be a long week," Phillips sighed.

<hr>

The story of how the Peach State turned purple echoes far beyond the state's boundaries and a historic election cycle that transformed little-known Georgians into polarizing national figures. The nation's gaze turned to Georgia not just because of its stunning presidential flip, fueled by a handful of formerly Republican strongholds circling Atlanta. And not just because of the two runoff elections that effectively determined whether Biden could muscle his legislative agenda through a Democratic-controlled Senate or whether he'd be stymied by Republicans. What local political insiders know well, and what the rest of the country began to realize in 2020, is that flipping control of Georgia may fundamentally realign national politics, giving Democrats an invaluable foothold in the Deep South and a bulwark against growing Republican strength elsewhere.

Democrats engineered the epic turnaround with a formula that could serve as a template for the party in once bright-red territories elsewhere. For parts of the last two decades, Georgia Democrats maneuvered for victories by trying to re-create the same coalitions that had helped keep them in power through much of the twentieth century: a tenuous alliance between Black voters in Atlanta and conservative white rural power brokers who ruled the state. Some campaigned as moderate versions of Republicans, heralding support for gun rights and opposition to abortion while running, screaming, from national party figures. Inevitably, the rural conservatives would shift toward the GOP—and no amount of messaging or proposals could draw them back.

In 2020, though, Georgia Democrats mostly abandoned attempts to pose as moderate "Republican-lite" figures and jettisoned all-out efforts to convert conservative voters with poll-tested talking points. Instead, leaders energized the party's core constituencies—including many who rarely cast ballots—with policies that just a few years prior would have seemed unthinkable: Gun control. Decriminalization of marijuana. An end to crackdowns on illegal immigrants. Progressive social and economic justice initiatives. An expansion of abortion rights. While President Trump characterized Democrats in Georgia and beyond as puppets of the "radical left," local candidates unabashedly embraced national figures they once avoided.

Republicans had watched as Democrats crept closer in election after election this decade, edging toward breaking the GOP monopoly on power. And they realized that the formula that helped them win in 2018—huge margins in rural and exurban areas to offset their defeats in suburban areas—would soon fizzle. The only question was when.

"I've been raising the flag for years that Democrats were closing the gap in Georgia—and now it's clear to anyone who wants to open their eyes and see it," said Brian Robinson, a veteran political aide who served as a key deputy to Republican governor Nathan Deal during his two terms in office from 2011 to 2019.

Flipped is an account of that transformation, based on my years of reporting the state's political metamorphosis at *The Atlanta Journal-Constitution*. In these pages, you'll meet a rich cast of characters who shaped the races. There's Governor Brian Kemp, who two years after his narrow victory over Abrams thought his biggest worry would be staunch Democratic opposition to his every move under Georgia's Gold Dome, the nickname for the state Capitol. Never could he have imagined he'd end the election cycle as the prime target of Trump's fury.

A former home builder with vast political ambitions, Kemp won office by mobilizing the same rural white base that helped Trump capture the state—and that ensured no one could outflank him to his right. That meant airing an ad featuring him mockingly aiming a shotgun at his daughter's faux boyfriend, "Jake," in a TV spot promoting his gun rights support, thirty seconds of material that generated heaps of outrage on the left but praise and attention from the right. And that meant holding fiercely to strict voting rules while he was Georgia's top election official that Democrats charged were archaic and discriminatory.

The governor was certain he had reinforced his conservative credentials by signing into law sweeping antiabortion restrictions shortly after taking office and barnstorming for Trump around the state. But as the vote count continued after November 3, Kemp was forced to make a decision that could put his political future in jeopardy: heed Trump's demand to call an emergency legislative session that could overturn the election, or grudgingly accept Biden's victory.

Kemp's handpicked appointment to the US Senate, Kelly Loeffler, was supposed to be the Republican answer to the growing ranks of college-educated white women who sided with Democrats: a political novice with a successful background in business and civic life who could offer wavering Republicans a different brand of conservatism. Instead, she wound up veering to the party's extreme right flank, trying to curry favor with a skeptical president while facing open hostility from state Republican leaders who labeled her an inauthentic stooge.

A mild-mannered former Illinois farm girl, Loeffler worked her way up the corporate ladder until she landed at a little-known startup in Atlanta, where she met her future husband, Jeff Sprecher, an amiable wheeler-dealer whose company, Intercontinental Exchange, wound up buying the New York Stock Exchange. Her political ambitions came at a steep price, including an open revolt by the WNBA team that she proudly co-owned. Simply getting past the first-round voting cost her a fortune—she and her husband spent more than $30 million on her race—only to land her in a runoff that put every facet of her life under the microscope. As the 2021 showdown neared, some of her confidants wondered: Was it worth the price?

Her opponent, Raphael Warnock, the magnetic pastor of Atlanta's famed Ebenezer Baptist Church, grew up borrowing Martin Luther King Jr.'s speaking cadence and style—and later inherited his pulpit. He was raised in public housing in Savannah, the eleventh of twelve children—he liked to quip that his parents, both preachers, took to heart the Bible's command to be fruitful and multiply—and the first to graduate from college. Warnock also followed in King's footsteps by attending Morehouse College, where he embraced Atlanta's civil rights legacy and championed a message of Black empowerment and advancement through civic engagement.

After stints at churches in Harlem and Baltimore, Warnock landed his dream job in 2005, becoming the youngest senior pastor in Ebenezer's history, and continued to put the church at the intersection of political activism and civil rights. Backed by Abrams, he launched his first political run for Senate in 2020 and instantly became the top Democratic contender in a wide-open race. Warnock's charge to "remain the reverend" was put to the test as he was pummeled relentlessly on Georgia's airwaves over his past sermons and stances.

Jon Ossoff, the would-be millennial senator, started his climb into politics at the age of sixteen with a letter he wrote to John Lewis after he read the civil rights icon's memoir. That note yielded a summer job in Lewis's congressional office and, later, helped him land work as an aide to Congressman Hank Johnson, who represented a neighboring district. The two put him on the national map in 2017 when they endorsed his special election bid for a wide-open suburban district heavily favored to stay in Republican control.

Ossoff ran a by-the-books campaign for the seat, left vacant when Trump tapped the incumbent for a cabinet post, and was careful not to alienate moderate and independent voters. While he entered the race to muted fanfare as an unknown "make Trump furious" candidate, he finished it with a relentless focus on the middle and few harsh words for a president who branded him the worst of the worst. The strategy didn't work. He was narrowly defeated by his Republican opponent, making him the first high-profile Democrat to lose a political race in the Trump era. As 2020 turned to 2021, his mission was to ensure he wouldn't also be the last.

David Perdue, a temperamental former executive who clung to his outsider image despite six years in the nation's chummiest of clubs, had a humble upbringing in middle Georgia as the son of a schoolteacher and a public school superintendent. After graduating from Georgia Tech, he plunged into the corporate world, eventually rising to become the chief executive of Reebok and later Dollar General. When a US Senate seat opened in 2014, he called his first cousin Sonny, by then a former two-term governor, and encouraged him to run. Sonny flipped the script and urged David to jump in the race instead.

Even with the backing of one of the state's most powerful networks, Perdue was an underdog in a field of veteran Republican politicians. At one political event in rural Georgia, then-governor Nathan Deal walked right past him, taking Perdue to be just another face in the crowd. The unintentional snub forced Perdue to confront a cruel reality: as high as he'd risen in corporate America, he was a nobody in Georgia's political world. The truth was, he didn't like politicians or politics—or the way media covered the contests. His wife, Bonnie, talked him out of abandoning the race. Now, six years after his first victory, he faced another gut-check moment—this time with the fate of the Senate hanging in the balance.

Georgia's shift from one end of the political spectrum toward the other wasn't an overnight change but a long, intentional process built on the work of the politicians who drive the day's news and the efforts of hundreds of staffers, thousands of activists, and hundreds of thousands of newly engaged voters. Battle-hardened political veterans like to say Democrats had to pitch the "perfect game" to pull off the upsets, and there's no doubt that extraordinary fortune buoyed their hard work. In this book, you'll find the stories of the figures who drove the transformation, powering a dramatic upheaval that seemed so sudden from afar but was really the result of years of toil.

PART 1

⌃

GEORGIA ON THE VERGE

⌄

Chapter 1

WTF HAPPENED?

After President Trump's victory in 2016, Democrats in Georgia were angry—and ready to channel that fury into political energy. Georgia House minority leader Stacey Abrams had spent a lifetime preparing for just this moment.

The daughter of United Methodist ministers, Abrams grew up grounded in activism: she remembers boycotting a local Shell gas station as a child to protest the oil giant's ownership's ties to apartheid South Africa. As a teenager, she started a spreadsheet that meticulously charted each of her career goals, including a run for president as early as 2028. While a student at Spelman College, the famed historically Black institution in Atlanta, she led protests after the Rodney King verdict and challenged Atlanta mayor Maynard Jackson, the trailblazing first African American man elected to lead a major southern city, to work harder to help poor people of color. At Yale Law School, she worked at a legal clinic while writing the first of what would be a string of romance novels under a pen name. After a stint working for a prestigious Atlanta law firm and as a deputy city attorney, Abrams won a statehouse legislative seat and dedicated herself to becoming a political force—not by backslapping her way through the halls of Georgia's Gold Dome but by focusing on changing her party's direction from the inside out.

But if there was a defining story of her youthful foray into politics, it was the regrettable high school trip to the Governor's Mansion for a reception for valedictorians. It was one she spoke about to friends in quiet moments and, later, on the campaign trail to roaring crowds. Her family's car had broken down before the dinner, and Abrams and her parents had to take a bus to the formal event in Atlanta's most elite neighborhood. While her peers drove up in expensive rides, Abrams and her parents walked the winding driveway to the big black gates surrounding the estate. When they arrived at the guard station, a security officer glanced at Abrams's mom and dad and then back at her. "This is a private event," she remembers him saying. "You don't belong here."

Abrams's incensed parents soon had him regretting his words with a tongue-lashing, and they were eventually allowed into the reception. But that moment from 1991 would be seared in her memory. She didn't recall meeting then governor Zell Miller that day or celebrating with other elite high school students from across Georgia. What she did remember was that an agent of the state attempted to block her entry to the Governor's Mansion by insisting that she didn't "belong" there.

In early 2017, she had that story in mind as she began putting the finishing touches on a soon-to-be-launched campaign to convince voters that she belonged in Georgia's top office. Over the past three years, she'd founded a voting rights group, the New Georgia Project, whose goal was to engage hundreds of thousands of voters of color disconnected from state politics. She built a national fundraising operation to promote her vision of liberal policies in the South. She helped transform her often-warring Democratic colleagues in the Georgia House into a more effective fighting force. And she assembled a team of aides and advisers to help burnish her national profile and not-so-quietly make senior party officials aware that she was running for governor—with or without their support.

To some in Georgia's political class, though, Abrams was known as a behind-the-scenes operator knowledgeable in the nuances of legislation and skilled at picking apart Republican talking points—and not as a fiery orator who could energize the masses. Sure, she had proven that she could impress wealthy donors in closed-door meetings. But many in Georgia were scarcely familiar with Abrams's name, let alone her ability to motivate Democrats.

While Georgia Democrats lacked a clear leader after years of demoralizing defeats, Abrams had been one of Trump's most outspoken critics in Georgia. His surprise White House victory gave her the chance she needed to funnel Democratic outrage into results—and cement her claim as the leader of the party's resurgence.

On a weekday afternoon in January 2017 in downtown Atlanta, not far from the spot where baseball legend Hank Aaron belted his 715th home run, a crowd of five hundred or so activists, politicians, and onlookers gathered at a union hall. A former beauty queen angling to run for office wore a sparkling sash. Haggard parents turned campaign leaflets into makeshift coloring books to keep their little ones occupied. Once and future candidates crammed into rows of plastic folding chairs arrayed under fluorescent lights.

A hush descended over the room as Abrams delivered her vision of how Democrats could win Georgia. Over the course of about fifteen minutes, she spoke of mobilizing liberals by promising expanded access to health care, promoting a more equitable economy, and a push to register, and then engage, overlooked Georgia voters. Above all, she made the case that Democrats could win back Republican-held territory if they embraced authenticity rather than set aside their priorities to try to win over wavering moderates. She wanted to be both a salve and a spark to angry, hurt, and frustrated Democrats; she promised them there was a tangible path to flipping Georgia, that resistance wasn't futile.

Like her or not, many of Abrams's fellow Democratic lawmakers saw her as a no-nonsense leader capable of navigating the messy mash-up of compromise and the shrewd triangulation of power under the Gold Dome. To her most loyal supporters, she was a prophet of voting rights, a visionary intent on building an ascendant political coalition with her promise of being an "unapologetic progressive." To her critics, she was a threatening new force in state politics whose promise to energize liberals could upend decades of a conservative-leaning status quo. But most hadn't seen her like this before: uncompromising, inspirational, and demanding. The audience, eager for a statewide standard-bearer in the Trump era, interrupted her speech frequently with applause and at the end rewarded her with a booming ovation.

The speech heralded some of the challenges that awaited Abrams as she rose in political stardom. An avowed introvert who once happily went to the grocery store and local haunts unrecognized, Abrams wasn't used to so openly wearing her heart on her sleeve. That day, in an aside, she said only half-jokingly that "if I could cry, I would"—a window into a no-nonsense and sometimes brusque style that had Democratic rivals whispering that she was the wrong fit for a party looking for a new champion.

As her message gained traction, it soon became clear that Abrams's political strategy would set Democrats on a course toward a new kind of battleground politics that would bring unprecedented spending, visits from a constellation of political stars, constant attention from national media, and a clash of ideologies between two parties diametrically opposed on most every major policy debate, each eager to use the other to energize their bases. As the audience trickled out of the union hall that day, many left confident that Abrams could awaken a dormant wing of the party.

There was, however, good reason to be skeptical. As 2017 dawned, Republicans controlled every statewide office in Georgia and both US Senate seats and enjoyed commanding majorities in the state legislature. Just a few years earlier, in the 2014 elections, a Republican ticket led by first-term governor Nathan Deal and Senate candidate David Perdue swept every statewide office easily, brushing aside younger, well-financed Democrats who had storied last names.

This had not always been the Georgia way. For most of the twentieth century, Democrats controlled every lever of power in the state with the unwavering support of rural white voters, stoked by crowd-pleasing populism, who backed segregationist and racist measures that disenfranchised Black residents. It was a monopoly built on a revulsion toward Reconstructionist policies promoted by Abraham Lincoln's Republican successors and, later, on the durability of Franklin Delano Roosevelt's New Deal coalition, one that united labor unions, poor white farmers, and minority voters.

Even as national Democrats championed civil rights legislation, partisans in Georgia and elsewhere in the "Solid South" mostly opposed the reforms, an agenda that helped them keep their grip on state power. Though their support might have seemed counterintuitive, Black voters reliably lined up behind Democratic candidates. Like its neighbors in the Deep South, Georgia was essentially a one-party state where victory in a Democratic primary was tantamount to election in November. To wield any sort of electoral power in Georgia, Black leaders had to wade into Democratic waters—or not bother at all.

Jimmy Carter came from that political tradition. He portrayed himself as a reliable southern conservative on his way to a gubernatorial victory in 1970 only to stun his supporters by delivering an inaugural address that demanded an end to racial discrimination in Georgia. He then remade his image into that of a moderate reformer who reorganized state government and appointed an unprecedented number of women and minorities to key agencies and judicial posts—a record he invoked during his triumphant 1976 run for president.

One of the first chinks in the state's Democratic armor emerged during Carter's doomed 1980 reelection bid, when he easily carried Georgia but was shellacked in much of the rest of the country. Bobby Kahn, then a young Carter staffer, left the president's election party in Atlanta about fifteen minutes after the polls closed, dejected over the White House defeat. But he drifted to sleep that night believing that at least Senator Herman Talmadge, the cigar-chomping, scandal-plagued four-term Democratic incumbent, would win. As he strolled to his law school class the next morning, a late run of *The Atlanta Constitution* declared Republican Mack Mattingly the winner. (An earlier edition of the paper inaccurately asserted that Talmadge "walks away with it.") Kahn, a stalwart Democrat who would go on to lead the state party, was astonished: "It was the wake-up call."

A wave of suburbanite returns that had streamed in overnight had won Mattingly, the Reagan revolutionary and woebegone chair of the state GOP, a seat as the first Republican elected to the Senate from Georgia since Reconstruction. His victory by just twenty-seven thousand votes exiled Talmadge, the hard-drinking scion of a political dynasty and self-proclaimed champion of the rural South, known to friends and foes simply as "Hummon."

Talmadge's loss also seemed to mark the start of a shift in power away from the countryside and toward metro Atlanta, where his opponent amassed a commanding edge. "Everyone sort of thought I was crazy," Mattingly later observed of his quiet eighteen months of campaigning. Everyone, that is, except the supporters who bought into his message of limited government, low taxes, strong military defense, and individual responsibility. So stunning was Mattingly's victory that newly elected president Ronald Reagan quipped to him: "Your coattails weren't long enough to drag me in" over Carter in Georgia.

But dreams of a Republican renaissance would be short-lived. Six years later, a congenial congressman and onetime Atlanta councilman named Wyche Fowler, known as the "night mayor of City Hall" for his owlish ways, rebuilt the Democratic alliance between rural white conservatives and Black voters in the cities to oust Mattingly. And the rise of Zell Miller, a bullheaded, mountain-bred college professor, arrested a broader GOP takeover with the help of far-reaching education initiatives that would forever change the state.

Frustrating his allies and enemies alike with diverging policy stances—he earned the derisive moniker "Zig-Zag Zell" early in his career—Miller was at times a liberal, a moderate, and a staunch conservative. His rivals griped that there wasn't a single position that Miller hadn't stood for at one time or another. "He wanted to ride a bicycle in a parade," former governor Lester Maddox once said of him, "but they wouldn't allow him because he was declared a danger with all his zigzagging all over the place."

He was also a shrewd tactician. After sixteen years as lieutenant governor, Miller was elected to the state's top job in 1990, defeating civil rights leader Andrew Young for the all-important Democratic nomination with a pledge to establish a state lottery to fund prekindergarten programs, technology improvements, and a college scholarship for students who maintained B averages.

He made good on the promise by signing into law the HOPE Scholarship, which has been responsible for sending more than 2 million students to colleges and tech schools. Weeks before his 2018 death, Miller told his former chief of staff Keith Mason at their final face-to-face meeting how proud he was that his legacy was still intact: "You know what I like about this lottery? It makes this old face still look new."

For a generation after Miller's stint as governor, Democrats ran on safe-guarding and expanding the program. Before it had become a runaway success, Roy Barnes had hired a TV crew in 1989 to capture him delivering an anti-lottery speech from the Senate floor; when the smooth-talking trial lawyer ran for governor in 1998 after Miller's two terms, he pledged to expand the program on his way to a narrow victory.

By then, the Democratic coalition that had endured through much of the century was clearly starting to fray. Though Bill Clinton carried the state in 1992, Republican Bob Dole narrowly captured its thirteen electoral votes four years later. The growing Atlanta suburbs, filling in with newcomers with no allegiance to the Democratic Party, tilted increasingly toward the GOP. And conservative rural Democrats found themselves marginalized by the shifting leftward tides of the party in Atlanta and Washington. The revolution really took wing, though, when an irascible party-switching state senator named Sonny Perdue won an upset victory in 2002 to become the first Republican governor in Georgia since Reconstruction.

Perdue had given up his powerful job as the state Senate's second-in-command shortly after his father had suffered a grave heart attack. As he spent three weeks of soul-searching in an austere middle Georgia hospital room, watching his eighty-four-year-old father, a lifelong farmer, slip away, he challenged himself to look inward: "Are you going to do what's right in your own heart?" he asked himself. To Perdue, the honest answer to that question meant risking the power he'd accumulated in the legislature and switching in 1998 to the moribund Republican Party.

Quite quickly Perdue became a daily testament to what happened to Democrats who bolted the party: he was stripped of power and authority, lost his coveted committee assignments, and watched in vain as nearly every piece of legislation he hoped to pass was relegated to the dustbin. His time as a backbencher made him resolved to take on a bigger challenge, this time against "King Roy," the moniker he gave the supremely powerful Democratic governor. He had little else to lose, he reasoned, so why not take a shot at the highest office in the state?

Over the eighteen months leading to the 2002 election, Perdue capital-ized on outrage from teachers stung by the Democratic governor's education overhaul and conservatives upset by Barnes's redesign of the state flag that minimized the Confederate battle emblem. A long shot to most, Perdue was outspent by Barnes by more than six to one. The Democrat also had the backing of almost every significant political network in the state, and endorsements from Georgia's most important power brokers. Barnes led every major preelection poll, including one that showed him with an eleven-point advantage a few days before the vote.

Many at Perdue's victory party at the Grand Hyatt in Buckhead were there on a lark, expecting more of the same: a valiant Republican effort swept aside by another Democratic win. But the sense of impending doom was erased by a burst of deafening applause at around 8:58 p.m. That's when Perdue took the lead for the first time—an edge he wouldn't relinquish. Perdue wound up winning by five percentage points.

His stunning victory accelerated the shift of rural white voters away from Democrats, a realignment that would propel conservatives to power over the next two decades. State Democrats, beset by party-switchers who followed Perdue's lead, were soon in shambles. Months after Perdue's victory, state Democratic Party executive director Jeff DiSantis passed around a yellow legal pad at an organizational meeting and asked activists to write down the names of their local county chairs. Party leaders had been so comfortably in power that for years that no one had bothered to keep a list. Even years later, Barnes's defeat still stung. "When did I get over it?" said Kahn, who was Barnes's top aide. "I'll let you know when that happens."

One election cycle after another, Democrats tried—and failed—to draw upon the same formula that had kept the party in charge of Georgia for generations. Party leaders thought they had their best shot in 2014, when Jason Carter, an energetic state senator and grandson of the former president, and Michelle Nunn, a policy-oriented nonprofit executive and daughter of former US senator Sam Nunn, both tried to build an electable coalition.

Nunn followed in her father's centrist footsteps, pushing such noncontroversial and nonpartisan ideas as banning former members of Congress from becoming lobbyists, adopting new transparency requirements, and meeting with every senator her first year. Carter centered his campaign on bolstering the "vanishing" HOPE Scholarship, boosting education funding, and pursuing the expansion of the Medicaid program. He also voted in the legislature for a broad expansion of gun rights—in part, he later explained, because he didn't want Republicans to make the polarizing debate a wedge issue for the rest of the campaign.

Both avoided President Barack Obama when he came to visit shortly before the election. And both followed what was then seen as the shrewd conventional wisdom for Georgia Democrats by steering clear of some of the state's most contentious social and cultural issues. Their goal was to win back former Democrats who had fled to the GOP without turning away the party's most loyal supporters.

"In 2014, there was no justifiable path to victory by relying just on the base. It had to be a 'both, and' strategy," Carter said, looking back on the election. "We had to energize Black voters and win over persuasion voters."

Both lost by about two hundred thousand votes—roughly eight percentage points. Democrats fared even worse in 2016, when they couldn't recruit a top-notch challenger to Senator Johnny Isakson, a popular two-term incumbent who helped usher in the modern-day Republican era in Georgia. Vulnerable Republican incumbents in down-ballot state legislative seats that year often faced ill-prepared Democratic challengers—or none at all. One GOP state lawmaker who represented the northern suburb of Dunwoody pleaded guilty to driving under the influence with a gun on his hip and four teenage exchange students in his car just months before the 2016 election. But even he won another two years in office easily because no Democrat had bothered to qualify for the seat by the deadline.

The Democrats failed to take advantage of a massive political shift as the bedroom communities that once surrounded Atlanta like a scarlet ribbon turned blue in 2016. Trump carried Georgia by about five percentage points without so much as a campaign rally in the state during the closing months of the race. But in an electoral shock, Hillary Clinton won Gwinnett County, marking the first time a Democrat captured the fast-growing area northeast of Atlanta since Jimmy Carter's 1976 presidential run. Likewise, Clinton was the first Democrat since Carter to carry Cobb County, the northwest Atlanta suburb that was the launching pad for the careers of Georgia's modern-day GOP elite.

Trump's victory in Georgia was expected. But his once unimaginable triumph over Clinton in the national election sent Democrats reeling—and became a powerful motivational tool. Adrienne White was a hardened veteran of grassroots organizing, gathering month after month with the same solid but unchanging group of a few dozen activists. Once, she was elated to learn she had been accepted to a prestigious training program for a Georgia-based women's advocacy group—until she realized that there were so few applicants that everyone who applied was approved. The crowds at grassroots meetings she helped organize became so familiar to her that she often felt as if she was speaking in an echo chamber.

Trump was the best recruiting draw White could ask for. About three weeks after the November election, the Red Clay Democrats group she helped lead gathered at a funky bar called Sister Louisa's Church of the Living Room and Ping Pong Emporium on Atlanta's bustling Edgewood Avenue. The room was filled with fluorescent crosses and borderline blasphemous religious symbols, and the event was dubbed "WTF Happened?" White and other organizers expected a crowd of a few dozen of the regulars, plus a handful of curious onlookers. Instead, hundreds piled in, cramming the bar's upper floor and spilling onto the stairs and street below. She finally had the electorate's attention, a chance to bring in new voters to revitalize the party. The message she delivered that night was a simple one as she reminded a crowd that needed no reminding that Trump was about to take office.

"This is what happens when you're not engaged."

Trump or no Trump in the White House, Stacey Abrams was ready to make her mark. Even if it meant a brutal clash over the direction of the party between those who believed the path to victory relied on winning back moderate white voters and those, like Abrams, who desired to do away with the tattered "old playbook" that ignored communities of color, particularly among the state's roughly one third of Black voters. She believed Democrats should reject false choices between chasing moderate white voters and "unlikely" Black Georgians who rarely participated in elections. She had a hopeful way of describing those unaligned voters: they would be Democrats if only "we ask them to speak up."

Over the next few months, Abrams and her aides finalized a plan to hand those voters a megaphone. She had cemented her decision to run for governor after an exhausting legislative session seven years earlier, in 2010, that ended with a vote, just before midnight, to eliminate tax credits for hundreds of thousands of poor Georgians. The measure's sponsor hadn't even mentioned the changes he had tacked onto an otherwise innocuous measure when he presented the bill to fellow lawmakers, and Governor Perdue didn't explain why he signed the $22 million cost-saving measure into law a few weeks later. For Abrams, the infuriating swipe at struggling Georgians crystallized the beginning of what she saw as a ten-year project to rebuild the party.

At around the same time, she stepped into a void in the party's upper tiers to run for House leader, and her victory in the internal vote made her the first woman and first African American to head the House Democratic caucus. She gained the job after the party was shellacked in the 2010 elections, losses that left Democrats at their lowest point in the political order since Reconstruction. Her mission was to turn the sixty-three-member caucus—a mix of conservative rural white old-timers, moderate Black members, and a handful of more liberal newcomers—into a fighting force. Her leadership style ruffled feathers, so much so that one of her top deputies switched parties after he wanted more of a say in decision-making. It was a shock to Abrams, particularly because he was so liberal that, she later joked, he would have voted for "fluffy unicorns" if they came up for debate. But she always knew she would face internal friction steering the party in a new direction.

In her new role, she raised funds for robocalls to mobilize voters in their districts, staged press conferences to tout long-shot measures they sponsored, and held "shadow" hearings for them when Republicans refused to do so. When a senior Republican accidentally wandered into one of those meetings, mistakenly believing it to be for a key vote, Abrams felt vindicated. In her first two years alone, the caucus exponentially increased its output, more than doubling the number of town halls and tripling the number of press conferences—metrics that fast became part of a thirty-one-page slideshow shared with deep-pocketed donors.

As Abrams planned her campaign for governor, she and her aides determined that success would depend on building a national footprint to raise large amounts of out-of-state cash, while also cultivating a homegrown operation that relied on in-state media—even if it meant being portrayed as a "celebrity" candidate. Early on, Abrams decided she would spend the bulk of her campaign account hiring staff, corralling volunteers, and seeding field offices around the state rather than saving it for a TV blitz close to the time of the vote. And she would wage battle against those within her own party who felt that Black voters were "congenitally predisposed" to vote and that therefore mobilization efforts weren't necessary.

Abrams was also helped by a crucial demographic shift she was sure she could harness. In 1970, Georgia had been roughly three-quarters white. By 2018, white Georgians scarcely made up half of the state's population. And while wealthy whites moving from other parts of the country accounted for some of the state's explosive growth, nearly half of the 1.9 million eligible voters added to Georgia's rolls between 2000 and 2019 were Black. The share of eligible Black voters in Georgia overall increased by 5 percent over that time span—the largest percentage-point increase among Black voters in any state during that period, according to the Pew Research Center. Since Black voters overwhelmingly favored Democrats, that was all good news to Abrams—so long as she could encourage more of them to show up to vote.

Abrams's chief partner in the campaign was Lauren Groh-Wargo, a battle-honed strategist who relocated to Atlanta from Ohio to work with Abrams. Groh-Wargo was introduced to Abrams in 2011 after she read a glowing profile of the politician and surprised herself by picking up the phone to dial her up out the blue. The two met for lunch not long after, in what Groh-Wargo joked felt like a round of "political dating," and decided to join forces. Though they came from wildly different backgrounds—Groh-Wargo was a white gay daughter of the Midwest—the duo quickly became what each described as "thought partners" who, to their friends and deputies, seemed as if they spoke from the same mouth.

A veteran of the rough-and-tumble politics of a perennial battleground state, Groh-Wargo imported her hard-won lessons to the South. First, she recognized, Democrats had to understand, at a forensic level, that they were losing in Georgia partly because of an assumption that disenchanted former supporters would eventually make their way back into the fold. To win them back, she urged, they needed sharp, calculated policies instead of what she called an "overstuffed manifesto" of grab-bag proposals. That meant a platform based on economic security, bolstering education, and expanding access to health care. And they needed a strong state party apparatus to build a bench of talented politicians and strategists.

The two women made an unlikely alliance to help reconstruct the state party with DuBose Porter, a backslapping newspaper publisher and throwback to the yesteryear of Georgia Democrats. A longtime state legislator from the farming town of Dublin in the eastern part of the state, Porter had often supported conservative issues over nearly two decades in the state House, including a vote to ban same-sex marriage. But he had become increasingly progressive during his failed run for governor in 2010.

With Abrams's help, he won the party's leadership post in 2013, inheriting a state apparatus in full retreat. The previous chair had been forced to resign amid an activist revolt and legal problems that would send him to prison. The party didn't have enough cash in the reserves to pay the utility bills, let alone hire an extensive on-the-ground network of staffers. Congressman Hank Johnson cut a $10,000 check from his campaign account just so the organization could keep the lights on. As the party rebuilt its coffers, Porter went to work restoring ties with key constituencies. At an LGBTQ caucus meeting not long after he won the party chairmanship, Porter highlighted how he transformed from an opponent of marriage equality to an avowed advocate of gay rights. Sometimes, he said, to make your case to a different audience, "you need a bald-headed fat redneck."

All of that was important to Abrams and Groh-Wargo. But most essential to them was a commitment to building a grassroots network capable of identifying, registering, and mobilizing the untapped pool of voters central to her campaign. This was no easy sell. At a donor briefing in 2017, old-guard Democrats insisted that the only way the party could win in Georgia was by getting 30 percent of the white vote—and Democrats were barely cracking the

20 percent mark. To succeed in 2018, they maintained, Democrats needed to run even harder to the middle and give Georgians a moderate alternative to Trump.

Groh-Wargo couldn't stifle a chuckle during the meeting. Just look at voter participation and registration figures over the past decade, she told the group, and see the huge numbers of voters of color—not just Black voters, but also Latinos, Asian Americans, and other minorities—who weren't engaged. It was hard for her to stomach the opposition from fellow Democrats who believed Black turnout was already maxed out in Georgia when her metrics showed so many voters of color were still on the sidelines. "It was a radical, disruptive threat to say things out loud that were so obvious in the data," she said.

That strategy shaped Abrams's platform priorities. Yes, she embraced liberal issues that Democrats competing statewide in earlier elections would have avoided. She backed a hike in the minimum wage, supported gun control measures, opposed abortion restrictions, railed against new crackdowns on illegal immigrants, and endorsed the removal of the enormous carving of Confederate war leaders from the face of the state-owned Stone Mountain. At her early campaign events, Abrams told of her brother's struggles with drug addiction to underscore the need for a criminal justice overhaul.

But she also saw herself as a pragmatist who, as the top Democrat in the state House in the early 2010s, had to keep together a fractious caucus. She pledged to expand Medicaid under the Affordable Care Act—a notion that polls showed had wide support among Georgia voters—and boost funding for public education. And she made increasing access to the ballot a key part of her campaign, highlighting an issue that often got short shrift on the trail.

Even as Abrams waged her bid to become the nation's first Black female elected governor, she prepared to run a quieter, parallel operation that she and Groh-Wargo saw as just as essential. They also had to convince the political class—skeptical pundits, high-powered donors who wouldn't return her calls, party king- and queenmakers who didn't believe her vision could flip the state—that she had a legitimate shot at winning.

Even Groh-Wargo's most trusted deputies needed some convincing. In February 2018, Groh-Wargo reached out to Seth Bringman, a veteran operative who had worked for her a decade earlier at the state Democratic Party in Ohio, which at the time was the quintessential presidential battleground. As he replaced light fixtures in his newly purchased home in Ohio's capital city, he initially politely but firmly rebuffed her invitation to join Abrams's team— not because he didn't believe in the candidate's message, but because he didn't believe Democrats could yet win in Georgia.

Groh-Wargo and Abrams knew they needed a shadow campaign that mirrored the press conferences, rallies, and headline-grabbing events that mark any sophisticated run for office. They had a phrase for the mission: "a concurrent campaign of belief."

Chapter 2

WHO IS THIS GUY?

The name was the easy part. After Donald Trump won the presidency, Becky Butler and her partner, Pat Byrd, invited a group of friends over to seek comfort after what they saw as a world-shattering loss. Before they knew it, about sixty people jumbled into the airy living room of their house near Emory University's bustling campus on the eastern side of Atlanta. They came to be known as "Necessary Trouble"—an upstart group that borrowed its moniker from the favorite philosophy of its beloved congressman, the civil rights hero John Lewis.

Butler asked each of the attendees two questions. The first relied on her background as a social worker and specialist in Taoist meditation: "How are you calming your nervous system down?" One woman talked of planting daffodil bulbs. Another mentioned a book she'd been reading about the French Revolution. A third offered a story of self-soothing involving painting a totem pole.

Then Butler asked a more pointed question: "What are you doing about it?"

Almost no one in the room had an answer.

Butler did. Her parents were blacklisted during the McCarthy era, so she knew what it was like to get on the government's wrong side. She lived in a deep-blue part of town where Democrats had no need to worry about Republican opposition, but she had marshaled friends and neighbors to "adopt" candidates running in other parts of the state. Butler saw her organization, a mostly white group, as a "rear guard" to the Black-led advocacies that had been promoting political change in Georgia for decades.

One of the first political meetings she attended just weeks after the election was an LGBTQ caucus gathering in downtown Atlanta in January 2017. Stacey Abrams was there, exhorting the crowd with a call to action. So was a less familiar face: a tall, brown-haired twenty-nine-year-old wearing a dark, slightly oversized suit. Butler watched curiously as he circled the room shaking hands and introducing himself as a candidate with just his first name. She thought, *Who is this guy?* After he made the rounds, Butler pulled the young man aside with some friendly advice: "Say your last name—and what office you're running for."

No one in the room could have realized then, of course, that Jon Ossoff, the rookie candidate standing before them, was on the cusp of a battle for Congress in Atlanta's northern suburbs that would draw explosive national attention—and attract a mind-boggling $60 million in spending—as the first national test of Trump's popularity and a bellwether of the political trends that would define his presidency.

The Sixth District, which included a wealthy slice of Atlanta's bedroom communities, wasn't exactly fertile ground for a skirmish that would captivate the nation. For a generation, it had been a launching pad for high-profile Republican talent. Congressman Tom Price, a curmudgeonly orthopedic surgeon who once was viewed as a potential future House Speaker, had won another two years in his seat there by twenty-four points just weeks earlier. Before Price, the suburban stretch was represented by two other Republican standouts: Newt Gingrich, who held the seat while he was House Speaker, and Johnny Isakson, who graduated to the US Senate after seven terms representing the district. It was such a surefire GOP lock that when Trump tapped Price to be his secretary of health and human services, media lists of his potential successors didn't include a single Democratic name.

Ossoff set about to change that. Shortly before Christmas 2016, he gathered a small group to share a decision that surprised even some of his closest friends. He was planning to run for the seat, even though he had almost no name recognition or visibility. He told them he was unfazed by Price's dominant performance weeks earlier. The Democrat that Price bested raised no money and didn't even bother to create a campaign website. The more important number, he told them, was Trump's slim 1.5-point margin of victory in the district. Since it was a special election, Ossoff knew there would surely be a glut of Republicans battling each other for the nomination, giving a Democrat an opening if one could consolidate support. He was confident he could be the unifier, for he had an advantage that no other Democrat could boast: the backing of two of Georgia's liberal lions, congressmen Hank Johnson and John Lewis.

While a nineteen-year-old student at Georgetown University who had envisioned a career in diplomacy, Ossoff had worked for Johnson as a speechwriter and press aide during his nationally watched 2006 campaign to oust fellow Democratic congresswoman Cynthia McKinney. After Johnson beat the controversial incumbent, Ossoff split his time between being a college undergraduate and a legislative aide in the freshman congressman's Capitol office, at one moment singing in a campus a cappella group and at the next writing a successful House resolution that urged peaceful negotiations to end a growing crisis in Uganda. Johnson would later refer to Ossoff as an "idea factory."

As importantly, Ossoff cultivated a special bond with Lewis. While in high school, he had read the civil rights icon's biography and was so inspired by the stories of young people who made a lasting difference for social justice that he penned a letter to Lewis's office to ask for a meeting. It led to a coveted post there the following summer, where Ossoff made a lasting impression on the congressman, who helped him land the job with Johnson. Years later, Lewis told Ossoff that his note triggered memories of a remarkable episode from his own youth. As a seventeen-year-old in rural Alabama, Lewis had written a letter to Martin Luther King Jr. and, to his eternal gratitude, was sent back a round-trip Greyhound bus ticket to Montgomery to meet with him, "and it changed my life."

Like other Democrats devastated by Trump's victory, Ossoff felt the nation was being rocked by a political cataclysm. He just wanted to pick up the nearest banner and charge. When the big Democratic names who could have cleared the field didn't make a move for the congressional seat, Ossoff seized the initiative. He talked to Johnson, his old boss, who wholeheartedly encouraged him to go forward with a campaign. Then he sat down with Lewis in Atlanta, armed with thick files of precinct-by-precinct data, meticulously prepared to talk through his case for and against a run. Lewis cut his former intern off mid-pitch.

"Jon," Lewis assured him, "I'll support you."

The endorsements gave Ossoff instant cachet, a guarantee that even though his candidacy seemed out of nowhere, two of the party's most trusted Georgia figures believed in him. When he entered the race on January 5, 2017, with a boast of $250,000 in cash commitments already lined up, plenty were still skeptical of the millennial newcomer who wouldn't turn thirty until February. But party leaders knew that the surest chance they had to flip the seat was to consolidate early behind the candidate with the best chance of winning—even if that meant rallying to someone who was initially running his campaign out of his parents' basement.

Sally Harrell, a former Democratic state legislator, was talked into abandoning her campaign in the face of Ossoff's overwhelming resources. At the time, she credited his ability to "utilize Washington connections." Another candidate, Josh McLaurin, quit his bid not long after beers with Ossoff. McLaurin, a local attorney with a Yale Law School pedigree, arrived at the bar alone, wearing jeans. Ossoff was dressed in a crisp suit and came ready to talk of his latest fundraising exploits. It was financial firepower that McLaurin—and every other would-be contender in the Democratic race— simply couldn't match.

The son of a Harvard-trained publishing executive and an Australian-born businesswoman and activist, Ossoff stood pencil-straight and spoke in sometimes meandering tones, with a cadence that reminded some of President Obama. At his earliest events, such as at a synagogue to highlight his Jewish faith, his stump speeches generated polite applause but not ground-shaking ovations. Nor did his pensive personality match the sound and fury of a political firebrand. He was so consistently on message that his critics easily mocked him as robotic; when asked at one of his first events to name an oddball thing that voters should know about him, he hedged. "Let me get back to you on that," he finally answered, wary of a journalistic "trap" question that could come back to haunt him.

Mindful that his lack of an extensive record was both an asset and a weakness, Ossoff quickly tried to establish his credentials. He framed himself as a former "senior level staffer" with top-secret national security clearance, thanks to his post as a mid-level committee staffer for Johnson, a claim that drew cackles from Republicans, who considered it a hyperinflated boast. And he touted his private sector experience as an investigative journalist, owing to his job at the helm of the investigative journalism company Insight TWI.

Ossoff's journey to that position epitomized the audacity of his personality. He'd met the company's founder, the former BBC journalist Ron McCullagh, as a teenager while at a dinner party during a 2003 trip to southeastern France with his mother. Later McCullagh recruited him as TWI's chief executive when Ossoff was twenty-six. The company's investigations into assassins in El Salvador, death squads in Kenya, and Islamic State terrorists in Iraqi deserts became Exhibit A of Ossoff's corruption-fighting credentials during his campaign.

As stiff as he could seem at some early events, he tapped into a hunger that invigorated his supporters. Jen Cox was one of a few dozen Democrats at a Cobb County meet and greet in January where Ossoff promised to channel their fears and anxiety over Trump's administration into a liberal comeback story. She readily admitted she initially would have preferred to support a female contender, but none felt compelling to her. Instead, to her surprise, she was wowed by a young man who seemed to have the passion and political ability to match his high-flying ambition. She texted a friend immediately: "We have our candidate."

Cox had moved to an affluent part of Cobb County just northwest of Atlanta in 2009 and made it a personal "salvation quest" to find fellow liberals in the very incubator of the Gingrich Revolution. It wasn't easy. Around 2016, she heard of an underground Facebook group called "Liberal Moms of Roswell and Cobb," a confidential outlet for these women to vent about politics without jeopardizing their social lives, their jobs, and their families' standing—no small concern in deep-red society. During a bawdy round of Cards Against

Humanity with about thirty friends, Cox encouraged them to come out of hiding, so to speak, and hold events for Hillary Clinton. Even organizing a sign-waving for the Democratic presidential nominee at a busy intersection before the November 2016 vote was a hush-hush affair. It took two weeks of quiet canvassing to pull off the event, and Cox was thrilled by the turnout. More than two hundred people showed up, some in disguise lest they be outed.

Luisa Wakeman was so concerned about being revealed as a Democrat that she showed up in deep cover with a hat and sunglasses; two years later she would run for public office. A driver in his seventies pulled over in his sedan with tears in his eyes, telling Cox that he'd "never thought he'd see this" sort of liberal outpouring in his backyard. Many, many others asked how they could get involved. To Cox, it was an inflection point, the moment she realized that "we were onto something," that suburban Democrats could make a difference. Clinton's narrow victory in Cobb in November 2016 further proved the point. Now she and her growing organization of women activists, Pave It Blue, were ready to channel their might behind Ossoff.

Ossoff became the first congressional candidate to harness that newfound liberal energy to counter Democrats' darkest nightmares about Trump's presidency. One early ad he ran featured a clock ticking down from thirty seconds as it insisted that the president "is not only embarrassing us on the world stage, he could start an unnecessary war." After pledging to "make Trump furious," Ossoff brought that position to life when he showed up at Hartsfield-Jackson Atlanta International Airport with congressmen Johnson and Lewis to console Georgians detained in the chaos of the president's executive order that closed US borders to travelers from certain majority-Muslim countries. Some of his consultants, Ossoff said, had warned him not to take so public a stand and to play it safe in a conservative-leaning district. He rejected that advice, believing it was the "wrong moment in history" to back down.

Ossoff was the main source of his own campaign strategy, often shaping his message and image with his advisers in a makeshift office dotted with beanbag chairs and cutout photos of volunteers. His working theory was that he had a grassroots army at the ready, eager to be mobilized to fight back against Trump. He just needed to keep them energized without doing anything to interfere with their commitment. In short, he deduced that he needed to be circumspect on some hot-button issues, outspoken on others—and always careful not to say anything too controversial that could alienate his core supporters.

His early protest against the travel ban helped Ossoff draw attention from the fundraising gurus at the liberal Daily Kos group, which helped generate hundreds of thousands of dollars from national donors, crucial early support that helped raise his visibility. That triggered an ongoing cycle that brought both local and national attention to his fledgling campaign, which in turn yielded even more money from donors looking for an outlet to stick it to Trump.

But that push and pull between Ossoff's instincts and the conventional wisdom of campaigning in a Republican-leaning area foreshadowed the friction ahead. As the campaign drew more notice, Ossoff's image as a Trump-fighting candidate conflicted with an increasingly guarded message from the candidate on the trail. Ossoff's later TV ads were focused on job creation and turning the district into a tech hub—not relentlessly jabbing a thumb in Trump's eye. His campaign's data showed that even if he wrung every vote he could from solid Democrats in the area, Ossoff still needed to win a significant portion of independents and moderates who typically vote for Republicans. When Trump attacked Ossoff directly, he resisted the urge to issue a scathing response. Instead, the Democrat offered more tepid push-back, saying he wasn't concerned with the comings and goings of "Washington figures."

Ossoff's strategy helped him get off to an incredibly fast start in the eighteen-candidate special election. Seizing on the national attention, he built a formidable fundraising machine that more than dwarfed his closest opponents in the eighteen-candidate race. He was praised by House Democratic leader Nancy Pelosi and endorsed by top state Democrats and liberal figures from afar. Alyssa Milano, an actress and activist, even ferried Ossoff supporters to the polls in a black SUV on the first day of early voting. His jaw-dropping fundraising advantage—a record-setting $8.3 million haul in the first quarter—enabled him to flood Democratic-leaning households with multiple mailers a day, but also to target other voters outside the party's orbit, including some who typically voted in GOP primaries and others who rarely cast ballots at all.

Still, that financial firepower didn't mean that the national party—or even the local voters—would automatically embrace him. Ossoff hired a campaign manager, Keenan Pontoni, who was brutally honest and meticulously data-driven. During their first interview, Pontoni flatly admitted, "I don't know, I'll have to get back to you" repeatedly to questions about door-knocking strategies and TV buys rather than take a guess without the metrics to back it up. That honesty, along with his sharp answers in a follow-up, intrigued Ossoff, who entrusted Pontoni to build one of the largest field operations Georgia had ever seen. He rallied volunteers and donors traumatized by Trump's victory to Ossoff's side, and soon the campaign had legions of supporters fanning out across the suburbs.

"We didn't know what we had. All the upswell that came as a reaction to Trump's election was still in the beginning stages, and we had no idea the power of what was being harnessed at that point," said Sacha Haworth, one of Ossoff's chief campaign deputies. "I don't think the party itself knew how to tame it. No one was prepared for the attention about to be poured into the race."

That included Republicans caught flat-footed by Ossoff's out-of-nowhere success. Quickly, they dreamed up ways to counter his rise in the polls. They framed Ossoff as a "carpetbagger" who didn't understand the district and pilloried his thin résumé. They also exploited the Democrat's college escapades, which were readily found on the internet, and featured videos of Ossoff dressed as Han Solo, the swashbuckling rebel leader in the *Star Wars* franchise.

"Imagine you had thirty seconds to make a life-or-death decision," an incredulous-sounding narrator offered in a Republican attack ad over a grainy clip of Ossoff competing in a drinking game with another *Star Wars* character. "Would you really want this guy making those decisions for your family?"

Soon Ossoff and his allies countered on the space opera theme, depicting him as a rebel insurgent painting a target on the Trump Death Star. One response ad declared "District 6 has a New Hope," and, soon, *Star Wars*–themed "Resistance" pro-Ossoff placards popped up on front lawns. Cox was adamant about the need for more yard signs to prove to skeptical Sixth District residents that other Democrats lived nearby. At an early campaign meeting, she made her case to Ossoff: "If we put them in this deep, dark-red suburban district, they will start to change psychology."

=====

Republican contenders were fractured and divided, spending more time battling one another instead of trying to dampen Ossoff's rising poll numbers. They bickered about the most trivial of matters—social media hashtags and doctored Facebook posts—and feuded over the degree of their loyalty to Trump. One contender snatched up the staffers of a rival after a group quit the campaign en masse. Another candidate's ad depicted him with a shovel cleaning up the mess left behind a pack of donkeys and elephants—including one pachyderm wearing the signature string of pearls of the GOP frontrunner, Karen Handel. In response, she took to pointedly wearing the necklace at her events.

The Republicans believed they could afford to ignore Ossoff because of the gusher of spending from outside groups bent on keeping his poll numbers from soaring too high. The Congressional Leadership Fund, a high-powered super PAC with ties to Speaker Paul Ryan, spent more than $7 million on the GOP effort to thwart Ossoff and sent one hundred staffers across the district. What's more, few believed Ossoff had a shot at an outright victory at the April 18 special election. Georgia law requires victorious candidates to notch a majority of the vote in congressional elections, and conservatives were confident they could keep him under the 50 percent mark and then unite behind whichever Republican emerged to defeat Ossoff in a head-to-head runoff matchup nine weeks later.

Ossoff's campaign was also starting to generate more enthusiasm among Republicans who saw the vote as the first electoral performance review for Trump's new administration. The Hollywood types who helped foster glowing media coverage for Ossoff became evidence for conservatives that he was out of touch with "Georgia values." Republicans rarely missed a chance to link Ossoff to Pelosi, one of the most reviled political figures in the district. At one event after another, Ossoff sidestepped questions about whether he'd vote for Pelosi as House Speaker should Democrats flip the chamber in the 2018 midterms. All the while, leading Republican figures from Ryan to Trump weighed in repeatedly: the president called Ossoff a "super-liberal Democrat" and boastfully predicted that Republicans would easily win the runoff.

Ossoff continued to steer clear of controversial social issues. As the vote neared, he spent far more time on the campaign trail railing against spending excesses by both political parties and promising to work with Republicans on a health-care overhaul or immigration reforms than hammering GOP policies. Strategists framed the race as a proving ground for a key emerging constituency—not the disillusioned Rust Belt voters who had earned so much scrutiny a few months earlier for fleeing Hillary Clinton, but the denizens of upscale offices in well-educated bedroom communities who felt alienated by both presidential contenders.

"When part of your win strategy is to persuade Republicans, it doesn't help to insult them after they just voted for Trump," said Haworth. "And we thought a Democrat couldn't win this district without Republican votes."

But there was a catch: that sort of bland bipartisan message worked against a fundraising strategy that relied on the skyrocketing donations from liberals that Ossoff needed to flip the seat. The campaign found itself torn between the dueling narratives. "You want to persuade Republicans without pissing them off," Haworth said. "But the only way we got there was because of the resources we earned because he promised to 'Make Trump Furious.'"

———

That Ossoff was even this competitive in the district was remarkable. Mitt Romney had won it by an overwhelming margin in the 2012 presidential contest, and many Democrats hadn't even bothered to stand for legislative seats or local offices in much of the territory in November 2016. The way Republicans viewed it, the left was never expected to put up a fight in the Sixth District, let alone win.

The district's conservative roots stretched back four decades, when a little-known college professor named Newt Gingrich won the seat in 1978 on his third try to represent a territory that then extended from parts of south Atlanta to the Alabama line. It was a vast stretch that encompassed the home of Georgia House Speaker Tom Murphy, an ultra-powerful politician with a legendary temper who proudly called himself a "yellow dog Democrat"—someone so loyal to his party that he would rather vote for a canine than a Republican. He hated the fact that Gingrich represented him and so masterminded the redrawing of the district in 1991 to shift its borders closer to the suburbs, making Cobb County the new centerpiece of the territory, in hopes of forcing Gingrich out. Instead, Gingrich moved to Cobb and easily won reelection, eventually using the new district as a springboard for the 1994 "Republican Revolution" that flipped control of the chamber and made the Georgian speaker of the US House.

In 2011, when a Republican-controlled statehouse armed with fresh US census data redrew Georgia's political boundaries, conservatives etched them with a precision that would make Gingrich proud: they packed urban Democrats in fewer congressional districts around the state while bleaching other outlying areas to make them whiter and more conservative.

Even with that endeavor, Price's district became significantly more competitive, losing the expanse of exurban Cherokee County to pick up a swath of more moderate DeKalb County. Why would conservatives in the Georgia legislature make life more difficult for an incumbent Republican? While Governor Deal never publicly admitted it, the new maps could have been payback for what he considered an unforgivable affront. Price had been one of Deal's first supporters in the 2010 race for governor, but he later flipped to Handel as it looked like her chances in the election improved. Known for his typically civil disposition, Deal's response to the snub was about as cutting as it got. "As a native Georgian, I was brought up to believe that a person's word is his bond," he said then, swiping at both Price's disloyalty and his Michigan upbringing.

The new boundaries were a setback for Price—but not a debilitating one. "Our majorities were so bulletproof that we could afford to mess with each other," one of Deal's aides said. Even under the new, more challenging map, Price won landslide after landslide after landslide. A month before the 2008 election, Price even put his reelection campaign on hold to serve on jury duty for a homicide trial, never overtly worried about an upset defeat. State Republicans weren't shy about their intent for the district's design. "I'll be very blunt: These lines were not drawn to get Hank Johnson's protégé to be my representative. And you didn't hear that," said State Senator Fran Millar, a free-speaking Republican, at a local GOP breakfast a few days before the April special election. "They were not drawn for that purpose, OK? They were not drawn for that purpose."

Suddenly Millar and other confident Republicans faced an intense struggle just to keep Ossoff under 50 percent. New ad campaigns pummeled him as an inexperienced pretender. Local conservatives set about reminding their base to show up and vote for someone, anyone, who wasn't Ossoff.

"They are trying to embarrass us, but let's show them this district is Republican red," said Attorney General Chris Carr, who lived in the Dunwoody community on the eastern edge of the district. GOP chair John Padgett dismissed Ossoff and other Democrats as "little blue-headed folks" ripe for an electoral beating. Handel, the leading Republican in the polls, sought to project an aura of inevitability. "Look, we're a little fractured right now," she acknowledged to a group of supporters in suburban Sandy Springs. "When all the votes are counted, we will all come together on the morning of the nineteenth and get ready to kick some Ossoff."

On the April 2017 election night, hundreds of Ossoff backers crowded into the Crowne Plaza hotel at the edge of Atlanta's northern boundaries, where big-screen TVs flashed early returns as his supporters floated about the room with cautious optimism. Internal polls showed him hovering around the midforties, and Ossoff aides downplayed expectations by predicting that the fierce Republican counterattack worked just well enough.

They were right. With returns showing Ossoff hovering just below the 50 percent mark—he would finish with around 48.1 percent of the vote—he delivered a speech to supporters just before midnight, asserting that there would be a "victory for the ages" in the runoff vote in June. "So, bring it on," he said with bluster. "Because we are courageous. We are humble. And we know how to fight."

Privately, though, Ossoff's camp was deflated. The candidate and his aides knew his best shot was a knockout blow in the first round. Now they had to contend with the full might of a united GOP. And Handel seemed born for the fight.

———

One of the GOP's most notorious scrappers, Handel had experienced a series of ups and downs that had been a part of Georgia's political firmament for nearly two decades. Her second-place finish in the April vote meant that her rough-and-tumble personal narrative would once again be front and center. While most Georgians had never heard of Ossoff before he entered the race, Handel was known to just about everyone who followed politics in Georgia. That wasn't always a positive. Her critics and admirers alike called her stubborn, petty, and vindictive. She could be charming one moment, cold-blooded the next.

"If I'm ever going to be in a bar fight, I'd ask her to clear her schedule so she could be there," said Brian Robinson, a GOP operative who worked for and against Handel over the years. Her friends and allies described her as a substantive, solutions-oriented candidate who combined a knack for street fighting with a keen grasp of wonky policies. Handel had always viewed the backbiting from the critics as the price of admission of being a successful Republican woman in the chauvinistic world of Georgia politics. And she had the scars to prove it.

Handel had fled a troubled home in Maryland when she was seventeen, after her alcoholic mother pulled a gun on her, and she graduated from high school while working two part-time positions. She never finished college, holding positions at Hallmark and then with Marilyn Quayle, the wife of then vice president Dan Quayle. Her husband, Steve, brought the couple to Atlanta in 1993 when he landed a job in the tech industry. Her career took off with the move, and she was hired as CEO of the Greater North Fulton Chamber of Commerce and worked as a deputy chief of staff for Governor Sonny Perdue. By 2003, her political star rising, she won a special election to chair Fulton County's cantankerous commission before she was elected Georgia's secretary of state in 2006—becoming the first Republican to win that post in state history. Her capitol office featured an oversized portrait of a frontier woman holding off a group of frightened male British sympathizers who invaded her Georgia home during the Revolutionary War. It wasn't meant as a symbol of her own hard-earned political rise in Georgia, she'd tell visitors in a pitch-perfect deadpan. Not a single one believed her.

Handel attempted to use her experience as the secretary of state as a springboard to higher office, but her lofty ambitions were repeatedly thwarted. Her 2010 gubernatorial bid ended in a narrow runoff defeat to Deal and she finished in third place in the 2014 GOP primary for the open US Senate seat that David Perdue ultimately won. But even her time in political exile prepared her for a comeback. Handel's short-lived stint at the Susan G. Komen for the Cure foundation made her a darling to religious conservatives—and an enemy to liberals—when she resigned from a leadership role after it reversed its decision to cut ties with Planned Parenthood. Her book about the episode, *Planned Bullyhood*, scaled up her national profile and stoked old rivalries. A passage in the book that invoked ethics allegations against Deal led Robinson, then the governor's spokesman, to declare her criticisms "sadder than the end of *Old Yeller*."

Throughout the first phase of the 2017 congressional campaign, Handel lived by a motto: "Be focused, do my level best not to make an unforced error, and be authentic." But the nine-week sprint to a runoff brought new pressures. By now, the head-to-head matchup had become the most competitive race in the nation since Trump took office, and a Democratic victory threatened to be both an embarrassing setback for Republicans and a devastating rebuke to the president.

During the entire first round, Republicans had downplayed Ossoff's appeal, arguing that he benefited from a rare combination of epic fundraising, soaring enthusiasm, and distracted rivals. Now the GOP had no excuse if Ossoff pulled off a runoff upset. "Tomorrow, we start the campaign anew," Handel said the night of the first round of voting, as results showed she had landed the second spot in a runoff. "Beating Ossoff and holding this seat is something that rises above any one person."

She hardly had time to celebrate. The call for unity was just the first item on a lengthy to-do list. Handel's campaign hired dozens upon dozens of staffers in the span of two weeks, including a new campaign manager to replace an adviser forced to quit because of a family emergency. The media attention was stifling, with dozens of reporters from England to Japan trailing the candidates at every stop. The National Republican Congressional Committee sent a junior aide to monitor Handel to make sure she was meeting the party's demands; she sat quietly in stale rooms with Handel for hours as the candidate made fundraising calls.

"Everybody wanted a piece of the campaign," Handel said. "They wanted a piece of me. Everything went from a hundred miles an hour to two hundred miles an hour overnight."

Handel let the strain of the campaign show, especially with the press. One reporter for a national magazine, she said, duped her into an interview by pretending to honor her for an award. Handel stormed out in disgust when it was apparent she had been tricked. Days later, she bolted from a TV interview with the local CBS affiliate after a few acidic exchanges. Every word she uttered was under the microscope.

Just as Ossoff was wary of sounding too liberal, Handel walked a tightrope in accepting Trump's support. No longer the antiestablishment candidate of her earlier statewide runs, she now cast herself as a traditional conservative who generally backed the president's policies but had a muscular independent streak. As she welcomed Trump, Vice President Mike Pence, and House Speaker Paul Ryan to campaign events, she declared an "all hands on deck" approach to any Republican offering help.

Outside the public's view, the high-pressure campaign was taking its toll on her. About two weeks before the runoff vote, Handel felt as if she had reached a breaking point. Without telling her aides or her husband, Steve, Handel hopped in her car, turned off her phone, and drove down Interstate 75 with no particular destination in mind. She got as far as Macon, about eighty-five miles south of Atlanta, when she stopped for a cup of coffee at Starbucks, gave herself a pep talk, and hightailed it back home.

"I told myself: Get your shit together. People are counting on you. Get your ass back to the office," Handel later said. The entire ride back, she played Helen Reddy's feminist anthem "I Am Woman" on repeat. For her, the song wasn't about the women's movement—it was about being counted down and finding a way to bounce back stronger. She returned home and let Steve, worried sick that she hadn't picked up her phone, know that she was safe, sound, and ready for the homestretch.

Finding that strength from within was critical for Handel in the final days of the runoff. She pummeled Ossoff as a front for out-of-state liberals and tied him to the party's most liberal figures. But one of her strongest arguments revolved around a fateful decision Ossoff had made before he got in the race. Though he was born in the Sixth District, Ossoff and his soon-to-be wife, Alisha, decided to live near Emory University, where she was attending medical school, rather than move a few miles north into the boundaries of the district. For the entirety of the campaign, he was labeled by Handel and other Republicans as a carpetbagger who didn't understand local issues. And their internal polls showed the attack seemed to be popular with local conservatives.

As the runoff grew more intense, so did more serious threats. Six days before the vote, a gunman opened fire on a Republican congressional baseball team during a practice, striking US Congressman Steve Scalise and three other people. Handel's phone rang with a call from her aides to return to her office immediately. When she refused, one of her aides insisted that she listen to a profane rant about Handel that the gunman had posted on his social media page. She couldn't bring herself to comprehend it. "I didn't think I'd be on someone's radar screen like that."

A few days later, her husband, Steve, was sent a message from neighbors in a private chat group who had received envelopes containing suspicious white powder. He told them to call 911 immediately. One of the recipients told authorities that the envelope he was sent read: "Your neighbor Karen Handel is a dirty fascist," and to take a "whiff of the powder and join her in the hospital." Soon the neighborhood was cordoned off by police as helicopters buzzed overhead. Every dog within a five-mile radius seemed to be barking as Handel and her husband nervously waited in their basement until they got the all-clear sign.

By the eve of the June 20 runoff, the candidates and voters were exhausted. Both Ossoff and Handel were inescapable on the airwaves across metro Atlanta, and many who didn't even live in the district mistakenly thought they could vote in the election. At Ossoff's final election rally, hundreds piled into an indoor entertainment complex in Roswell, where blue-shirted volunteers gathered steps away from a high-octane go-cart track and a noisy arcade. Over the course of the campaign, Ossoff had matured as a candidate. He was now practiced in the art of revving up a crowd, injecting a dash of personality into his events, and connecting with his audience. And he shifted to a new closing message, one focused on shared values of respect, civility, and decency, which was meant to be an unsubtle dig at Trump without so much as mentioning his name. "Politics does not have to be about fear and hate and deception and division," he said to howls from a crowd hanging on his every word.

"We are courageous," he announced to an explosion of cheers. "We are kind," he said to more applause. "And we know how to fight."

As the runoff arrived, the unanswered questions that shadowed the campaign were to finally be resolved. Was Ossoff but a temporary mascot for angry Democrats seeking revenge on a president they never thought would win? Or was the campaign he built the vanguard of a lasting political realignment that could serve as a model for Democrats to compete in once solidly Republican districts?

Voters trudged to polling sites through soggy weather that drenched subdivisions and strip malls, while a record number of others had already cast their ballots during a three-week early voting period. A flurry of text messages rebounded among Handel's supporters with the encouraging news that the online election market PredictIt projected she would be victorious. Early returns that began to trickle in after polls closed at seven o'clock that night seemed to reinforce that idea among Ossoff backers camped out at his campaign party at the Westin Hotel.

With the crowd growing restless, Congressman John Lewis came onstage for a pep talk, promising to his supporters—and the more than fifty reporters on hand to cover the event—that the state "will never, ever be the same if Jon Ossoff is elected." But he also gave the attendees, some of whom were growing despondent as the returns came in, something to ponder if his former intern was defeated. Ossoff, he said, had inspired a remarkable wave of volunteers. "So, I say to you, more than ever before, we need a leader. We need someone like Jon Ossoff. We need his kindness. We need his leadership. For these are the times that try a man's soul." Before he left the stage, Lewis told the crowd that no matter what happened that night, they had made a "huge down payment on progress."

Trailing by four points around 10:15 p.m., Ossoff called Handel to concede the race. He was concise and gracious in congratulating his adversary. About ten minutes later, he hopped up to the stage beside Alisha, as hundreds of supporters raised smartphones to document the final moments of his candidacy. The campaign, Ossoff said somberly, "showed the world that in places where no one thought it was even possible to fight, we could fight."

Across a stretch of suburbia at Handel's victory party, the scene was pure jubilation. Cheers of "Trump, Trump, Trump!" replaced the upbeat Bob Marley tunes that were on blast as Handel thanked the president and other prominent Republicans for their support. Then she praised Ossoff for being courteous in his concession call. "My pledge is to be part of the solution to focus on governing, to put my experience to work to help solve the very serious issues we're facing in this country." Later, while Handel was on the phone with a reporter at the *Journal-Constitution*, she had to interrupt the conversation to answer a call that beeped in: it was Trump.

"He said he knew I was going to win," she recounted. "I'm glad I did."

To win such a high-profile contest, Handel had had to wage a nearly spotless campaign. She avoided any game-changing gaffes and stayed on message depicting Ossoff as a naive rookie funded by out-of-state interests. Her victory made her one of the nation's best-known members of Congress. Vindication was hers, if only for a short time. She had won the right to fill the eighteen or so months left on the remainder of Price's term, which hardly left her space to decompress before mounting a reelection campaign. "I was ready to get to work," she said later. "And I knew we'd have to do this all over again."

Handel allowed herself a victory lap or two. And she took a special delight in proving wrong all those who counted her out, not just Democrats but the Republicans who quietly cheered her political demise and the media she delighted in ribbing. Not long after she set up shop in Washington, her husband pinned an article to the door of her office in a corridor of the Longworth House Office Building. It was front-page coverage of a *Journal-Constitution* poll that showed Handel trailing Ossoff by seven points a few days before the race.

Ossoff's loss was a gut punch to Democrats. They had been determined to prove that even voters in Republican strongholds wouldn't stand by Trump or his allies. Instead, they wound up sending a different message to Washington, one that demonstrated how Republicans in newly competitive districts could still win by embracing the president's agenda. For his part, Ossoff found himself in the middle of a fresh round of soul-searching from party figures tired of what they saw as moral victories. Congressman Seth Moulton, a Massachusetts Democrat on the party's progressive flank, was among those who blasted Ossoff's approach. The Georgia race, he said, "better be a wake-up call for Democrats—business as usual isn't working."

The critics had plenty of post-election Wednesday morning quarterbacking advice. They argued that Ossoff should never have abandoned his early, more muscular attacks on Trump—and that he should have been more upfront in his support for progressive issues. Neera Tanden, then the head of the liberal Center for American Progress, tweeted a twist on Michelle Obama's catchphrase not long after the Georgia polls closed: "One important lesson is that when they go low, going high doesn't f**king work." Closer to home, DuBose Porter, the rural white liberal who led the Democratic Party of Georgia, blamed gerrymandering for an uneven playing field. "Make no mistake— there is a seismic shift on the horizon that will send shock waves from the US House to the courthouse."

It just wouldn't take place in that election.

Ossoff's advisers insisted, even years later, that his campaign strategy was the only course to win the district. They blamed, in part, the antipathy stirred up around Pelosi and her image as a California liberal. One of the most effective anti-Ossoff attack ads didn't include any barbed words: it featured hipsters and hippies against a backdrop of Pelosi's hometown of San Francisco that described Ossoff as "one of us," hitting a nerve among Georgia Republicans protective of the state's political independence and wary of "outsider" interference. But they took solace in the fact that they had managed to shift the district by a double-digit margin from the November election, and set the stage for more gains in the suburbs in future elections.

Ossoff hinted throughout his concession speech that he wouldn't stray far from the political spotlight—and no one doubted that. His campaign had broken staggering fundraising records and stayed on message to come within striking distance of a momentous upset. That funding had kept his image on the airwaves and enabled him to build a vast campaign apparatus, including six field offices scattered about the district, which targeted the "unlikely" voters Abrams said were essential to any successful Democratic campaign. And he mobilized a passionate legion of more than twelve thousand volunteers, many of whom would stay engaged in politics long after his defeat.

"This was not the outcome any of us were hoping for," he said in his speech, broadcast live on national TV. "But this is the beginning of something much bigger than us."

Chapter 3

STACEY VS. STACEY

Despite Jon Ossoff's defeat, many Georgia Democrats continued to believe that running to the middle could work in a statewide race. And the leadership of that movement fell to Stacey Evans, the straitlaced white state representative from the rural hinterlands whose challenge to Stacey Abrams made for a bruising battle over the direction of the party.

Like so many state Democratic candidates before her, Evans put the HOPE Scholarship at the center of her campaign. But for her, the fate of the program was more than just about preserving a popular policy. It was the cornerstone of her identity. Her mother, Kim, was a seventeen-year-old high school senior when she found out she was pregnant and refused veiled hints to have an abortion. Instead, she hocked her engagement ring to cover living expenses and found a job at a carpet mill in North Georgia. She was a hard worker and strong mother, but her choice in men was questionable, and her mistakes would come to shape Evans's life.

The two hopped from one run-down home to another throughout Stacey's childhood. The worst was a white trailer in the deeply conservative rural mountain town of Ringgold. Evans would film an ad outside its tidy wooden porch, calling it "one of the sixteen homes I grew up in that I'd rather not remember." When Evans was twelve, she called the police from the bedroom of that trailer to report that her mother was being abused by her stepfather. The authorities, she said, shrugged off her complaint and insisted that the man "wouldn't hurt a fly." They never bothered to stop by, she said. Her mother's second marriage ended in a 1994 divorce filing that included an alleged assault that left Kim with broken ribs and a dislocated jaw.

Even with all the troubles at home, Evans excelled as a student and filled her schedule with clubs, activities, and side jobs. But it was only when Governor Zell Miller, the godfather of the HOPE program, visited Ringgold High School's cafeteria to speak at a National Honor Society banquet that Evans grasped the life-changing potential of the program. The scholarship, granted to students who maintained a B average, was her paid ticket to the University of Georgia—and a new life.

In the northeast Georgia town of Athens, where a cast-iron arch separates a lively downtown from an idyllic college campus, Evans realized she was a rare first-generation UGA student—and committed to make herself feel less like a "unicorn." She plunged into the local chapter of Young Democrats, then law school, then moved to the suburbs and joined a legal practice where she developed a specialty in complex business litigation. When a Georgia House seat came open in her suburban Cobb County district in 2010, she successfully ran on a promise to defend the beloved scholarship. At the time, the program was in great peril, teetering during the Great Recession as lottery sales plummeted and demand for awards soared. In Evans's first year in office, Republican governor Nathan Deal brokered an agreement with Abrams, the newly elected House minority leader, to slash the program's burgeoning price tag.

Under the new system, the HOPE Scholarship was still available to students who maintained a B average, but it paid less toward tuition. To be eligible for a full free ride to college, most students would have to earn a 3.7 GPA in high school and register a 1200 on the combined math and verbal SAT test. The new program was called the Zell Miller Scholarship, and only about 10 percent of HOPE recipients were eligible for the awards. Abrams pitched the deal as a last-ditch effort to keep the program afloat and stave off more onerous cuts. "If we do nothing, HOPE goes away," she wrote in a 2011 email to fellow Democratic legislators.

Evans was then a minor player at the capitol. But she viewed Abrams's pact as a shocking betrayal. She had struggled with the SAT in high school and knew that other students in rural or poor areas could also suffer under the new rules. When it came up for a vote, the freshman lawmaker turned heads by stepping to the center of the House floor and delivering a passionate speech against the overhaul, what she called the "most devastating day" of her political career. Her aide and confidant, Seth Clark, put it this way: "The governor of Georgia in the 1990s saved Stacey's life. And the governor of Georgia, twenty years later, cut the program that saved her life with the help of Democratic lawmakers."

After a few more terms in office, Evans had built enough of a statewide profile—and a fat bank account, thanks to her share of a nine-figure Medicare legal fraud judgment—that she was often being mentioned in the same breath as Abrams as a gubernatorial candidate. But it wasn't until a bipartisan HOPE-related measure she sponsored was pulled from the voting calendar in 2017 that she decided to run for governor. A Republican lawmaker told her that evening, "We're not writing any more future campaign commercials for you," effectively clinching her next step. If she was going to be sidelined as a legislator, Evans thought, she might as well aim higher.

A few days later, in March 2017, Evans leaked word that she was planning to run, causing a sensation in the state capitol that also deepened the chill between her and Abrams. Earlier in the year, Abrams had urged the fellow Democrat to wait until mid-April after the legislative session to announce her decision, to avoid splitting the caucus into camps at a time she felt the party needed to be united to challenge Republican-backed measures. The moment Democratic lawmakers learned of Evans's plans in a *Journal-Constitution* report, they started picking sides.

Evans also beat Abrams to the punch in May with her formal announcement for governor, pledging to make technical colleges tuition-free and to put "hope"—the scholarship and the concept—at the center of her campaign. Though Abrams hadn't yet officially entered the race, her role in the HOPE compromise was clearly on Evans's mind as she laid out her plans from her high-rise office in midtown Atlanta. "It gutted the program that was responsible for everything that's good in my life," she said upon announcing her bid. "The Stacey Evans born today doesn't have the same opportunity that the Stacey born in 1978 had."

To Evans there was no other "pro–HOPE Scholarship voice" in the running. And she felt she could reach Black voters—by far the largest bloc of the Democratic electorate—by demonstrating how the cuts disproportionately affected Black students. She leveraged the support of several African American state legislators, who publicly criticized Abrams for a "follow the leader" approach that left little room for questions or discussion. As Abrams was not yet the nationally known political star that she would become, Evans regarded her as a formidable—but beatable—rival.

―――――

Abrams couldn't let her opponent get too much of a head start—and she couldn't lose her advantage with Black women voters. When she launched her campaign in June 2017, it was at a carefully calibrated event aimed at the backbone of the Democratic electorate. Rather than holding a boisterous rally around the corner from her townhouse in Atlanta's quirky Kirkwood neighborhood, where her base of support ran so deep that sightings of her spawned text chains about her latest whereabouts, Abrams trekked to the southwestern Georgia city of Albany, the heart of a predominantly Black rural area whose residents often felt overlooked.

At a steamy park dotted with boardwalks that crisscrossed pungent cypress swampland, Abrams threw a barbecue that attracted about one hundred supporters—and the usual swarms of flies that hover south of Georgia's Gnat Line—to celebrate her kickoff. She told the audience she had picked Albany because it reminded her of her upbringing in rural Mississippi, where her parents raised her and her five siblings with three priorities in mind: go to church, go to school, and take care of one another. "I'm from a town that is about one hundred and fifty miles from the capital," she said. "Sometimes that one hundred and fifty miles is a lifetime away. I'm from a place that can also be forgotten because it's not where we think politics and business should happen."

From the very start, she embraced the historic nature of her bid to become the first Black woman elected governor in the nation—and along with it a willingness to accept a brand of identity politics often shunned in Georgia. If voters marginalized by generations of systemic racism and structural inequality wanted to reclaim their place in American politics, Abrams argued, they had to recognize and embrace their role in society whether they wanted to or not.

It was a strategy that worried some fellow Democrats, who feared her tilt to the party's left would make her more vulnerable against a Republican. Former governor Roy Barnes, now a thriving lawyer with a mammoth office in the suburb of Marietta, endorsed Evans just a few weeks after Abrams launched her campaign. "Georgians aren't laying up worrying about what Washington, DC, wants or some national party divide," Barnes said. "They're worried about how they're going to pay for their kids' and grandkids' college."

Abrams might as well have yawned in reaction. There were two main paths Democrats could pursue, she said on the same morning she learned Barnes had endorsed her rival: one was to attempt to re-create a coalition that hadn't existed since the late 1990s; the other was to harness an emerging alliance that was racially, economically, and geographically diverse.

In short, she was saying that the politics that defined Barnes's heyday in the 1990s no longer existed. For Seth Clark, a write-up of Abrams's response in the *Journal-Constitution* that morning crystallized to him that a different sort of Democratic fight was at hand. The headline: STACEY ABRAMS ON ROY BARNES' SNUB: IT'S NOT 1998.

"I read that," Clark recalled years later, "and literally responded, 'Shit.'"

The Evans campaign heard another alarm bell a few weeks later during the Netroots Nation conference in downtown Atlanta. The annual gathering of leading progressive candidates and activists had become a symbol of the left's frustration with the national party, and in past years both Bill Clinton and Joe Biden had been heckled and interrupted onstage by demonstrators upset that they didn't do more to meet their demands. Just a year earlier, activists even shouted down then presidential candidate Bernie Sanders, an icon to many in the party's left, while he was trying to deliver a speech. "If you don't want me to be here, that's OK," Sanders grumbled.

The August 2017 conference was the first time Netroots Nation had been held in the South, a strategic decision by organizers to bring attention to the growing clout of progressives in Georgia and across the region. Abrams kicked off the event with a story she had rarely shared before about a small "strike team" she and several other Democratic legislators had formed in 2008 to ruffle Republican feathers. Their mission had been to help cultivate back-bench legislators, to prepare challenging questions to test GOP lawmakers, and to generally complicate the passage of the measures they opposed. There was one more pointed step she took, adding to the delight of a crowd that admired her insurgent streak: she didn't clue in the party's leadership on their efforts. "Not because they might object, but because we didn't need or want their permission," she explained. "Because resistance demands independence and flexibility."

Two days later, it was Evans's turn to appear at Netroots Nation. She had seen Abrams's name on the agenda, and when her campaign reminded the conference's organizers that she, too, was running, she was awarded a prime Saturday morning slot. Evans knew she was not likely to find a friendly audience after a heads-up from organizers that pro-Abrams demonstrators were planning a disruption. But she wanted this speech to be her most significant campaign address yet. Over weeks of work, Evans and her advisers framed her remarks as a way to bridge the gap between the old brand of Democratic politics in the South and an ascendant new coalition, making the argument that the same forces that had made the civil rights movement possible could now be harnessed again to elect someone like Evans to Georgia's top office. It was, she thought, to be a piece of memorable oratory—"one for the shelves."

The crowd never got to hear it. Almost as soon as Evans began to speak to hundreds of attendees in the spacious ballroom, roughly two dozen Black protesters sprang into action. They fanned out in front of the stage, holding brightly colored posters that read NO ONE CAN WIN WITHOUT US. Out in the audience, other demonstrators handed out flyers that likened Evans to Betsy DeVos, Trump's education secretary. Taken aback by the commotion, Evans attempted to speak over the din, but the protesters suffocated her words with chants of "Support Black women!"

Evans pleaded with the room for quiet: "Do we want to drown out each other, or do we want to drown out Trump? I want to drown out Trump! Who is with me?" The chants only grew louder, and Evans stood in awkward silence before trying, and failing, to start her own rallying cry of "Hope, hope, hope!" throughout the room. As the chaos around her grew, Evans weighed her two best options: walk off the stage or continue to give her speech. *I'm not going to back down*, she told herself. She plowed forward, however much the cacophony drowned out her words.

Laura Register had a front-row seat to the spectacle. A Democratic activist from the rural hamlet of Cairo, a South Georgia town best known as the birthplace of Jackie Robinson, Register was in Atlanta for the weekend to run errands and decided to bring her twenty-five-year-old son to the convention. Seated at a table with other Abrams fans—she had brought pro-Abrams T-shirts with her—Register was curious to hear Evans out. When the protesters surrounded her table to shout Evans down, Register briefly, and unsuccessfully, tried to stop them before a few turned on her. She left, shaken, and called Evans not long after to pledge her support. "It was traumatizing to me," she recalled, "and I was so impressed with how Evans handled it."

To many in the crowd, the signs and chants made the protest seem more like a pro-Abrams demonstration. Several organizers later said they were voicing their concern with Evans's support for a Republican-led effort to give the state new authority over struggling schools. No matter the root cause, it was a resounding embarrassment to Evans during one of the first showcase events of the race for governor. A flood of "Stacey vs. Stacey" headlines followed, each invoking the hecklers that disrupted Evans's speech.

Some Abrams supporters reveled in the demonstration that had so thoroughly humiliated her opponent, though they insisted they had no role in it. Abrams likewise denied any involvement but refused to "condemn peaceful protest" organized by marginalized communities; she told aides that, had it happened to her, she would have handed the group the microphone and let them have their say. In fact, at one of her appearances in rural Georgia, an angry man had burst into the room spouting racist comments to try to silence her. Abrams stopped in the middle of her remarks and calmly asked him to "go ahead and say what you need to say." He was so surprised, he rambled for a bit and then left. "Protest is disruptive. It's uncomfortable," Abrams said at a forum a few weeks later. "But for communities who have been silenced, it's sometimes the only way they can be heard."

———

The Netroots event cast a harsh spotlight on the depth of the rift between the two women. At its heart the tension wasn't over a broad split on policy. Both advocated for stronger gun control and decriminalizing marijuana—two issues that previous Democratic candidates had seen as deal breakers in a statewide race. They both called for the expansion of Medicaid, supported making technical college tuition-free, and promised to champion measures to help bring economic equity for poor and disenfranchised Georgians.

Instead, the contest turned into the very proxy war over the fate of the party in the South that many strategists predicted it would be. Abrams staked her claim to office on a plan to maximize African American turnout and aggressively register voters that she pledged would yield an ascendant coalition of LGBTQ communities, union forces, voters of color, and liberal whites that would transform the state. Abrams regarded Evans's strategy as a redux of the same approach that had failed Jason Carter and Roy Barnes earlier in the decade. "We've ignored so many Democrats that we've forgotten if we can just get them to vote, we can win," Abrams said. Often she'd add that moderates would come, too. Evans, meanwhile, told every crowd she could that simply energizing reliably Democratic voters was not enough. "We have to go to the suburbs and get moderate Republicans and independents to vote for us," she said.

As Abrams marshaled resources for a May 2018 primary, her campaign boasted of its immense "structural advantage" and early work building out a field operation, a step that candidates traditionally launched closer to the general election. The early focus caught some voters unaware. At one stop by campaign canvassers in late 2017 near Abrams's east Atlanta home, a woman shrugged when asked whether she would vote in the upcoming primary. "It will be for one of the Staceys," she deadpanned.

To build the network, Abrams leaned on the web of organizational events she had put together since she was elected to House leadership eight years earlier: town halls and educational hearings that flew under the media's radar but helped create a sense of party unity in smaller communities. Once, Abrams started her day helping to show a prized cow at a state fair, then rushed to a gas station where she changed into an evening gown to end the day at a fancy county gala.

Her strategy started to pay off by early 2018 with rising poll numbers and media attention. The pressure on Evans only compounded as national and state leaders begged her to drop out. As the primary neared, Abrams had wiped out Evans's early fundraising advantage and was benefiting from a relentless flow of national media coverage. Doug Jones's stunning flip of an Alabama US Senate seat in December 2017, a win fueled by Black women unified behind his candidacy, was another reminder of Evans's vulnerabilities. Jason Carter, the party's nominee for governor in 2014, sat down with Evans on Martin Luther King Jr. Day to discuss her options as qualifying day loomed. It was only January 2018 and there was still time, he suggested, to drop out and announce for another position before the deadline. Maybe run for lieutenant governor or another statewide office? Carter was a fan of the HBO series *Game of Thrones*, whose heroine, Daenerys Targaryen, sought to harness fire-breathing dragons to conquer a shattered kingdom. In this scenario, he told Evans, Abrams wielded the ultimate weapon: "She has dragons."

But Evans wasn't prepared to quit. Her internal polling showed that, with four months to go, most Democratic primary voters were still undecided, and the pressure from the party's elite only made her want to stay put. Besides, she wasn't a *Game of Thrones* fan, and the dragons reference was lost on her. "Why would I get out?" she asked Carter.

Abrams and her aides weren't worried a bit. In the days before the election, they built momentum with a string of big-name endorsements that culminated with an announcement of support from Hillary Clinton on the eve of the primary. "In the beginning we were running against a flailing campaign that was trying to build the plane while it was taking off," Clark, the Evans adviser, would later say. "By the end of the campaign, we were running against a national, well-oiled machine."

Abrams's advisers accurately predicted a blowout. But even some of her closest supporters were stunned by the shellacking she dealt Evans. It was a 53-point victory that wasn't just a satisfying thumping of her rival. It proved Abrams could build a robust network that mobilized young and non-white Georgians in a way that had eluded generations of candidates. Not only did Abrams win, but her strategy prevailed as well.

Now it was time to see if it could work in a general election.

Chapter 4

"GAME OVER"

As Georgia Democrats moved toward the left, Republicans raced in the opposite direction. A field of five GOP candidates formed to succeed Nathan Deal, a mild-mannered two-term governor who had staked his legislative agenda on something that few Republicans before him would have bragged about: a sweeping overhaul of criminal justice laws that made it easier for low-level criminals to seek counseling and other treatments rather than prison time.

His would-be successors had little intention to follow in his footsteps. One, State Senator Michael Williams, traveled the state in a dilapidated gray-painted "deportation bus" adorned with a message to "fill this bus with illegals"; fittingly, it would break down just before his last-place finish and, months later, he apologized for having run at all. Another candidate, State Senator Hunter Hill, filmed an ad of himself firing a round into a far-off target like a sharpshooter, then boasting that "I won't give an inch on our Second Amendment."

But the real focus was on the Republican front-runner, Lieutenant Governor Casey Cagle, a lean fitness fanatic who had never lost an election—and who had been preparing to run for governor for a decade. Cagle had a rapturous ambition that baffled even his closest friends, marked by a constant: he hated losing more than he liked winning. Growing up in a single-wide trailer in a rural North Georgia community where his family had lived for seven generations, he channeled that energy into sports, with dreams of playing professional football. But when a leg injury forced him out of the game, he moved back to his hometown, ran a tuxedo business, and founded a small bank before delving into local politics.

In 1994, at the age of twenty-eight, he waged a long-shot bid for a Georgia Senate seat against a popular Democratic incumbent and won, becoming the youngest member of the chamber. He used that platform in 2006 to launch another tough campaign, this time for the state's number two job. In that race, Cagle faced a Republican primary against Ralph Reed, the former Christian Coalition executive director once described by *Time* magazine as "the Right Hand of God." Many viewed Reed's campaign as the first rung in a ladder that would inevitably lead to the governor's office and beyond, a path to power that would be sustained by his squeaky-clean image and the might of Georgia's evangelical voters. But Cagle pulled off a stunning upset, tarnishing his opponent by relentlessly tying him to a growing scandal involving Reed's connection to disgraced lobbyist Jack Abramoff. His easy general election victory a few months later made him the first Republican lieutenant governor in Georgia's history.

In his new position, Cagle made little secret of his ambitions to run for governor—and filed paperwork in 2008 to do so. His surprise announcement a year later to abandon the race, citing urgent surgery to remove bone spurs in his spine and repair a degenerative disc, upended the contest. Though his dreams were delayed, Cagle's political ambitions had not yet been shelved. He was easily reelected as lieutenant governor in 2010 and 2014, and he used the powerful position to consolidate his power and collect IOUs. His critics branded him "Campaign Casey," hoping to damage him in an era of outsider politics, but Cagle leaned into his experience as a major player who had a hand in many of Georgia's biggest success stories.

He amassed an early fundraising advantage, took a lead in the first polls of the race, and collected a long list of endorsements. Still, front-runner status was a curse as much as it was a blessing in Georgia Republican politics, where being labeled part of the establishment had doomed many before him. At every turn, his rivals amplified his ties to the party's insider wing. Cagle came to see the contest as a laborious footrace. "Everyone behind you has a rope tied to you, and they're pulling you back," he said later. "Every tug is disruptive, and it is painful."

Then came what Cagle called the "tweet heard round the world." Slipping in the polls, he vowed to "kill" a jet-fuel tax exemption for the state's dominant private employer, Delta Air Lines, in a naked political maneuver to prove his conservative credentials and separate him from his rivals. The tax break was originally adopted in the mid-2000s during a time when the airline was struggling, but lawmakers nixed it in 2015. With support from Governor Deal, who said it was crucial to keep Atlanta competitive with other airline hubs, Delta's executives were confident they could restore the incentive in 2018. That was until the company, responding to a mass shooting at a Florida high school, ended a group discount for National Rifle Association members. In swift fashion, Cagle orchestrated the defeat of the incentive as payback for its rebuke of the gun rights group, costing the airline a tax break that would have saved Delta an estimated $40 million a year.

In a sense, the gamble paid off: the NRA awarded Cagle its coveted endorsement, and he now had ammunition to respond to far-right conservatives who whispered that he was secretly a moderate at heart. But his allies worried the Delta snub would undermine the pro-business brand that Cagle and other Georgia Republicans had happily cultivated for years and further an unnecessary divide between the state and one of its prized Fortune 500 giants. It also conflicted with the chummy corporate record that Cagle had honed over the years and alienated his longtime allies—starting with Delta chief executive Ed Bastian, once a close Cagle friend. "He understood my position, and I understood his," Cagle said years later, still sounding torn over the decision. "But we had to agree to disagree."

In the end, the dramatic move didn't give Cagle the insurmountable advantage he hoped it would. Polls showed him stuck in the low forties, far ahead of his next closest rival but still short of the majority-vote mark he needed to avoid the crapshoot of a runoff. Cagle underestimated the magnetism of the "outsider" candidate in Georgia's first full election cycle in the Trump era. And his chief Republican rival embraced that label in a way the lieutenant governor never could.

On paper, Brian Kemp was about as much of an insider as the lieutenant governor. He had two straight statewide victories as Georgia's secretary of state under his belt and an office across the rotunda from Cagle at the state capitol. But Kemp was quicker to embrace Trump's nativist brand of politics. It started with his April Fool's Day entry into the race in 2017, when Kemp promised a "Georgia first" strategy to crack down on illegal immigration and took swipes at "fake news" and the political status quo. "It helped that, unlike many, I never ever became a full-time politician," he told a suburban crowd gathered on the weekend morning he announced his entry, never mind the fact that he drew a six-figure salary as a statewide officeholder.

Kemp always considered himself distant from Georgia's ruling political class. He grew up working on a farm outside Athens, the liberal college town in northeast Georgia surrounded by a ring of tidy suburbs full of left-leaning professors and university bureaucrats, and then circled by another orbit of rural hamlets and farmland where conservatives reigned. Business and farming are rooted deeper in his family tree than politics, though Kemp's ancestors include a veteran of the Revolutionary War who helped establish his beloved University of Georgia. A fourth-generation graduate of UGA, friends joke that "Brine," as they call him, would probably bleed the school's signature red and black if he was stuck with a needle. His college roommate and best friend might as well have been campus royalty: Daniel Dooley, the son of legendary football coach Vince Dooley.

After graduating, Kemp dug ditches and poured concrete as he built a business in the construction industry, rambling around northeast Georgia in a sturdy pickup truck. His up-and-down fortunes occasionally had him on the brink of financial disaster. Often, he'd say, the construction workers framing houses and putting up drywall at his sites had more cash in their wallets than he did. At campaign events, he'd share memories of stressful Friday nights when he hardly made payroll, let alone repaid vendors. He recalled asking himself more than a few times, "Are we going to make it through?"

As his business grew, so did his frustrations with local commissioners who oversaw construction and zoning regulations. Rather than run for county office, he decided to aim for a bigger target. Doug Haines, the Democrat who represented Athens in the state Senate, was up for another term in 2002, and Kemp felt a political realignment was in the air.

Despite warnings to wait another cycle or two, when the climate might be better for Republicans, Kemp raised cash from longtime friends of his family and local business owners. He juggled political paperwork while sitting on a backhoe, in jeans and his heavy work boots, and trekked to just about every event he could, whether it be a gathering of seniors on Tuesdays at the local Hardee's or a library club on the edge of downtown. He doled out his cell phone number like candy, taking calls at all hours.

Kemp's energetic approach wasn't the only hint of his campaigns to come. Haines at first wanted to ignore his Republican challenger, but Kemp went negative early, slamming him over his votes in the legislature. Haines didn't effectively strike back, a regret that would haunt him years later. Kemp won the seat by just 489 votes out of more than 34,000 cast, joining a wave of Republicans elected to Georgia office in a watershed GOP year that was topped by Sonny Perdue's victory in the race for governor.

Four years later, a restless Kemp lost a tough Republican primary for agricultural commissioner and returned to Athens full time to expand his business. But the failed bid gave him a taste of statewide campaigning he couldn't shake, and after Secretary of State Karen Handel stepped down in 2009 to run for governor, Kemp joined a heated Republican primary to fill her seat. Most Republicans had figured Governor Perdue would tap a placeholder to the job who wouldn't run for a full term, paving the way for a wide-open election contest. But Perdue upended that assumption by appointing Kemp, giving him a gift of incumbency that gave him a leg up in the race for the Republican nomination and, months later, an easy general election win.

In his two terms there, Kemp focused on bringing the secretary of state's office into the digital age, building a new technological infrastructure that enabled Georgians to register to vote and renew business licenses online. He also intensified a battle over voting rights that would come to define his tenure: he backed the state's requirement that voters show a photo ID to vote, canceled more than 1.4 million inactive voters, and put tens of thousands of voter registration applications on "pending" status because of discrepancies in registration information. It was a taste of what was to come: while Kemp presented himself as a defender of the integrity of the vote, his critics vilified him as an unabashed agent of voter suppression.

As he climbed the ladder, he honed a personal touch that helped distinguish him from other politicians. Kemp rose early each morning at his place in Atlanta, plodding to a computer in a ratty T-shirt, Crocs, and gym shorts as he scanned local newspapers, tapping out condolences to families he spotted in the obituary section of the *Journal-Constitution* and congratulatory notes to folks honored in the Walton County paper. He made efforts to attend the funeral of every law enforcement officer killed in the line of duty, often appearing in the back pews of a church with no notice, and kept his calendar full of fish fries in Tifton and barbecues in LaGrange. Everywhere he went, even the most remote towns off dusty backroads, he seemed to have a friend willing to throw him a fundraiser—and then put him up for the night in a spare bedroom or on an air mattress.

The first week of March 2017, Kemp gathered with his advisers for a two-day meeting in Athens to assess whether he had a legitimate shot at winning the race for governor. His team laid out his biographical advantages in the unsettled race: he was a small business owner seen as an outsider. He had solid statewide name recognition. And poll numbers suggested that Cagle wasn't the unstoppable juggernaut that some insiders assumed he was. Kemp didn't need much convincing; he was already leaning toward a run.

Just as important, he had secured the blessing of his wife, Marty, and their three teenage daughters after warning them of the trials that were sure to come. He told them the media and his political opponents were sure to seize on his vulnerabilities, from sour business dealings to his political connections, and they needed to be prepared for a venomous race. Because once he announced, he reminded them, there was no turning back. After taking stock of the risks and rewards, his family agreed to the idea. And by the end of the two-day meeting, Kemp was determined to be the first major Republican candidate in the race.

Those early weeks were a slog. His campaign team wasn't gelling, fundraising came in fits and starts, and even some of his close friends were slow to return his calls. Each night around nine-thirty, he phoned his political adviser, Ryan Mahoney, to take account of the day's stumbles. Another well-known Republican was about to endorse Cagle. Another survey had Kemp trailing the field. Going into the race, Kemp knew he wouldn't be the favorite, but he also didn't expect it to be so hard to gain traction.

Kemp had every reason to call at night and berate Mahoney for his lagging poll numbers. But by late 2017, he turned the calls into pep talks, insisting that his campaign would be fine so long as they just worked harder, spoke to more people, scheduled more events. Mahoney would patiently listen as Kemp talked himself out of his despair. "You know, we just got to keep chopping," Kemp said during one particularly down moment. "Keep chopping" became the unofficial motto of the campaign. "And if the numbers were tight—which they always were—he'd say we needed to get back on the road," Mahoney recalled.

That wasn't all he needed. Kemp's campaign funneled much of its campaign bankroll—about $500,000—to a tough-talking TV ad in March 2018 that fell flat. Instead of impressing Republicans with a pledge to stand behind Trump's call to "secure the border and end sanctuary cities," Kemp's internal poll numbers actually dropped. About six weeks before the primary, he fired his media firm, his pollster, and his general consultant. A revamped team of campaign aides took the reins, and one of the first orders of business was to redefine Kemp's image to conservatives.

The television ad that rolled out in late April 2018 opened with Kemp sitting leisurely in a living room surrounded by enough guns to stock an armory—assault rifles are propped against the back wall, handguns displayed casually to his right, another long gun on the coffee table in front of him. The camera panned back to show Kemp cavalierly cleaning a shotgun as a nervous-looking visitor fidgeted to his left.

"This is Jake, a young man interested in one of my daughters," Kemp said, fingering the weapon. "Jake asked why I was running for governor."

Eyeing the gun, Jake ticked through Kemp's platform of capping government spending, slashing regulations, and improving the state's business reputation. Then Kemp quizzed him on what it would take to date his daughter: "Respect," Jake said.

"And?" Kemp asked.

"A healthy appreciation for the Second Amendment," Jake replied, pausing for a half beat. "Sir."

Kemp snapped the shotgun into place, aiming it toward the young man. "We're going to get along just fine."

When the ad was filmed, Kemp didn't have high expectations. He thought another TV spot featuring a promise to toughen penalties on illegal immigration was far more controversial. Some of his advisers worried the pro-gun messaging went too far, though the candidate urged them not to fret. "You can get by with a lot more than you used to," he told them, a reference to Trump's say-anything political approach.

The reaction to the "Jake" ad was swift and overwhelming. Kemp felt as if his campaign had managed to bottle lightning—and used it to electrify the party's base. The thirty-second spot both raised his profile around the state and made it more difficult for his Republican rivals to capture attention. Smiling through an appearance on Fox News, Kemp gleefully took stock in another side effect of the ad: "it's driving the liberal media crazy."

Indeed, it triggered an outpouring of outrage that generated him plenty of free media attention. Stacey Abrams joined in with an appearance on *Late Night with Seth Meyers*. "What I would say, as someone who learned how to shoot when I was growing up in Mississippi, the first thing you learn is, 'You don't do that,'" she said, pointing at a freeze-frame of Kemp training the gun toward Jake. "Firearm 101 is, 'Don't point at people.' Because Firearm 102 is, 'You go to prison.'"

The newfound conservative supporters drawn to his campaign, in part thanks to the $1 million it put behind the ad, helped power Kemp to a second-place finish in the May 2018 primary. Though he trailed far behind Cagle's 39 percent showing, Kemp kept the lieutenant governor well under the majority vote needed for an outright win. And the nine-week runoff campaign offered a chance to reset the race, one that Kemp felt he could turn in his favor despite his fundraising deficit. From the outset, Kemp had pledged to be the more honest, transparent, and conservative candidate—the guy Georgians could trust to do the right thing "when no one was looking."

As it turned out, the tagline couldn't have been more fitting.

Shortly after the first round of voting, Cagle received a call from one of his vanquished rivals to discuss endorsing him in the race against Kemp. A muscular former Stanford swimmer and ex–Navy SEAL with a shock of blond hair, Clay Tippins was a first-time candidate who had never really proven himself as a top contender. He mixed military machoism and policy nerdery, spending most of his time talking about issues—like an expansion of medical marijuana or improving third-grade reading levels—that were an odd fit with the red meat of gun rights expansions, abortion limits, and anti–illegal immigration screeds that lit up the rest of the GOP field.

With a fourth-place finish behind him, Tippins asked Cagle for a private meeting at the lieutenant governor's campaign office in northeast Atlanta, just beyond the tangle of highway interchanges known as Spaghetti Junction. But before he stepped into Cagle's sparse conference room, Tippins surreptitiously turned on his iPhone's recorder and tucked it into his front jacket pocket. The entire ninety-minute meeting between the two men was secretly recorded, and there was no aide in the room to interrupt, parry, or deflect Tippins's questions—or nudge Cagle to bite his tongue. By the time it was over, an ecstatic Tippins left convinced that what Cagle had just told him could end his campaign. A few days later he called television reporter Richard Belcher and me with a promise of the seismic scoop.

During their sit-down, the lieutenant governor told Tippins that he had helped pass tax credit legislation that was bad "a thousand different ways" because he hoped it would deprive another opponent in the gubernatorial primary of a gusher of financial support. "Is it bad public policy? Between you and me, it is," Cagle acknowledged to Tippins. He laid bare the underbelly of Georgia backroom deals, telling Tippins, "It ain't about public policy. It's about fucking politics."

The details of the tape went public in June 2018, just a few weeks before the runoff. It led the nightly newscast on WSB, Atlanta's most-watched broadcast station, and dominated the website and the front page of the *Journal-Constitution*. For Kemp, it was as if the clouds parted to grant him a game-changing gift. He had long tried to paint Cagle as a phony conservative;

now he could use his own words against him. Furious, the lieutenant governor vented to his aides at the betrayal, knowing he had reinforced exactly what Kemp and his allies had been saying about him: he was an untrustworthy insider who put his own personal interests ahead of conservative principles. It was exacting a toll on the campaign trail, too; Cagle's poll numbers soon took a beating.

Tippins was unapologetic. He explained earnestly that he disclosed the private conversation because he wanted to provide Georgians a window into Cagle's true character. "I hope voters are furious," he said. Some blasted Tippins as a self-absorbed cretin. Others, he said, told him they couldn't believe Cagle was "that damn stupid."

Cagle was livid—at both Tippins and himself. He had let his guard down and trusted a former adversary he hardly knew in what he thought would be a confidential conversation. That lapse in judgment now jeopardized his entire decade-in-the-making campaign. Years later, he still seethed at Tippins's betrayal: "It was the most unethical move that you could make. It took a pretty sick individual to do that. And as a man, he doesn't want to meet me in a dark alley."

Inside Cagle's campaign there was a conflict about how to respond to the treachery. Encouraged by his three adult sons, Cagle desperately wanted to paint Tippins as a weak-kneed liberal in disguise and a saboteur. His strategists convinced Cagle to take a different route. He told voters he had nothing to hide, and that he had simply answered Tippins's questions "openly and honestly." Voters, Cagle argued, should look to his decades-long record in public office—and not a snippet of secretly recorded conversation—for all they needed to know about his character. Going into the last two weeks of the race, Cagle felt there was still a chance he could steady his campaign and win the nomination.

All the while, the lieutenant governor's attacks turned more frantic, slamming Kemp over his troubled investment in a failed Kentucky seed-crushing plant and questionable campaign contributions. At one campaign event, Cagle said "there's no question" Abrams would win in November if Kemp was the GOP nominee. About a week before the runoff, Cagle received Governor Deal's endorsement, though it came in the most understated way: during a question-and-answer session at an unrelated economic development announcement. Cagle's campaign cast it as a turning point, hopeful he'd regained momentum in the final days of the race. "We had a winning strategy," Cagle later would say. "And it would have been a very winning strategy had it not been for outside influence."

———

Six days before the July 2018 runoff, Kemp held a press conference at his campaign headquarters near the gallery of Steve Penley, whose "patriotic art" and portraits of statewide officials hung in the capitol offices of Georgia's GOP elite. He was feeling optimistic. Polls showed him with a roughly six-point advantage over Cagle and, in a telling sign, lobbyists were rushing to write checks to his campaign. Kemp's goal for the final stretch before the runoff vote was to avoid any unforced errors and keep the pressure on his opponent.

The event he held was humdrum enough as Tippins joined Kemp at a podium to formally offer his blessing. Few reporters even bothered to show up, since the endorsement was seen as a given. The real action, however, was about to take place off-camera. As Kemp began to speak, Ryan Mahoney peered down at his phone as it blew up with a barrage of texts and calls. The longtime Kemp aide scrolled through the messages and saw a name he couldn't ignore: Brian Jack, the Georgia-bred political director for President Trump.

Mahoney had spent the last two months phoning and texting Jack with updates on the runoff. Now Jack was the one calling him, urging him to check Twitter. Immediately. "You're going to like it. Call me back."

Right there, on his feed, was a tweet from Trump giving Kemp his "full and total endorsement." Mahoney brimmed with anxious energy, catching the candidate's eye as he hurried through his speech. Other aides seemed like they were bouncing off the walls with excitement. Kemp powered through his remarks while he wondered to himself, What the hell are they doing? When the event was over, he hustled over to check his staff to see why they seemed about to explode. Mahoney showed him the tweet.

"For real?" Kemp asked, worried that maybe it was some trick. Told it was legit, he couldn't hide a growing grin. "Wow. We need to get into the office now." Soon, his staff had lined up for him a blitz of TV interviews, donor calls, and social media posts to amplify the president's endorsement. By the following day, he was up twenty-one points in the campaign's latest tracking poll. By the end of the week, that had grown to a thirty-point edge.

"It was game over," Mahoney said.

Cagle also hadn't had any clue that the endorsement would happen. Trump's advisers had assured the lieutenant governor that the president wasn't going to pick sides, and Cagle had taken that promise to the bank. At the hilly campus of University of North Georgia, Cagle was mingling with a crowd of veterans after finishing up his stump speech when an ashen-faced aide pulled him aside and bluntly told him, "Trump just endorsed Kemp." So certain that Trump would stay out of the race, Cagle thought it was a joke. "Yeah, right," he chuckled.

When he was shown the president's tweet, Cagle knew immediately that it was his campaign's death sentence. "From that point forward, it was virtually impossible. I'm a fighter and I went around the state and tried to make our case," Cagle said later. "But we saw it internally. I didn't think there was ever going to be a bottom to the cliff that we were falling off."

He was right. But that didn't mean Cagle would go down quietly. He tied himself to Deal, who had done little publicly for Cagle even after he endorsed him. He downplayed the president's snub, telling a sparse crowd of supporters at a tiny railroad town that Georgians don't "need someone else deciding who our governor's going to be." He and his allies escalated the negative attacks on Kemp, including a final, scathing round of ads that accused his rival of abetting sex offenders. And his advisers put forth long-shot scenarios where Cagle could prevail if voter turnout took a drastic dive.

Behind the scenes, though, the pulse of his campaign was hardly beating. As he prepared for a last hoorah—an election-eve fly-around tour—the ever-confident Cagle sounded a strange wistful note. He didn't lament the secret recording or the Trump endorsement. Instead, he vented about the negativity that had dominated the nine-week runoff, much of it from his campaign.

Just why Trump weighed into the race remained a mystery for a few weeks. "I did that for Sonny Perdue," he told a *Daily Caller* reporter in September 2018. The former Georgia governor was one of the president's first cabinet appointments, and would wind up serving faithfully as his agriculture secretary his entire term in office. Just as Perdue had elevated Kemp to an open secretary of state seat nearly eight years earlier, his influence again cleared the way for his ally's rise, this time convincing the president to guarantee him the GOP nomination.

After the meeting with Sonny Perdue, Trump dictated the tweet to endorse Kemp directly to Dan Scavino, his social media director. "I have to really respect the candidate, I have to like the candidate," Trump told *The Daily Caller* later, "otherwise I'm just not going to get involved."

Sonny Perdue had his own reasons for wading into the contest: he admired Kemp's work ethic and thought he was the only Republican who could beat Abrams. Just as important, Perdue was no fan of Cagle, who was backed by kingpins known derisively as the "Gainesville mafia" based in the foothills of North Georgia who often competed for influence with Perdue's formidable inner circle. And he and his cousin, Senator David Perdue, worried Cagle didn't have what it took to beat Abrams in November.

The former governor also had a long, long memory: in early 2003, Cagle gave an impassioned speech denouncing a watered-down tax proposal backed by Perdue that would help fill a budget shortfall, leaving the new Republican governor feeling betrayed by his own party. From that point forward, tensions between the two only seemed to grow.

It helped, too, that Trump told aides he genuinely enjoyed Kemp's TV ads, a portfolio that by now had grown from the gun-toting "Jake" spot to include thirty-second commercials featuring chain saws, explosions, and a pledge that he would "round up criminal illegals" himself in his dusty old truck.

Sonny Perdue didn't stand alone in Kemp's cheering corner. Years later, Trump would also say David Perdue encouraged him to take Kemp's side in the race, though the senator downplayed his role to friends. Long after he was bypassed, Cagle still laid the blame squarely at someone else's feet: Nick Ayers, the savvy strategist and thirtysomething cousin of the Perdues who had risen to become Vice President Mike Pence's top aide and an adviser to Trump. Cagle believed that Ayers had orchestrated the endorsement as part of a plot to reap the dividends of another close ally in power.

"The master plan of Nick Ayers came into fruition," Cagle claimed. Ayers dismissed the suggestion. Certainly, he had vouched for Kemp, Ayers said, but he was only part of a chorus of voices who had advised Trump to back the secretary of state over Cagle. He also rejected claims that he benefited financially from campaign spending after Trump made his selection.

With Trump in his corner, Kemp was just getting started. Outside his campaign party in his hometown of Athens, an aide parked his two-tone gray Ford F-350 pickup and loaded a chain saw into the bed of the heavy-duty vehicle. Well-wishers stopped to take selfies in front of both, as if they were mascots for his candidacy, anxious for a picture of the heroes of his TV commercials.

Inside the hotel, a full-on celebration raged as the race was called about ninety minutes after the polls closed. Kemp won all but two of Georgia's 159 counties, trouncing Cagle even in his own backyard. Just as Stacey Abrams had humbled her primary opponent to unite Democrats, there was no question that the Republican Party was unified behind Kemp. As the balloons dropped and supporters crammed into a ballroom that suddenly seemed too small, Kemp and his family took the stage in a corner of the room, his three teenage daughters each wiping tears from their eyes.

Kemp couldn't resist a callout to a famed University of Georgia tradition usually reserved for a football win.

"I was gonna ask y'all how it's going, Athens? Are we ready to ring the victory bell tonight?"

Despite the celebratory mood—and the party would soon spill over to the bars of downtown Athens for his younger supporters—Kemp was focused, already, on the next round.

"Here's the question: Do you really want a governor who is bought and paid for by liberal billionaires and out-of-state socialists? Do you want a governor that's gonna answer to Nancy Pelosi and Hillary Clinton? Do you want a governor who thinks government is the answer to every challenge we face?"

"NOOOO!" the supporters blared in unison so loudly that some of the older folks covered their ears.

"Of course you don't. This is the state of Georgia. We are a red state."

Chapter 5

IS THIS THE MOMENT?

Stacey Abrams and Brian Kemp had never squared off against each other on the ballot, but they were like two boxers who had been circling each other for years before getting a chance at a championship bout.

Even as Abrams battled Stacey Evans in the first days of the race, she also pummeled Kemp at campaign stops as someone who treated "voter suppression as a way of life," earning reliable explosions of applause from those who saw the secretary of state as an emerging supervillain. And Kemp often looked past Casey Cagle to raise campaign cash and curry favor with conservatives by branding Abrams as the ringleader of a band of "left-wing agitators" that would stop at nothing to tilt the playing field.

Their animosity had deep roots, starting with a fundamental disagreement over voting rights laws. Kemp amplified the threat of illegal voter fraud to justify requirements such as ID laws, even though his office acknowledged there were no instances of systemic irregularities at the ballot box. And Abrams accused Kemp and other Republicans of supporting legislation that would disenfranchise poor, Black, and elderly voters.

One of the most serious clashes came in 2014, just as an Abrams-backed organization called the New Georgia Project was scaling up its ambitious plans to bring eight hundred thousand minority voters onto the rolls within a decade. The organization swamped local elections offices with about eighty-five thousand voter registration forms as Democrats Jason Carter and Michelle Nunn ran for governor and US Senate. But a few months before the vote, Kemp's office launched an investigation of the group, saying that he suspected forged signatures and incomplete forms. He filed a far-ranging subpoena demanding troves of internal records, an exhaustive request that Abrams's camp saw as state-sanctioned harassment.

In the end, Kemp's investigation of the New Georgia Project fizzled—though it did uncover problems with independent contractors who handled the registration forms. But the investigation exacted a different toll on Abrams's inner circle. Lauren Groh-Wargo, her top deputy, was shuttling back and forth from Ohio at the time to be with her pregnant partner, and lived in fear of trumped-up charges from Kemp's office. "Republicans were gunning for us. And we never knew when the other shoe would drop," she said.

Groh-Wargo and other Democrats saw the investigation as just the latest attempt by Kemp to misuse his state office to harass left-leaning voting rights activists. They traced the pattern back to 2010, when Kemp's office launched an investigation into activists in Quitman, a speck of a town near the Florida border. Upset at local education policy, Black residents organized an absentee ballot drive that helped African American candidates flip control of the Brooks County school board, a political turnabout that drew the suspicions of local Republicans. Investigators questioned more than four hundred people, and a dozen Black organizers were charged with more than one hundred election law violations. They became icons among Georgia's voting rights advocates, earning the moniker "Quitman 10+2," named for the ten initially arrested and the two later charged. None was convicted of electoral wrongdoing, and the case collapsed a few years later.

In 2012, after the Atlanta-based Asian American Legal Advocacy Center asked Kemp's office for help in ensuring that many of its newly registered clients were on the voter rolls, organizers found themselves the focus of an investigation questioning whether it had violated state registration laws. Helen Ho, the group's director, handed over reams of documents to investigators and hired a lawyer. The case was closed with no action taken in 2015.

Outraged by what they regarded as another sham probe, Abrams and other supporters of the New Georgia Project gathered in September 2014 before a specially called meeting of elections officials to present thirteen plastic bins filled with copies of registration applications they said hadn't been processed. The Reverend Raphael Warnock, the pastor of Atlanta's landmark Ebenezer Baptist Church who was growing his reputation as a voting rights advocate, turned heads with his indictment of Kemp: "You don't have to wear a hood or be a member of the Ku Klux Klan to be engaged in voter suppression."

———

While Kemp was still scrapping with Cagle over the nine-week runoff, Abrams was free to gear up for the general election by wooing independent voters, recruiting more volunteers, and scaling up her fundraising. After Kemp won the GOP nomination, he set about focusing the full force of his campaign on the Democrat. He was well aware what a tough opponent she would be—though his advisers weren't shy about reminding him.

At Kemp's first meeting after his July 2018 victory, Kemp and his consultants acknowledged that the very same maneuvering that had won him the runoff—the blustery ads, the promise to be a "politically incorrect conservative," and of course the Trump endorsement—would make it that much harder to win a general election with more independent voters. Pollster Glen Bolger soberly laid out his findings to the campaign hands: Abrams had an early eight-point advantage. "You're in a bad spot, and it only gets harder from here."

The campaign's polling showed that voters held Abrams in high regard and, worse for Kemp's November hopes, found many voters considered her to be a moderate. She was in prime position to embrace a dual narrative that could sink the Republican's chances: that she was a bold African American female running as an "unapologetic progressive" in a southern state, and that she was also a pragmatic mainstream candidate.

The first step to dent her public image came down to highlighting Abrams's stances on illegal immigration and gun control, and reminding voters of the tax bill of roughly $54,000 she still hadn't paid off. (At the time, she said she was chipping away at the debt incrementally after deferring her 2015 and 2016 taxes to help pay her parents' medical bills.) The provocative conservative ads that earned so much attention earlier in the summer were replaced with peppy TV spots that introduced Kemp's wife and daughters. Others that focused on education, health care, and public safety soon followed. Campaign researchers hunted for anything to damage Abrams's popularity among more moderate voters. "We might not be able to convince people on our own," Kemp adviser Ryan Mahoney told other staffers at the meeting, "but what we can do is take her own words and use them against her."

Republicans soon put that strategy into action. At a stop in Jonesboro, Abrams said the promised "blue wave" of Democratic voters was comprised of "those who are documented and undocumented," giving Kemp an opening to mischaracterize her remarks as pushing for "illegals to vote" for her. When Abrams told a group of students in Statesboro that "people shouldn't have to go into agriculture or hospitality in order to make a living in Georgia," it quickly became a Republican attack claiming that she didn't understand the plight of farmers despite her immediate efforts to rephrase her remarks.

So did Abrams's appearance on *Meet the Press* shortly before the election, when she mispronounced the name of one of Georgia's 159 counties, calling it Glasgow instead of Glascock. Kemp made the most of each of these gaffes in rural parts of the state. Not long after greeting a crowd of one hundred gathered outside a livestock barn off Pig Jig Boulevard in the South Georgia hamlet of Vienna, Kemp silently surveyed the crowd, letting a pregnant pause build tension. "We have been all over the state," he said, before waiting another beat. "And we have yet to find Glasgow County."

Abrams was not afraid to embrace other potential vulnerabilities. At a town hall in Dalton in North Georgia, a woman asked her why she supported removing the hallowed carving of Confederate leaders on the massive state-owned Stone Mountain monument—a symbol of the Old South that sparked revulsion in some Georgians and reverence in others. Abrams answered by referring to recent acts of violence sparked by white supremacy, along with a traumatizing childhood visit to the home of Jefferson Davis, the Confederate leader who fought to keep her ancestors in slavery.

"Will I ever say that Stone Mountain is a good thing? That celebrating the terrorism that was visited upon not only African Americans but Jews in the state of Georgia is a good thing? Absolutely not," she told the audience. "And if I was willing to say that, then you should not want me to be the next governor of Georgia."

Kemp had his own weaknesses. Having refused to step down as secretary of state, he was attacked for all the voting issues that marred the final months of the campaign—some that were his direct responsibility, others that were caused by local county elections boards charged with administering the voting. He and his aides had decided early on that, unlike Karen Handel and other predecessors who ran for higher office, he wouldn't resign his post. They reasoned that he'd still be blamed for any problems at the ballot box regardless, and that quitting would be viewed as a sign of weakness. Besides, he wanted to stay in the job he was elected to carry out, and to keep a title that gave him political cachet and a high-profile platform.

Some of Kemp's allies wound up regretting that decision. The revelation late in the campaign that his office's strict exact-match policy stalled more than 47,000 voter registrations because of discrepancies in government records became a rallying cry for Democrats. So, too, did the fact that on his watch more than 1.4 million voter registrations were canceled, including a batch of 534,000 Georgians removed from the rolls on a night in July 2017. It was the largest single removal of voters in US history.

As a three-week early voting period arrived, troves of absentee ballots were rejected because signatures didn't line up or key information was missing. Early voting sites were plagued by long lines and equipment malfunctions; some simply didn't have enough power cords to keep machines running. Poorly trained poll workers contributed to long lines in other places.

In the closing stretch, Abrams and her allies seized on these voting obstacles to paint the Republican as both a bumbling bureaucrat and a malicious suppressor who abused his position to help his election chances. Kemp leveled increasingly critical attacks on Abrams's voting rights stances and warned that the spate of lawsuits Democrats and their allies filed seeking last-minute changes would only gum up the system.

Some of these controversial state voting policies implemented under Kemp's oversight escaped federal scrutiny because of a 2013 US Supreme Court ruling that Abrams and other Democrats saw as a fundamental threat to the right to vote. The *Shelby County v. Holder* decision tossed out the nearly fifty-year-old requirement that Georgia and other jurisdictions with histories of voting discrimination pre-clear with the Justice Department any changes to electoral measures. The court ruled that the justification for increased federal oversight in the South, which was introduced in the 1960s, was now outdated, leaving it to Congress to update. Gridlock and a lack of political will prevented any progress on that front in Washington.

Confounding local decisions only raised the temperature. Elections officials in west Georgia's Randolph County proposed in August to close all but two of its nine polling places, prodded by a consultant suggested by Kemp's office who promised the changes would save money. Though the polling sites remained open after a national outcry, a *Journal-Constitution* analysis found that hundreds of other voting locations had been closed since 2012, often in sparsely populated rural areas where access to the polls was more difficult.

On the first day of the early voting period in October, a group of forty Black seniors who lived in a county-run center in rural east Georgia were told to get off a bus headed to a polling site. Local officials called the Black Voters Matter busing event a "political activity" not permitted on government property. LaTosha Brown, the group's cofounder, saw something more nefarious: an intimidation tactic targeting older Black residents who had endured the injustices of the civil rights era.

Even Abrams's own trip to vote early went awry. She arrived to cast her ballot at South DeKalb Mall about two weeks before the election and found a lengthy line stretching beyond kiosks along the building's busy corridors. When she reached the early voting site, trailed by a dozen or so journalists, a poll worker out of earshot of the press quietly told her she couldn't vote because she had already requested an absentee ballot.

Abrams, who was privately mortified, spoke with the voting location's manager and the matter was quickly resolved—even the journalists on-site were unaware what had taken place. She made a snap decision not to make an issue of it, worried about bringing negative attention to staffers who so clearly wanted to ensure she could vote. Still, it revealed to Abrams a deeper flaw in the voting system. As an attorney and legislator deeply involved in elections law, even she had to struggle to ensure she could cast her ballot. What about the countless other Georgians, she wondered, who could never have so quickly fixed their problem?

———

The tension was front and center in late October 2018 at the studios of Georgia Public Broadcasting in midtown Atlanta, where Abrams and Kemp met for what would be their first televised debate. With national press on hand, both seemed unusually anxious as they took their places behind the podiums adorned with the logo of the Atlanta Press Club. Within minutes of the opening bell, though, they both settled into a familiar, if brutal, back-and-forth. Abrams accused Kemp of systemically hampering minority voters from casting a ballot, charging that they'd been "purged, they've been suppressed, and they've been scared." "Voter suppression isn't only about blocking the vote," she continued. "It is also about creating an atmosphere of fear, making people worry that their votes won't count." Kemp countered by calling her claims a "farce" and arguing that the blowback was engineered by Democrats trying to score political points.

Their bludgeoning of each other came to an abrupt halt when a fire alarm sounded just as Libertarian candidate Ted Metz was answering a question. The television feed was briefly pulled off-line as organizers investigated the cause, but the broadcast resumed less than five minutes later.

Metz, who had lost an ear in a battle with cancer, had no shot at winning the race and hadn't been seriously campaigning. He had even posted an online fundraising appeal asking frustrated voters to "put your money where your mouth is" and help pay his medical bills if they wanted him to drop out of the race, before quickly deleting it and declaring it to be a joke. But with polls showing Abrams and Kemp running neck and neck, Metz knew he could play the role of spoiler by forcing the race into a runoff with even a tiny fraction of the ballots. At the debate, he aimed for the fringe vote, centering his answers around the wonders of industrial hemp, which he believed would replace the need for oil and curb global warming. "Everything can be done with hemp!" he declared.

Abrams and Kemp, meanwhile, touched on just a few of the issues that had marked their gaping policy divide. Abrams wanted to repeal abortion restrictions, ban assault rifles, expand Medicaid, and block a controversial "religious liberty" policy opposed by gay rights groups and corporate boosters. Kemp pledged to adopt the nation's most stringent abortion limits, expand where people could carry weapons, block Medicaid expansion, and sign the "religious liberty" measure into law.

But their split went far beyond those attention-grabbing policies, extending to fiscal agenda, criminal justice, and a basic core philosophy. Kemp's Trumpian "Georgia First" strategy took hard-line stances on illegal immigration and violent offenders to pile up votes in rural strongholds and outer exurbs where Republicans reigned. Though he no longer boasted of being a "politically incorrect conservative," Kemp steadfastly stuck by Trump, calculating as the campaign dragged on that energizing conservatives in Republican strongholds far outweighed the risks of driving away independents in the suburbs.

So long overlooked in political races, Georgia was now the constant focus of nationwide attention as both campaigns raced to motivate their political bases rather than try to persuade the few remaining undecided voters. John Legend took selfies with students clad in pro-Abrams gear in a stuffy Georgia Tech classroom, while the rapper Yung Joc marched beside the Democrat in a get-out-the-vote rally along Atlanta's historic Edgewood Avenue. Abrams's star-studded endorsers included actor Will Ferrell, hip-hop magnate Ludacris, and talk show icon Oprah Winfrey, who stumped for the Democrat the Thursday before the election. "No one even asked me to come here," Winfrey told a packed crowd in suburban Marietta. The very same day, Vice President Mike Pence headlined a string of visits strategically planned to drum up attention outside Atlanta. At his stop in the manufacturing hub of Dalton, Pence nodded to the pro-Abrams celebrities. "I'd like to remind Stacey and Oprah and Will Ferrell, I'm kind of a big deal, too," Pence told a crowd of thousands. "And I've got a message for all of Stacey Abrams's liberal Hollywood friends: this ain't Hollywood."

The next day, the Friday before the election, a line wrapped around a gym on the campus of Morehouse College near downtown Atlanta to hear former president Barack Obama, who had recently returned to the campaign trail.

His voice growing hoarse, Obama drew a comparison between Kemp and national Republicans who pushed to "take away the right to vote" from Georgians. "How can you actively try to prevent citizens from your state from exercising their most basic right?" he asked incredulously. When his speech wound down, Abrams's exhausted aides saw on Twitter that early voting lines still stretched for hours at nearby voting sites. A group went to a polling location in the South DeKalb Mall, the same shopping center where Abrams had had trouble casting her ballot, where they found people waiting in the dark, some cradling children in their arms, as they stood in slow-moving lines to cast their ballots. As the staffers handed out warm pizza and bottles of water, one Abrams deputy broke down in tears.

＝＝

The Sunday before the election was to mark another crucial moment: a long-scheduled second and final televised debate on Atlanta's highest-rated TV station, WSB, a last chance for the two candidates to meet face-to-face. But those plans were upstaged, and the debate scrapped, to the outrage of Abrams and her supporters. Compelled by the pleas of Senator David Perdue, President Trump agreed to stage a final rally for Kemp at an airport near the midsized city of Macon just two days before the 2018 vote. "This is a base turnout election," Kemp said of Trump's visit. "And he's definitely someone the base is excited about." Trump was determined to turn the race into a referendum on his presidency, a bet that Republicans were willing to make given the president's five-point victory two years earlier.

But even as his supporters lined up outside the airfield Sunday morning to get a better vantage of the president, a stunning accusation from Kemp's office the morning of the visit overshadowed the rally. Just before 8:00 a.m., Kemp's office announced an investigation into what it called "possible cybercrimes" targeting voter registration systems by the Democratic Party of Georgia. Not long after, a Kemp staffer said the FBI was seeking information on a Democratic volunteer. His campaign in prompt fashion then alleged that Democrats were maliciously trying to manipulate the election—a "fourth-quarter Hail Mary pass that was intercepted in the end zone." It was an astonishing charge that first confused, and then enraged, Democrats in the final hours of the campaign. "Team Kemp is losing their minds," the state party said on Twitter.

A state investigation later revealed that the online activity that Kemp's office described as a "failed hacking attempt" was in fact just a series of scans by the US Department of Homeland Security, which a Kemp deputy had approved three months earlier. And the volunteer was simply passing along an email she had received a day earlier from a Georgia voter who described how he had discovered a vulnerability in the state's website that could allow anyone to download confidential voter information. He wanted to make sure authorities could patch up the lapse. After receiving an email summarizing his findings, the volunteer sent it to a supervisor, who then asked two Georgia Tech cybersecurity experts to have a look. Soon the warnings about the vulnerability were forwarded to law enforcement officials and journalists, and Kemp's office seemed to rush news of an investigation before a media outlet could beat them to the punch with an embarrassing story about the potential lapse.

The Georgia Bureau of Investigation would later conclude there was no "evidence of damage" to the secretary of state's office's network and computers, and that there was no proof of theft or loss of data. At the time, though, the charges brought even more chaos to the campaign's overheated final stretch. As Republicans prepared for a jubilant rally, Democrats rushed to purchase hundreds of new laptops for staffers in case their computers were confiscated by authorities probing Kemp's claims. Cameras were hastily set up in offices to monitor in case investigators burst through the doors to rifle through key documents. Down in Macon, Trump made little mention of the cheating allegations, but revved up thousands of supporters by claiming a Democratic victory would hurl a "wrecking ball" into the nation's economy.

On Election Day, Kemp returned to his hometown of Athens, this time rejecting a cramped hotel ballroom for his campaign party in favor of an expansive downtown convention center. As returns rolled in, he clung to a slim but steady lead, and his aides grew more optimistic throughout the night as turnout soared in rural areas. "Make no mistake: the math is on our side," Kemp told his supporters after the polls closed.

Former governor Sonny Perdue, who bounded between Kemp's war room and the rollicking party at the convention hall, said it was "mathematically impossible" for Abrams to win. As he wandered by a back exit, he leaned over to me: "Call this thing. It's over."

But it wasn't. In Atlanta, Abrams told voters to prepare for a "do-over" with a runoff against Kemp, and her campaign pointed to tens of thousands of absentee ballots still to be counted in vote-rich metro Atlanta counties. As each trove of ballots was tallied, she drew a tad closer to forcing Kemp into overtime. "Votes remain to be counted. Voices waiting to be heard," the Abrams campaign said in a dispatch at 4:00 a.m. on Wednesday, which made the case for why she wasn't about to concede.

As the week wore on, and the ballot counting continued, so did the standoff. Kemp hustled to the state capitol with Governor Nathan Deal for a press conference where he claimed a "clear and convincing victory" and introduced key staffers for his incoming administration. He also resigned as secretary of state, drawing howls from Democrats who had pleaded with him for months to step down from the post. "We won the race," Kemp announced, "and we're moving on."

Abrams remained insistent that there were enough outstanding votes to make up the difference and put together a litigation team. Over the next few days, Kemp's lead dwindled as more absentee and provisional ballots trickled in. But as larger left-leaning counties completed their vote tallies, Abrams and her allies were running short of options. She and her aides kept insisting there were thousands of outstanding ballots remaining to be counted, but they never materialized. Her campaign also filed lawsuits to force local officials to accept some previously rejected ballots and won an order that required elections officials to review thousands of additional provisional ballots. But it left Kemp's lead virtually unchanged.

As state officials prepared to certify the vote, Abrams briefly considered a long-shot legal challenge to contest the outcome in court. But state law establishes a high standard for a successful court challenge, and her aides knew it would be difficult to meet. Other Democrats outside Abrams's circle worried that drawing out the election further would distract attention from two other statewide runoffs for down-ticket seats that the party hoped to win.

On Friday, November 16—about ten days after the election—Abrams summoned reporters to her campaign headquarters for an announcement. As many expected she would, she formally ended her bid for office, acknowledging that Kemp would be the next governor and that she wouldn't contest the outcome in court. But this was no typical concession speech. In fact, Abrams didn't concede at all. Her scathing remarks would be lionized by liberals who saw Kemp as a voter-suppressing menace and condemned by conservatives anxious to paint her as a sore loser.

"To watch an elected official who claims to represent the people in this state baldly pin his hopes for election on the suppression of the people's democratic right to vote has been truly appalling," Abrams said. "So, let's be clear. This is not a speech of concession. Because concession means to acknowledge an action is right, true, or proper. As a woman of conscience and faith, I cannot concede that. But my assessment is the law currently allows no further viable remedy."

The campaign over, a relieved Kemp focused on the transition to office. He had collected about 1.97 million votes—the highest a gubernatorial candidate in Georgia has ever achieved, part of a surge in turnout that was closer to the level of a presidential election than a typical midterm. But it was the closest margin of victory in the race for Georgia's top political office in decades. Abrams came within about 55,000 votes of topping Kemp, and just as conservative parts of Georgia grew redder, the liberal bastions of the state were painted with an even darker shade of blue. Hillary Clinton won DeKalb County—the state's most important Democratic stronghold—with 79 percent in 2016. Abrams's support there in 2018 topped an astonishing 83 percent.

Both candidates had become national figures. The dramatic finish cemented their archrivalry in the minds of millions: Kemp as a cheating supervillain who abused the authority of his office to many on the left, and Abrams as a spiteful sore loser who undermined faith in the election system to many on the right.

Abrams took months to get over the loss and the swirl of emotions that ranged from anger to grief that followed. Her near victory amounted to the death knell of the Barnes doctrine in Georgia politics—that Democrats had to draw in rural whites to build a winning coalition. Now she and her supporters were at a crossroads. "It was a moment to decide what we wanted to do to respond: Do we agonize or do we organize?" said Jonae Wartel, who was Abrams's early-voting director. The answer, to Abrams's team, was obvious.

Abrams came to the same conclusion. The day before she ended her bid, Abrams's attorney and adviser Allegra Lawrence-Hardy pointed to a *Time* magazine cover story on the Democrat at the Atlanta campaign headquarters. Plans were already underway to launch Fair Fight, a group that Abrams unveiled during her non-concession speech that would battle to expand voting rights in the courts, in the statehouse, at the grassroots level, and in the media. In the coming days, the new organization would file a far-reaching lawsuit against the state "for the gross mismanagement of this election and to protect future elections from unconstitutional actions."

Maybe the silver lining of the campaign was this, Lawrence-Hardy told a visitor—a new movement to address the inequalities in the nation's electoral system. "We all thought that her victory was going to be the moment. But maybe this is the moment."

Chapter 6

THE MIRACLE

The biggest Georgia Democratic winner of the midterm election wasn't Stacey Abrams or another high-profile statewide candidate. It was Lucy McBath, a gun control advocate and Black daughter of civil rights activists, who channeled her grief over her son Jordan's shooting death to flip the same suburban Atlanta district that Jon Ossoff had narrowly lost a year earlier.

Her story of tragedy and then triumph led to the remarkable rise of a new power in Georgia politics.

"I always believe that God moves us," she said. "Whatever door he opens, I go through. How else do you go from being a flight attendant to a US representative?"

It was an ascent fueled by her love for her son, Jordan. Her miracle baby. She and her then husband, Ron Davis, had stopped trying to have children after McBath suffered two miscarriages and gave birth to a stillborn son in 1993. But a year later, as she was preparing to run the Peachtree Road Race through the heart of Atlanta on the Fourth of July, she learned she was pregnant.

For most of the next nine months, she remained at home under strict doctor's orders, fearful of taking any action that could upset the baby boy growing inside her. She spent her days cross-stitching, reading, talking on the phone—anything to pass the time. Afflicted with uterine fibroids, she almost died during labor and suffered through a case of septicemia for days after.

Jordan was healthy and perfect, blessed with a magnetic personality that drew a constant pack of friends to their middle-class home in Atlanta's suburbs. When the boy seemed to outpace his classwork, McBath homeschooled him for five years to make sure his math and writing skills were up to snuff. Like his mother, he wasn't afraid to question authority. When McBath sent him to Florida in 2011 to live with his father while she fought a recurrence of breast cancer, Jordan dug in his heels, not wanting to leave his friends behind at Marietta High School, where he was a popular sophomore. After arriving in Jacksonville, he felt like just another face in the crowd, struggling with bullies and schoolwork.

But Jordan pulled off a course correction with help from his demanding parents. By his junior year in Florida, he excelled in classes, got sparkling reviews from teachers, started dating a girl, and made a pack of new friends. His mom said he seemed "soul happy." When McBath last spoke to her son, on Thanksgiving Day 2012, they were at peace with each other.

The following day, Jordan and his friends were on their way to the mall to seek out Black Friday discounts when they stopped at a gas station. With music blaring in their car—the hip-hop anthem "Beef"—they crossed paths with Michael Dunn, a white man who pulled up in a black Jetta.

Dunn later testified that he cracked the window to politely ask the teens to turn the music down, though his girlfriend told authorities that he muttered something disparaging about "that thug music" just before she stepped out to buy snacks. Jordan's friend Tevin Thompson, sitting in the front seat of the red Dodge Durango, turned the volume down. But Jordan didn't want to reward the man's rude behavior so easily. He leaned over from the back seat and cranked the music back up, adding some choice words for Dunn. "You aren't going to talk to me like that," Dunn told the teens. Then he pulled a Taurus pistol from his glove compartment.

Just as Dunn took aim, one of Jordan's friends grabbed the wheel of the Durango and stepped on the gas. As their car peeled out of the gas station and toward a nearby shopping center, Dunn unloaded ten bullets at the careening vehicle. Three sliced through Jordan's door, striking him in the groin, heart, and lungs. His friends tried to stop the bleeding, and horrified witnesses dialed 911. An ambulance rushed the teen to the hospital, but it was too late. The seventeen-year-old died shortly after arriving. Dunn fled the scene, headed to a hotel with his girlfriend, and ordered in pizza. The next morning, Dunn was arrested after someone spotted his license plate, which had been plastered all over the media.

━━━

The trial attracted attention from a nation already shaken by the shooting death of another Black teen from Florida. In early 2012, the killing of Trayvon Martin led to a cultural reckoning. Now the shooting death of Davis by an armed white man who also showed no outward remorse resurfaced the swirl of outrage and angst.

In court testimony, Dunn claimed that he felt threatened by Jordan, and said he thought the teen had a shotgun or a stick. Dunn's girlfriend countered that she never saw anything of the sort. One of Dunn's lawyers claimed the pair thought they had encountered gang members. After a mistrial, in 2014 Dunn was found guilty of first-degree murder and locked up for life without parole. Upon sentencing, the judge declared the case "demonstrates our justice system does work."

As McBath grieved her son's death, the trauma galvanized her to do something—anything—to prevent another tragedy. She was no stranger to activism. McBath's father had led the Illinois chapter of the NAACP and owned an influential Black newspaper; she'd spent nights and weekends delivering it door to door with her mom. One summer she interned for the Washington office of the NAACP, and a few years later she clerked in the Virginia Senate for Douglas Wilder, the groundbreaking politician who would be elected the first Black governor in the South since Reconstruction. Later, she helped sate her wanderlust by becoming a Delta flight attendant in the 1980s and then moved to Atlanta, where the airline is headquartered.

"But still, in the back of my mind," she said later, "I always felt like maybe there was something else I was supposed to be doing."

After Jordan's shooting death, she and his father decided to tell their son's story without holding back. They were convinced that most Americans didn't understand the depths of gun culture and the power of the NRA, particularly in southern states where people like Dunn could use expansive stand-your-ground laws to try to justify shootings. One of her first forays into the public debate was a 2013 gun control event at the King Center near downtown Atlanta. Wearing a T-shirt with Jordan's face, she arrived carrying a copy of the *Rolling Stone* magazine that featured a story about her son's death. Arriving promptly at the start of the rally, she talked to anyone who would listen.

Not long after, Moms Demand Action asked if she would agree to become a national spokesperson for its growing efforts to limit gun laws. She was hesitant at first, but leaders of the organization, which formed after twenty-six people were killed at Sandy Hook Elementary School in Connecticut in 2012, assured her that she could shape the position however she wanted. McBath recognized that cultural movements in America worked best when they happened from the ground up, had a unifying message, and promoted inclusivity.

She decided her time would best be spent with different audiences in mind. She made her case for new firearms restrictions to the predominantly white suburban moms who seemed ready to embrace the issue. But she also spoke with faith leaders, communities of color, and others she felt were often left out of the discussion. As she grew in the role, so did her platform. President Obama invited her to the White House for an address on gun violence, she addressed the Democratic National Convention and testified before Congress, and she was an important surrogate for Hillary Clinton's campaign. But running for office herself had never been part of her plan—until she met with Renitta Shannon.

A first-term Democratic state legislator from southeast Atlanta, Shannon was a straight shooter with a knack for brevity. Over breakfast with McBath, she got right to the point. The Republican who represented McBath's slice of suburbia in the state legislature was more vulnerable than ever, Shannon said, and Democrats needed someone in their corner who could "fight the gun battle" in the statehouse. Would she run for the seat?

McBath had been asked countless times about a potential run for public office, but she'd always sidestepped the idea. Most of those encouraging her to run told McBath it was a natural "next step" for someone of her rising stature. Shannon, though, spoke persuasively to McBath about how elected office would give her "an opportunity to create the change you want to see." Before she knew it, McBath had answered, "OK." An ecstatic Shannon pulled out her smartphone and started making calls and lining up meetings before McBath could change her mind.

Just as McBath was gearing up her campaign in February 2018, the mass shooting in Parkland, Florida, refocused her attention. As she watched terrified students fleeing the campus of Marjory Stoneman Douglas High School, or emerging from buildings with their hands in the air as if they were criminals, McBath was struck by the realization they were about the same age as Jordan was when he was killed. Next came the predictable cycle that seemed to reoccur after every mass shooting: messages of regret, calls for sweeping changes, impassioned debate, and, inevitably, no action from a gridlocked Congress. What little hope she had for modest new gun restrictions evaporated after President Trump repeated the NRA's calls to arm teachers and increase security at schools rather than raise the age limit to buy rifles or require universal background checks. She grew even more furious watching Republican lawmakers tiptoe around the issue.

"You guys, seriously?" she raged at her TV screen. "No one is going to stand up to Trump? No one is going to stand up for our families and our communities and our children?"

At around that time, some of her friends urged McBath to aim for the US House seat that Republican Karen Handel had captured just a few months earlier if she really wanted a voice in the national gun policy debate. It meant a much more difficult campaign than a state House race, with all the fundraising pressure, media scrutiny, and political attacks that go along with competing for a district that a year ago was at the center of suffocating attention.

Terrified at the thought, McBath spent two days on the floor praying and crying over the decision with her Bible. But she found solace in the story of Queen Esther, the biblical heroine of the Purim story who intervened to convince her husband, the Persian king Ahasuerus, to prevent his evil minister from massacring the realm's Jews. She resolved to step into the arena. "I'm going to the king," McBath said to herself. "This is what I have to do for my people."

A few days later, McBath penned a letter to local Democrats that put the Parkland shootings at the center of her decision to run for Congress: "It's been much of the same response after every other mass shooting. 'It's not time to have the debate.' 'Let's wait and see.' 'It isn't the time to act,'" she wrote. "So, with much prayer and reflection, I've decided to listen to the voters I met and to those brave students from Parkland and run for Congress in my home district."

Though her reason for running was to curb gun violence, McBath was careful not to become a single-issue candidate. She tied Handel to Trump's more unpopular plans, such as an attempt to repeal the Affordable Care Act's preexisting conditions protections, and immigration crackdowns that resulted in family separations. It put Handel in a tough spot: she tried to shield herself from some of the president's most contentious policies, but she also couldn't afford to alienate him and his loyal supporters, still a formidable slice of the electorate despite the anti-Trump mood in the suburbs.

Above all, though, McBath's demand for stronger gun restrictions remained the North Star of her campaign—and it was an issue that was gaining popularity across Georgia. A few years earlier, insisting on stricter gun rules was a recipe for defeat in competitive districts. Even Democrats traveled the state trumpeting the NRA's approval. The spate of mass shootings helped turn the tide; now some state polls showed a majority of Georgians were in favor of new restrictions. It reflected the overall strategy that Abrams had helped pioneer, an argument that ideas once deemed too liberal for Georgia were now embraced by the mainstream.

⸻

The Sunday before the 2018 election, one of those glorious November days in Georgia made for T-shirts and jeans, McBath gave her stump speech on a supporter's crowded back porch in Marietta. It was one of the last in a string of get-out-the-vote rallies before the election, and her organizers had lined the heights of the screened-in porch with red-and-blue campaign signs. A mother handed McBath fidgeting twin boys as she posed for pictures with a smiling group of supporters, while others sipped lemonade and milled about the deck in search of fresh air.

There was an unfamiliar face in the crowd of well-wishers who approached McBath as she headed to the driveway en route to the next stop on a long itinerary. The tall, balding man in a brown jacket and black-rimmed glasses, his solemn eyes downcast, told her his name was Reuben Jones. His grandson, Bakeer Green, had been shot and killed the previous night in West Philadelphia. Jones was headed to his funeral.

"Then why are you here?" asked McBath, concerned and confused, as volunteers mingled around her.

"Because you're trying to keep families together. You're trying to keep families safe," he told her. "I felt like I needed to be here."

In the chaos of the campaign, it was often difficult for McBath to keep focus on her reason for running as she juggled all the other balls: staying on message, raising money, energizing volunteers, contacting activists, navigating the press. Here was a moment in which she realized how much her battle for Congress mattered.

"He came here to support me because I was fighting for him," she said years later, his story still embedded in her mind. "This is why we run."

McBath won the election by about three thousand votes, and her narrow victory was the biggest success story for Georgia Democrats after another round of statewide losses. Handel conceded a few days later, telling supporters that she hadn't been able to keep pace with the resources that gun control advocates had pumped into her rival's campaign, nor had she been able to account for the Democratic grassroots buildup in the district, which had started with Jon Ossoff's candidacy in the special election a year earlier. Years later, she still thought about her strategy after the 2017 race, when she decided to maintain a somewhat lower profile in Congress.

"There's something to be said about oversaturation, and I had gotten to that point. But maybe we should have just stayed on a full-court press. Would it have made any difference if we had gone the other way?" Handel said. Then she quoted something Sonny Perdue once told her, as if to rebut herself: "'You can only make the best decision you can make in the moment you have to make it.' There's no use second-guessing yourself."

McBath wasn't the only bright spot for the Democrats. A strategy of running viable candidates against Republican incumbents in suburban state legislative districts where incumbents long went unchallenged had paid dividends. Democrats netted eleven seats in the Georgia House and picked up two more in the state Senate, enough to make life more uncomfortable for their counterparts in the Republican-controlled legislature. And in the congressional district next door to McBath's, a budget analyst named Carolyn Bourdeaux came within a whisker of defeating Republican incumbent Rob Woodall. Though Democrats continued to struggle in statewide races, they were quickly making up lost ground in the bedroom communities circling Atlanta.

If Ossoff regretted passing up another shot at the seat—and he swore he didn't—he never showed it. Before the 2018 midterms, he was under tremendous pressure from local and national Democrats to mount a rematch against Handel, with a massive infrastructure and high-name ID at the ready. But he also felt he needed time to recover from the enormous strains of the national race. There was a wedding to plan with Alisha and a business to run. It seemed too soon for Ossoff to turn around so quickly and run again.

He wouldn't sit still for long, though. As McBath prepared to take her seat in Congress in December 2018, Ossoff prepared to tiptoe back into politics. First, though, he needed to test out a new message. On a gloomy weeknight he journeyed to a crowded library in a sparsely populated, deeply conservative area of northeast Georgia where Abrams had struggled to crack 15 percent of the vote just weeks earlier.

The one hundred or so people who showed up that night in Cornelia, a town of scarcely 4,000 people, heard a new sort of appeal from Ossoff: an urgent, populist message criticizing corporate influence in politics and a ravenous economy built on "debt and consumption." Lawmakers in Washington, he said, weren't lifting a finger to do anything about skyrocketing student debt, crumbling infrastructure, and an "unfathomably large empire that costs trillions of dollars."

As local Democrats raised their hands to vent to him about the loneliness of being a liberal in ruby-red territory, Ossoff told them to stay energized. As for his own next step, Ossoff was circumspect about whether he'd run for public office again. But anyone who knew him didn't doubt he'd be on a ballot again. He suggested as much before making the long drive back to Atlanta that night, when he cast his defeat as only a temporary bump in the road.

"This is a long fight. There will be triumph and heartbreak, near misses and wipeouts, and triumphant victories," he said. "But it's about every single battle."

The audience needed no reminding that a US Senate seat would soon be up for a vote.

PART 2

⋀

THE GATHERING
BLUE STORM

⋁

Chapter 7

A REPUBLICAN CALL TO ACTION

The rally at the Tillman Hangar in Rome is the type of annual must-attend Georgia political event that draws the top Republican figures in the state for a half day of political hype. But the combustible postelection environment in 2019 made it even more crucial for state GOP leaders to put on a show.

Plastic "freedom straws" adorned with Donald Trump's logo were arrayed next to sweating glasses of lemonade, and a Bikers for Trump phalanx paraded so loudly through the airport grounds that attendees plugged their ears, the thrumming of their engines temporarily drowning out a group of upbeat ladies welcoming guests with bumper stickers and party pamphlets. In the sweltering hangar, a trio of singers belted out catchy patriotic songs in August humidity so thick it felt like walking through pudding to reach rows of plastic folding chairs.

As political pep rallies go, though, the mood at this political ritual wasn't entirely joyful. This was no celebration of GOP power in Georgia. It was a call to action. One after another, Republican leaders took their turn at the microphone and bashed left-leaning policies, promoted Trump's agenda, and warned that the close midterm in 2018 was an ominous sign for next year's presidential race. Stacey Abrams had never really stopped running, each speaker reminded the audience, and was now channeling her energy behind a powerful voting rights organization. Even Governor Brian Kemp, fresh off his narrow election victory, was already raising the alarm. A private note he sent to top donors just after he took office might as well have been a head start on his 2022 reelection campaign, with an admonition to allies that resurgent liberals wanted to "stop our conservative progress" in its tracks.

Attorney General Chris Carr was on hand to deliver much the same message in person. One of the younger statewide Republican officers, Carr had boyish features that clashed with a balding pate. While other Republicans got their start catering to the party's most conservative wing, Carr was aligned with the party's mainstream establishment and stuck to a more pragmatic approach to policy. His base was in the northern Atlanta suburbs where he grew up rather than the small-town rural areas where so many other GOP officials started their careers. And he was a proud acolyte of another suburbanite, Senator Johnny Isakson, serving as his top aide for years in Washington at a time when the Georgia Republican was one of a vanishing number of legislators known for building bipartisan coalitions in Congress. When Governor Nathan Deal tapped Carr in October 2016 to fill a vacant attorney general post, he brought with him his pro-business sensibilities.

Earlier that same year, Carr was among the members of Deal's inner circle who urged him to veto a "religious liberty" measure that was painted by critics as discriminatory to the LGBTQ community and skewered by business leaders who threatened boycotts and other forms of economic payback. Deal's veto of the bill was one of the most consequential decisions of his eight years in office, and a few activist Republican groups responded by passing measures "censuring" him for the alleged betrayal.

On this day, Carr came to grassroots activists with a sense of foreboding. A few months earlier, he had squeaked by a young Democratic challenger named Charlie Bailey, a political novice who had campaigned as a county prosecutor who put gang members in jail. Carr's own close call, he knew, was a sign of things to come.

"My friends, we don't get to do what we do, we can't be successful, unless we win elections. The other side is desperate to win in Georgia," he told the restless crowd, many of whom were cooling themselves with flimsy Trump-branded fans. "They've got their targets set in Georgia, all the way down to city and local elections. We've got to get back to work."

Then Carr paused, preparing the audience to let his next words sink in.

"We can acknowledge that this is happening and do something about it and win," he said gravely. "Or not and lose."

═════

For much of the previous two decades, Democrats predicted that "changing demographics" would pave the way for an upset. And each cycle, they ended up empty-handed. That had changed dramatically by early 2019.

Without so much as a campaign stop in Georgia during the general election campaign, Hillary Clinton flipped the suburban Republican strongholds of Cobb and Gwinnett Counties for the first time since Jimmy Carter's presidency. Stacey Abrams captured 51 percent of the suburban vote two years later, outdoing Clinton's numbers by five percentage points. Suddenly the Republican road to ruling Georgia was much narrower. No longer were the bedroom suburban communities that had launched the careers of so many GOP stars—Isakson among them—central to the strategy.

Isakson used to joke that he was a Republican back when the party could fit into a phone booth, and that wasn't far from the truth. Long before out-of-power Democrats aimed for the New South's young and racially diverse constituency, a far different brand of Democrat controlled Georgia politics through racist schemes and gerrymandering that shut the GOP out—and often drowned out voices of moderation from within. It was premised on a "county unit system" that established a Georgia version of the Electoral College that gave majority-white rural counties more influence than dense, diverse cities. Before the scheme was tossed by the courts in 1963, the three least populous Georgia counties had the same number of "unit votes" as Atlanta's Fulton County, which in the 1960 census had a population of more than 550,000 people. For decades, Democrats gerrymandered legislative and congressional districts to maintain their grip on state politics, drawing maps that became ever more creative as their power waned. When Republicans took control of the statehouse in the early 2000s, they refashioned district lines with a similar intent.

But at the start of this new election cycle, Republicans could not ignore that their party was on the decline across vast stretches of metro Atlanta. Democrats carved a blue streak from the city limits up Georgia 400, the highway that stretches north across the traffic-snarled Perimeter Highway to the affluent suburban communities beyond before petering out near the rugged foothills of North Georgia. The towns of Dunwoody and Sandy Springs, inner suburbs straddling the highway that once voted reliably Republican, had fallen to Democrats. So had Gwinnett, the second-most-populous county in Georgia and home to burgeoning Indian, Latino, and Asian American communities.

When Brian Kemp took his oath of office on a frigid January afternoon in 2019 at Georgia Tech's McCamish Pavilion, he pledged to put partisan acrimony behind him and work with Democrats to bridge the widening rift between metro Atlanta and the rural heartland—a divide he helped stoke during the vicious campaign. Even the Bible verse he invoked during the swearing-in ceremony, Proverbs 16:7, was meant to send a more inclusive message: "When a man's ways please the Lord, He makes even his enemies to be at peace with him."

The geniality would not last. Despite the political warning signs—or maybe because of them—Georgia's new GOP regime began to tilt even more conservative. It was as if Republicans sensed a last gasp at unfettered power and decided to exploit their advantage while they could. At the dawn of Kemp's administration, Georgia Republicans were more willing to engage in partisan battles over cultural issues that party leaders had, for much of the previous decade, often avoided. And Kemp, the first lifelong Republican elected to the state's top office, was happy to lead the charge. The governor started a few weeks after his swearing-in by making a statement no politician in Georgia could ignore. He endorsed a strict "heartbeat" measure that banned abortions as early as six weeks—even though he and other supporters were certain it would be blocked by the courts.

The antiabortion bill was bewildering to Democrats, who viewed the focus on reproductive rights as a startling sea change. While Republicans had long trumpeted support for "pro-life" measures, they had not followed through with such sweeping legislative action. With politics so evenly divided in Georgia, Democrats were both confused and outraged that Republicans would try to use their thinning majorities in the legislature to further such an emotional divide.

Some who were encouraged by his inaugural address had genuinely expected Kemp to embrace more consensus-building measures after the tight election. One Democratic state lawmaker, Michelle Henson, complained that pushing "highly emotional and partisan bills" only alienated the handful of Democrats willing to give him the benefit of the doubt. Nikema Williams, a state senator who also chaired the Democratic Party of Georgia, predicted the swing to socially conservative legislation would backfire. "This is Brian Kemp's Republican Party, and he showed us exactly who he was when he was campaigning," she said. "We should have believed him."

Antiabortion groups, meanwhile, saw a small window to secure restrictions and lobbied Kemp and other Republicans to swiftly make good on their campaign pledges. Groups sprang up on both sides of the issue, with conservatives pledging to back "promise-keepers" who voted for the legislation, while abortion rights advocates vowed to take revenge on Republicans in swing districts who supported the crackdown. This was an especially fraught debate in metro Atlanta, where only a handful of surviving Republican legislators faced a difficult vote. Zac McCrary, a Democratic strategist, predicted that vulnerable Republicans who supported the new limits were effectively "committing self-immolation."

The legislative battle over the measure was the first major test of the Kemp administration—and the first gauge of the newfound clout of Democrats, who promised that anger and energy around the new law would lead to payback. Even though Kemp was well aware it could energize Democrats in a likely 2022 rematch against Abrams—he remarked during a helicopter trip to rural Georgia that she had somehow become more famous in defeat—he pressed ahead with his plan.

The final vote was preceded by such stifling pressure that its legislative sponsor conceded that his fellow Republicans were "terrified" of the backlash. One Republican from a liberal-leaning area was spotted in an emotional conversation on the floor of the Georgia House with Democrats who unsuccessfully pleaded with him to defy his party's leadership; others steered clear of the chamber altogether to avoid casting a vote that could come back to haunt them. Six wound up crossing party lines—five Republicans opposed the bill, and one Democrat supported it—and it passed with a single vote to spare. Kemp signed it into law a few days later, in May 2019, at his ceremonial office in the state capitol, surrounded by mostly women backers of the new limits. Outside, loud groups of abortion rights supporters chanted "Don't take away our care!" Kemp didn't flinch at the protests or the growing threats of boycotts from opponents of the new law. In his mind, none of the critics should have been surprised. He was keeping a promise he had made during the campaign.

That was the message he took to the annual meeting of Georgia Republicans a few weeks later, where he received a hero's welcome from hundreds of activists gathered on a Saturday in coastal Savannah. Along the crowded halls leading to the convention center, vendors of every variety hawked GOP paraphernalia: books about Trump's rise to power, life-size cardboard cutouts of the president, shirts and hats with his smiling face and slogans. Someone passed out bumper stickers that read "Isakson 2022," a reminder that yet another election campaign was looming after the presidential vote.

Inside, Kemp played to his audience, knowing that hated Hollywood celebrities were perfectly cast as the villain in his narrative. The very mention of actress Alyssa Milano's threat to stop filming in Georgia drew catcalls from the boisterous crowd. She had provoked particular animosity among state Republicans for traveling to the state capitol to hand deliver a letter urging the governor to veto the antiabortion law. One conservative lawmaker, Dominic LaRiccia, angrily accosted her, asking why she was objecting to a law in a state where she didn't live. Amid a crowd of supporters massed outside Kemp's second-floor office, Milano pointed toward the closed doors leading to his ceremonial desk: "These are the men that are voting on what goes on inside my uterus." Though Kemp didn't confront Milano at the statehouse, his response at the state convention would draw attention from Hollywood's gilded class. "We value and protect innocent life," he said, "even though that makes C-list celebrities squawk."

Those words were more than base-pleasing platitudes. They were also seen as a shot across the bow to establishment Republicans who had turned Georgia into a film mecca, thanks to a generous tax credit championed by governors Sonny Perdue and Nathan Deal that made the state one of the most popular TV and movie destinations on the planet. More than 250 projects were filmed in Georgia over the previous year, and analysts estimated the productions supported more than ninety thousand jobs and about $2.7 billion in direct spending. A month earlier, Kemp had appeared at the premiere of *Avengers: Endgame*, the Marvel blockbuster filmed in town, and promised to a theater full of executives he would remain committed to the lucrative incentives. Still, nervous local studio owners who had invested heavily in Georgia worried if the curtains were about to fall on the state's movie boom.

It was left to Abrams to trek to Hollywood to urge industry leaders to "stay and fight" the abortion restrictions rather than pull up stakes in Georgia. Former CBS chairwoman Nina Tassler organized a meeting between Abrams and dozens of executives, producers, actors, and rank-and-file staffers anxious about doing business in a state run by Kemp. "Many of us have projects in the state. I know it's complicated," Tassler wrote in an invite to the June 2019 meeting. "There's lots of money and jobs at stake—for us and for the people of Georgia."

Abrams was peppered with questions about why producers should keep planning projects in a state with such restrictive policies. She acknowledged the "moral pull" to punish Georgia with a boycott but countered that there's a "stronger effect by staying and changing the power structure that allowed this bill to pass." The threatened mass pullout never took place, though a smattering of individual projects bolted.

For Kemp, though, the celebrities who buzzed about withholding business from the state might as well have amounted to a campaign donation. Defiant, he promised the GOP audience another round of conservative legislation—perhaps a new crackdown on immigration. Rows full of activists from the Appalachian Mountains to the coastal lowlands rewarded him with deafening applause.

"We fought every liberal activist in the country—and we won. And I'll say it again for the folks in the back of the room: we won," Kemp said. "But make no mistake, we cannot rest on our laurels. We have to double down and do it again."

Kemp had an important ally who stood by him through the thicket of conflicts. Geoff Duncan was a fellow Republican who, at first glance, looked more like a reality TV star than a politician. A perma-tanned former Florida Marlins minor league pitcher, Duncan had a history of impulsive moves, perhaps none more rash than his decision to run for lieutenant governor. When he arrived at a cozy Caribou Coffee weeks after the November 2016 election, his beaming father straining to listen at a nearby table, he outlined to me a plan to run as a business-minded political outsider for Georgia's number two job despite the steep odds.

The favorite in that race was David Shafer, a powerful state senator owed plenty of favors—and who'd made plenty of enemies—over his sixteen years in the legislature. Some were angry enough they poured big money into secretive groups that financed volley after volley of ads that alleged "Shady Shafer" leveraged his position to get rich. Shafer denied the claims and, in keeping with the alliteration, set up a counteroffensive to damage "Deceptive Duncan."

In a runoff overshadowed by the race for governor, Duncan edged out Shafer in a nail-biter, and then he and Kemp worked in an odd-couple tandem on the campaign trail: the folksy Kemp, who talked up his farming roots, and the polished Duncan, a health-care executive who cracked jokes about his pitching arm. Duncan narrowly won his general election campaign, defeating Democratic logistics executive Sarah Riggs Amico, who years later would still sigh about her defeat: "You have no idea how difficult it is for a smart person to lose to someone that stupid."

Like Kemp, Duncan could be single-minded; his enemies alleged that he wasn't willing to put in the tedious work to build a statewide organization, that he was more obsessed with making it home for dinner than making the rounds at rubber-chicken fundraisers. Their families became so close that one of Duncan's three sons asked one of Kemp's three daughters to his high school prom, prompting quips about two-timing "Jake" from the shotgun ad. ("He seemed like such a nice boy," noted one political wag.)

Just as important, the two men genuinely liked each other. During a fly-around tour on the eve of the election, Kemp turned to Duncan to celebrate their former underdog statuses. They were both supposed to lose their primary races to powerful party favorites; now they were on the verge of statewide victories. "There have never been two men who have owed so little to the special interests," Kemp said to Duncan, who answered with an assured smile and a fist bump.

There was only one person in the Georgia GOP world who eclipsed them both. By 2019, David Perdue was one of the most popular figures in the Republican Party, a political rock star talked about as a potential White House candidate—if he managed to win a second term in 2020. He helped stamp out the "Never Trump" movement in Georgia during the 2016 campaign when he theatrically donned his faded blue jean jacket and Trump's bright-red MAGA cap to pledge loyalty to an outsider who is "saying what you and I say at home when Fox News is on air and we're throwing our socks at the TV." And then, in one of the simplest ways to explain Trump's appeal to his Georgia legions, he added: "He's saying what we feel."

Perdue always found it funny that he was granted such lofty status, that fawning conservatives waited in line for a selfie or a signature at GOP events. It wasn't so long ago that the Republican base regarded the globe-trotting former executive with mistrust, even disdain. He knew the love affair could be a fleeting one, that the activists now showering him with praise could just as quickly turn on him. He grew up in Houston County, where the Perdue name was a household one. But outside those friendly environs, he soon discovered just how little known he was.

The Republican field for an open US Senate seat in 2013 featured far more familiar names when he entered the race. His rivals included three veteran GOP congressmen and Karen Handel, who by then had served as secretary of state and narrowly lost a GOP runoff for governor. Perdue hardly registered in the early polls. He was overlooked or ignored at Republican events. His standing was so poor in those circles that Brandon Howell, one of Perdue's earliest volunteers, was confronted by an attendee when he wore the candidate's paraphernalia to an Atlanta Young Republicans meeting. "You're the first person wearing a David Perdue sticker that wasn't paid to wear one," Howell was told.

Before he ventured into the wilds of Georgia politics, Perdue had sought advice from his first cousin, Sonny Perdue, about a possible campaign. The former governor admonished him to not even think about a race until his wife, Bonnie, came to him on her own and urged him to run. About three weeks later, the couple was at his mother-in-law's house when Bonnie saw how restless and frustrated her husband had become watching Fox News coverage of the Obama administration.

With tears in her eyes, she resigned herself to the campaign ahead. She said later that she had a "sense come over me that David was supposed to do this," even though she certainly didn't envision spending her first months as a new grandmother in the back of a noisy RV filled with young aides, gobs of junk food, and cans of Coca-Cola. But, she concluded, it was a sacrifice worth making for her husband.

Perdue's business background was central to his political identity, and over the course of four decades he had built a career ranging from international consultant to senior executive with household brands like Sara Lee, Haggar Clothing, and Reebok. Then came a call from a corporate headhunter in 2002 to run a sputtering North Carolina manufacturing company called Pillowtex. Perdue was intrigued by the challenge and cast himself as a turnaround artist who could help the textile firm crawl out of bankruptcy through a stepped-up marketing campaign and outsourcing workers. Perdue later testified in a deposition that the deal "exploded in my face." He resigned in early 2003 and, not long after, the entire company collapsed, leaving about seven thousand workers out of a job. Perdue moved on to become chief executive of Dollar General—his most prominent posting yet—where he helped add more than twenty-five hundred stores to the family-owned chain's roster and collected more than $42 million in 2007 and 2008 after arranging the company's sale to private equity firm KKR.

To introduce himself to voters, Perdue launched provocative ads that made his GOP rivals out to be a bunch of crying babies and himself as the adult in the room. "Help me change the childish behavior up there," he said in one TV spot. Another ad showed him with the jean-jacketed, popped-collar image that helped establish his trademark "outsider" look. Adsmith Fred Davis met with him several times early in the campaign, and each time Perdue was wearing a bespoke suit with a power tie. Only during a TV shoot in Perdue's hometown of Perry did he dress down, trading the corporate attire for work boots and denim. When campaign research showed the look resonated with voters, Perdue started taking the faded blue jacket to his appearances, where it became a star attraction for the growing "selfie" lines.

Still, the campaign trail wasn't something he relished, at least not at first, as camera-wielding trackers logged his every move and much of the GOP establishment initially rallied around his rivals. The first-time candidate showed his naivete, too, with a sense of candor that could be both refreshing and off-putting. "This is not fun. I'm sorry," he told a small crowd at one of the first events in a grueling nine-stop day. "Somebody said, 'Aren't you having fun?' Yeah, if I get elected." That confession underscored a reality that would define Perdue's electoral career. Even years later, he never really liked campaign politics. He was never convinced he was ever good at it. And he never felt he had grown into it.

To Perdue, it was the mark of a true outsider to dismiss the stuff of a conventional campaign—carefully choreographed events, party gatherings, the backslapping and rounds of debates—as frivolous. He told voters all the time, "This is not the best job I've ever had." (His favorite gig was probably as a hard-charging Reebok executive in a high-pressure turnaround role.) As a candidate, you've got to show up to events you don't want to attend. You've got to answer leading questions. You've got to bend yourselves into pretzels on issues of the day. Perdue's reaction to much of this was: *Why bother?*

Perdue's rivals from both parties framed him as an out-of-touch rich guy. Sometimes he played into that depiction, such as when he denigrated Handel's lack of a college degree. "There's a high-school graduate in this race, okay?" he sniffed when asked which candidate had the best qualifications for office. It was a comment he came to profoundly regret, but in the moment it represented his lofty view of the Senate chambers as a place where the nation's elite hashed out the policies of the day.

There were times when he was just as insecure about his own credentials. To connect with everyday Georgians, he'd tout his background as a product of the public schools of middle Georgia and as someone who, his friends insisted, would rather eat at the local Waffle House than enjoy fine dining near his estate on exclusive Sea Island. But he'd also leverage his wealth, holding receptions and annual "retreats" for top donors at a five-star resort on Georgia's coast a short drive from his mansion.

Despite his business credentials, Perdue was no favorite of the establishment types who often ruled local political fiefdoms. He skipped many county party meetings after realizing many of the folks who showed up to pancake breakfast gatherings and Red Lobster lunches had already backed someone else in the primary. He lost his temper and walked out after ten minutes of an hour-long interview with the US Chamber of Commerce, telling leaders in a huff that "you've been waiting for a candidate like me for twenty years," then unloaded a scathing TV ad against the business group for backing his rival, Congressman Jack Kingston. After Perdue beat Kingston in the 2014 runoff to win the Republican nomination, activists would scratch their heads in wonder over how he won their county without support from the local party honchos. It was partly because campaign built out its own events, snubbing the "status quo" with every rally.

Years later, it wasn't lost on die-hard Republicans that he resembled another up-and-coming party figure: just like Trump, Perdue was an outsider businessman who thumbed his nose at the establishment before he came to embody it. And, just like Trump, he played up his wealth as an inoculant against the corrosive power of the Washington Swamp. "You've seen nice guys like me before, without a voting record, go up to Washington and lose themselves," Perdue told voters early in his campaign. "Here's why it's not going to happen to me: I've been there. They're not going to offer me anything I haven't seen before."

Still, even a consummate outsider needs a political veteran to help him navigate the inner workings of a premier statewide campaign. Derrick Dickey, his most trusted consultant in those days, was the rare operative who found a way to say to him, "You're right, but . . ." before explaining why he had to do the kinds of things he really didn't want to do. "My job was to remind him that in order to be the senator, you have to win the election, and there's a process that's often off-putting to get there," Dickey would later explain.

Dickey first met Perdue in February 2013 when he was summoned to

Sonny Perdue's corporate office to meet with an unidentified guest. The veteran strategist had never laid eyes on David Perdue, but he was intrigued by the idea of steering the campaign of an executive with no political record. Pretty quickly, though, he realized how much help the newcomer needed to prepare for a serious run for office. To Perdue, being a CEO was about building consensus. But political campaigns were all-out war. He had to be armed with talking points on issues he wasn't used to debating, like firearms loopholes and abortion exceptions, and he had to be convinced that trivial things mattered—the nuances of a policy response, the meet and greet with the dignitaries, the discipline it took to stay on message.

So often, Dickey discovered, Perdue had a caustic side, a knee-jerk tendency to dismiss certain mainstays of the campaign trail. He didn't hold an in-person town hall after his election, earning clucks of criticism from even die-hard supporters, and his temper was something to behold. The senator once snatched a student's cell phone at the Georgia Tech campus when he was being asked about possible voter suppression in the state.

He held his staff to exacting standards, obsessed with the minutiae. When his campaign RV kept bottoming out during one 2014 trip, the engineer in him surfaced, and he ruminated about the problem until he deduced that the vehicle's wheelbase wasn't evenly spaced. Only moments later he was already fixated on an off-kilter campaign mailer, questioning staffers about the minor printing error. "Every day, working with him is like Finals Week. You need to know what you're talking about. You need to be able to answer questions," said Howell, the longtime aide. "You're in the kitchen with someone who brings the heat—and you need to back it up."

That fiery personality could be endearing to his most loyal supporters. Years later, after Perdue voted to confirm conservative judge Brett Kavanaugh to the US Supreme Court, a group of protesters hounded the senator and his aides on his way back to his Capitol Hill office. As Perdue entered an elevator, a woman yelled, "Vote your conscience!" to his back. The senator turned around and, as the doors snapped close, responded: "I just did." As the elevator glided away, Perdue couldn't stifle a satisfied grin.

When he campaigned for a second—and what he claimed would be final—term in office, Perdue wasn't considered one of the most vulnerable

Republicans in the country, not nearly as imperiled as incumbents in places like Arizona and Colorado and North Carolina. But the senator himself wasn't as confident. Time and again, he cautioned that Georgia was closer than it appeared. As a businessman, he was accustomed to hearing out customers and monitoring the competition. As he tracked the Democratic ground-level energy and fundraising, he was convinced that Republicans were not adequately prepared.

In one private meeting, Perdue predicted he would need to garner twice as many votes as he had in 2014 to be reelected. His longtime ally Ginger Howard, one of the most prominent Republican figures in the state, gasped in horror. "The truth hurts sometimes," she said.

He'd share that truth at the same Georgia GOP gathering in Savannah where Kemp enthralled the crowd with his press for abortion restrictions. As Perdue spoke to the conventioneers, he presented them with an urgent challenge. "In 2018, the governor's race and lieutenant governor's race got a lot closer than it should have. The battle for the White House is right here in Georgia in 2020. If President Trump doesn't win Georgia, he won't win the presidency."

His other major problem? He still didn't know whom he'd face.

Chapter 8

BRICK BY BRICK

A soul food spot on the edge of the Flint River, the Grille House in Albany was known for its piping-hot oxtails, tasty collard greens, and live jazz. On Martin Luther King Jr. Day in 2019, it would also play host to an important political moment: the start of the Stacey Abrams comeback.

Abrams didn't call it that, of course. It was billed as a "thank you" tour organized by her new voting rights group, Fair Fight, which was rapidly expanding. Soon, Fair Fight would air a thirty-second Super Bowl ad that featured both Abrams and a local Republican official endorsing bipartisan elections legislation. By the summer, the group would branch out nationally, with chapters in other battleground states to promote increased ballot access. But the upstart group was not designed to be a vehicle for Abrams's political future. Rather, she and her inner circle envisioned it as an enduring force to fight for progressive causes that would outlast Abrams's time in Georgia politics. It was to be an organization capable of standing on its own even if, her aides predicted, Abrams one day won the presidency.

"We saw 2020 coming in December 2018, and we knew Georgia was the best place to see where the country is moving forward," said Hillary Holley, one of the core members of Abrams's brain trust who was deeply involved in the organization's start.

At this early stage, Holley had a simpler goal in mind. She was determined to keep the army of dedicated volunteers—folks who would knock on any door, send any text, make any phone call—engaged after Abrams's heartbreaking defeat to Governor Brian Kemp. And she and her colleagues wanted to get Abrams back in action after two tough months when the defeated Democrat said she cycled through stages of grief that "seemed to attack me all at once."

The first pangs of defeat, Abrams wrote in her book *Our Time Is Now*, were variations of anger and rage—visceral emotions that, frankly, caught her off guard. Abrams had always prided herself in staying calm and even-keeled during high-stress situations, and she saw sustained anger in others as a weakness. But after her loss, Abrams was mad—and she couldn't shake it. As she began to acknowledge about six days following the election that she wouldn't have enough votes to force a runoff with Kemp, Abrams started to channel her fury into another sentiment. She'd never seem to arrive at "acceptance." She called it the "plotting" phase. And on a yellow legal pad, she scribbled the basis for her post-defeat plans.

The planning stage fit Abrams well. She'd begun tracking her life goals on an Excel spreadsheet when she was eighteen, a chart that was both audacious and admirable in its ambition. She'd initially wanted to be mayor of Atlanta in her thirties and elected president by 2028. Abrams so meticulously mapped out each of her steps that she'd even applied for a permit in 1992, while a college student, before taking to the steps of the Georgia capitol to burn the state flag in protest of its Confederate emblem.

Of course, it was no accident that she now returned to the public stage at a restaurant in Albany, not far from the southwest Georgia park where she had kicked off her campaign for governor about eighteen months earlier. Abrams had easily carried the cluster of predominantly Black rural counties in the region in 2018, and she felt the path to retaking Georgia didn't flow just through the Chattahoochee River that meanders by Atlanta. It also swept down the Flint River, the lifeblood of southwest Georgia.

A few hundred supporters had crowded into the restaurant, expecting more of the fiery oratory that burned through the end of the gubernatorial campaign. They weren't disappointed. Abrams promised that Fair Fight would become a powerful new political force in Georgia, one that would build broad political coalitions, advocate for the expansion of Medicaid and voting rights measures, and, more broadly, keep alive the embers of her political agenda in Georgia. Just as she refused to concede the race to Kemp, she wasn't about to cede the political stage to him.

"The system is rigged, but now we know what they're doing, and we will get it undone," she said. "And that will only happen if they don't believe we are going to go home and sit still."

Abrams drew a line between the NFL referees who missed a blatant case of pass interference in that weekend's NFC Championship Game and Kemp's role as a secretary of state overseeing an election in which he was also a candidate. "There was a call that should have been made a long time ago in Georgia—you don't get to be the referee and the player."

Her top aide, Lauren Groh-Wargo, was even more blunt. The longtime Abrams loyalist was now chief executive of Fair Fight, and she pressed the crowd to sign letters addressed to the governor encouraging an electoral overhaul to make it easier for poor and minority voters to cast ballots. "We are going to give Brian Kemp living hell."

As for her own future, Abrams was as guarded as ever. She thanked her well-wishers for "challenging the status quo" but wasn't yet ready to say what her political future held. "I am running for office again. I don't know for what."

Privately, Abrams knew exactly what she *didn't* want. She didn't want to be a US senator—full stop, she told friends. Her climb up the political ladder bent toward the executive branch, ever since that spreadsheet she made as a teenager, and she was remarkably candid about her aspirations. She wanted to be considered as a vice presidential nominee. She wanted to one day run for president. But the most pressing priority in those days was to be Georgia's first Black governor.

Still, when Chuck Schumer asked for a meeting to talk about a Senate run, Abrams couldn't refuse the chance to hear him out. Curious about the Senate Democratic leader's pitch, she hopped on a flight to Washington in early 2019 for the sit-down with Schumer. Only a few minutes into their conversation, she came away with a clear impression: the New Yorker had done his homework.

She was impressed by how much Schumer and his aides understood Georgia and its potential for colossal political change. His advisers had come armed with reams of data—voter registration figures, polling analysis—that echoed the work the Abrams campaign had done to show Georgia was winnable for Democrats. He wasn't just complimenting Abrams's efforts. He built the case, brick by brick, that Abrams could energize Black turnout and break the region-wide Republican hold on the Deep South in a successful US Senate run by relying on the same strategy that she used to almost defeat Kemp.

He was making the same pledge to put Georgia on the political battle-ground map that Abrams had tried to establish for years, often fruitlessly, at donor conferences, strategy sessions, and appeals to Washington policy makers. Schumer vowed to see that promise to fruition if Abrams challenged Senator David Perdue in 2020.

He also keenly grasped what policies motivated her, making her a generous offer to be front and center on federal legislation that would make it easier for people to vote in elections, limit the gerrymandering of congressional districts, and strengthen ethics rules. It was a shrewd overture, the type of platform Schumer knew Abrams couldn't simply turn down out of hand. When the meeting wrapped up, Abrams promised Schumer she would seriously consider it.

While their back-and-forth continued over regular phone calls, others joined the pressure campaign. Senators Kirsten Gillibrand of New York and Kamala Harris of California both pleaded with Abrams to run. She met with Senator Catherine Cortez Masto, who helmed the Democratic Senatorial Campaign Committee, to explore how well-financed national groups could help. Back home, state Democrats cleared the way, envisioning her as a formidable force whose presence on the ballot could also ensure Georgia was in play in the presidential contest. Jon Ossoff, who was also weighing a bid, put it bluntly: "I'd like to see Stacey challenge Perdue." A *Journal-Constitution* poll added fuel to the fire: it showed Perdue's favorability ratings at about 45 percent—roughly seven percentage points behind Abrams.

The groundswell of support was building but Abrams wasn't buying into it. Still, as much as she wanted to rule out a run, she couldn't yet bring herself to tell Schumer and other Senate Democrats no. Deep down, she didn't like disappointing people.

Then in February came an unheard-of honor for a recently defeated candidate. Schumer tapped Abrams to deliver the Democratic response to President Trump's State of the Union address, both a nod to her growing stature in the party and yet another nudge to entice her to run. Abrams would be the first non-sitting public official to give the speech since the tradition began in 1966, and it afforded her a national platform to introduce herself to millions of Americans and promote her vision of expanding access to the ballot box. She'd also be the first Georgian and first Black woman to deliver the address.

The stakes were astronomically high. Bobby Jindal had been skewered for his animatronic response to President Obama's first speech to Congress in 2009. Florida senator Marco Rubio's ill-timed water break in 2013 drowned out any attention he got from his remarks. In 2018, the too-glistening lips of a Massachusetts Democrat dominated the news coverage of the speech, washing over the message he wanted to deliver. WAS THAT DROOL COMING OUT OF JOE KENNEDY'S MOUTH? a *Politico* headline asked.

Abrams told her friends she was "terrified" of squandering the moment, like so many had done before. "It's where political careers go to die," one aide nervously confided on the eve of the big speech. Schumer wasn't worried. "Donald Trump is the warm-up act for the real deal: Stacey Abrams."

Abrams wasn't going to leave anything to chance. She was at her best when she could feed off the energy and the enthusiasm of a live audience, and her team had about a week to line up a venue and vendors for the speech after a federal government shutdown was finally resolved. The International Brotherhood of Electrical Workers had been the first union to endorse Abrams, and leaders of the local chapter immediately agreed to allow her to use its union hall in downtown Atlanta—next door to the headquarters of the Democratic Party of Georgia—for the speech. It also offered a symbolic change of tone from the ornate US House chambers in Washington where Trump delivered his address, presenting viewers a subtle reminder of Democratic support for organized labor.

The event's planners scrambled to find idle construction crews to build a stage and operate the lights on short notice, as Atlanta had hosted the Super Bowl only days earlier, and most local contractors were fully booked. The Abrams camp invited about one hundred friends, relatives, and guests to pack the room, under strict orders to keep the site of her rebuttal top secret—a knack for being tight-lipped that was a hallmark of her team.

Abrams wrote the speech herself, finishing last-minute edits as Trump was still speaking, and quickly added wishes for a "happy Lunar New Year" at the urging of Asian American organizations. Before she stepped up to the podium, she also took advice from Rubio to heart: "Hydration is a very good idea. Trust me on this." Over the next ten minutes, she melded memories of her upbringing in Mississippi and a celebration of bipartisanship in Georgia with bracing criticism of Trump and the GOP agenda. Dan Pfeiffer, a former senior adviser to Obama, tapped out a viral tweet as she was still speaking: "Stacey Abrams should run for President."

In the weeks that followed, Abrams's self-imposed March deadline to make up her mind about a Senate bid slipped to April, though she still told both herself and her closest friends she wasn't interested in running. During one trip to Washington, she walked into Schumer's office determined to reject his invitation to run—and mindful that every day she remained non-committal gave other Democrats less time to build out their own Senate campaigns. And she walked out of the office undecided once again, after Schumer made another persuasive case that she run.

At a Vanderbilt University event in March, a sold-out crowd exploded in applause as Abrams told them of her two demands for every White House contender: "One, you have to tell me what you're going to do about voter suppression. And two, you have to believe Georgia is a swing state." Of her own future, she was cryptic as she confessed that the pain of the 2018 election still motivated her.

"Revenge," she added, with the tiniest hint of a smile, "can be very cathartic."

By April's end, she finally sealed her decision—and was ready to tell Senate leaders. Her instincts still insisted that she not run, and she concluded that nothing would convince her otherwise. She flew to Washington to tell Schumer in person—he was disappointed but, by then, not surprised—and promptly canceled a flight to New York to return to Georgia, where she let it be known publicly that the Senate race could move on without her.

There had been no "thunderclap moment," Abrams explained. She wanted the arguments for and against a run to percolate in her mind for a while. "We're responsible for doing the work we're best suited for," she said. And for her, she recognized, that meant steering a path toward the executive branch. "I enjoyed that time in the legislature. I think I was effective. But I believe in organizing systems and trying to address problems in a direct way."

She didn't like letting Schumer down, and her decision was made even more difficult as they had grown close over their regular conversations. It felt like she was failing a friend. But if there was a silver lining, it was that countless national Democrats had until then required prodding and cajoling to recognize that Georgia was a competitive state. Schumer no longer needed convincing. He was certain Georgia could be a top-tier battleground with the right candidates and investment.

Abrams was the only Georgia Democrat who could clear the field of other candidates. And the moment she opted out of the contest, the race against Perdue began in earnest. Teresa Tomlinson, the former two-term mayor of Columbus, had already let it be known she would run if Abrams passed, which rankled senior Democrats who felt she was trying to rush Abrams's decision. Almost immediately following Abrams's announcement, Tomlinson plunged into the race, saying that the party's defeats in 2018 showed that "winning Atlanta and its suburbs is not quite enough." She promised that her rural roots and record leading the west Georgia city would "help to expand the Abrams model and increase the likelihood of defeating Perdue."

Not long after, "the millennial mayor," Ted Terry, joined in, too. The thirty-six-year-old was the top politician in Clarkston, a town of about thirteen thousand people just east of Atlanta often described as the "Ellis Island of the South" because of its diversity. He had prodded his liberal city to support higher minimum wages and stricter clean energy standards and to decriminalize marijuana. If elected, he promised, he would bring similar policies to the national stage. He might have been best known in Georgia, however, for a recent role on the Netflix program *Queer Eye*, in which stylists forced him to prune a mangled "resistance beard" that he had let sprout from his chin like a gnarled tree stump after Trump's victory.

Another formidable candidate was Sarah Riggs Amico, who had run unsuccessfully for lieutenant governor a year earlier. The Harvard-trained executive launched her campaign in August 2019, just weeks after her family's car-hauling business filed for bankruptcy protection, and she framed her company's struggles as a symptom of the refusal by Congress to shore up troubled pension funds. Aiming for the union vote, one of her first events brought her to a picket line outside an AT&T hub in midtown Atlanta, where she joined strike organizers with a bright-red shirt that read WE WON'T BACK DOWN.

Each one of their debuts, however, was eclipsed by a bigger name. Jon Ossoff, now thirty-two, saw an opening to leverage his volunteer army, phonebook–thick fundraising list, and strong name recognition. He spent the years since his 2017 defeat to Karen Handel working on anti-corruption investigations that had won critical acclaim and testing bolder and more progressive policies. In April, he reinforced his leftward policy shift by headlining a student-organized town hall in Atlanta with a pledge to legalize marijuana, guarantee health insurance for all Americans, and work toward a debt-free higher education system—all policies he was reluctant to embrace as a more moderate candidate during his run for the US House seat. When Abrams announced she was out of the race, it seemed only a matter of time until Ossoff would jump in.

When Ossoff was ready to announce in September, he unveiled a full-fledged campaign platform that called for a "ruthless assault on corruption" in Washington and the mustering of a "grassroots army unlike any this state has ever seen." He launched his campaign from his cozy home in Grant Park—a diverse in-town Atlanta neighborhood where he and his wife, Alisha, had recently moved—with an interview with me in the *Journal-Constitution* and then a live segment on MSNBC. His entrance was punctuated by the highest-profile endorsement yet of any of the candidates. Congressman John Lewis, the famed civil rights icon, called Ossoff a "flame that is brighter than ever" and pledged to travel across Georgia to stump for his one-time intern.

To close Ossoff watchers, there was a new edginess behind his launch that was honed during his battle with the army of Republican opponents from two years earlier. In defeat, Ossoff said, he built something "special and enduring"—a framework of more than thirteen thousand volunteers and nearly five hundred thousand donors he could call upon. Now, he said, he was more prepared than ever to fight back. "I expect they'll bring all of that again because they recognize that I'm a threat," he said. "And I say bring it on."

Ossoff also thought himself better prepared to match up against Perdue than he had been against Karen Handel in 2017. During his brief exile from politics, he'd devised ways to sharpen the contrast between himself and the senator. And if 2020 was going to be the "election cycle to end all election cycles," as he half-jokingly predicted to his friends, he needed to be prepared for anything.

There was one more lesson that would guide his race. Looking back at his failed House bid, he concluded that Republicans had been able to shape the tone of the contest. This time, he would take the role of the aggressor against Perdue.

Define the race, he told himself, *lest it be defined for you.*

━━━━━

Democrats had a strong cadre of candidates. Still, there was a glaring absence. A year after Abrams nearly became the first person of color to win the race for governor in Georgia history, none of the top-tier candidates in the US Senate contest were Black. Atlanta mayor Keisha Lance Bottoms and Congresswoman Lucy McBath both passed on the race. So did Michael Thurmond, a former state labor commissioner who was chief executive of DeKalb County. Thurmond said the problem wasn't whether a strong Black candidate could win the Democratic primary. After all, he had easily won the party's nomination in the 2010 race against Senator Johnny Isakson. To Thurmond, the problem was whether a Black candidate could overcome the steep fundraising curve and beat Perdue in November. What often went overlooked, though, was the strong political ecosystem that was already taking shape in Georgia, an infrastructure built by women of color to advance and expand the state's growing Democratic coalition.

After a decade in the political trenches, Adrienne White was elected in January 2019 as vice chair of candidate recruitment for the Democratic Party of Georgia. She had put enormous pressure on herself to prevent Trump from winning the race for the White House in 2016, as if her work as a party operative and consultant would single-handedly decide the election. And when Hillary Clinton lost, she felt genuinely wrecked by the outcome.

The looming 2020 race brought resolve. She set about recruiting what would become the largest slate of Democratic candidates across the state since Reconstruction, mustering contenders even for the deepest-red districts around Georgia. Her days were packed with online meetings and strategic discussions that revolved around a belief that Black women voters like herself were key to the party's hopes. And she'd do everything she could to energize them. The name of the private weekly discussion group with other Democratic operatives summed up her mission perfectly: Win with Black Women.

Genny Castillo's introduction to politics came through an early meeting with Abrams, who hired her to be a liaison to the Hispanic community in 2011. In her first weeks, Castillo helped create a new internship program and translated into Spanish a GOP proposal to crack down on undocumented immigrants. During long car rides to and from grassroots assemblies, she built an unshakable bond with Abrams. She also taught her a bit of Spanish along the way. When Abrams became comfortable enough with the language to accept an award in Spanish, the event's organizers asked Castillo in hushed backstage whispers if Abrams was somehow her tía—her aunt—which always tickled the young operative.

As she grew as a political organizer, Castillo used her natural pep and energy to coax volunteers into stepping out of their comfort zone. A text was a start, and a phone call was better, she'd tell them, but a door-knock was the ultimate in personal communication. She was often tapped as the emcee of events because of her skill at enlivening crowds of strangers, whether it be on an elaborate stage before thousands of attendees or a social media livestream posted to her Instagram page.

LaTosha Brown grew up in a family in Selma, Alabama, with a reverential respect for voting rights. Her grandmother, banned most of her life from voting, donned her church outfit when she finally had the right to cast a ballot. Her grandfather kept a crinkled poll-tax receipt with him, an enduring reminder of racist Jim Crow laws. She lived not far from the famed Edmund

Pettus Bridge where, in 1965, John Lewis had led more than six hundred marchers who were brutally beaten by state troopers in what became known as "Bloody Sunday"—and a pivotal moment in the civil rights movement.

But it was her own bid for office, rather than stories of towering civil rights giants, that blazed her path toward advocacy. In 1998, Brown ran for an Alabama State Board of Education seat in a Democratic primary so close that the victor couldn't be decided for days. When elections officials finally certified the race, she trailed her opponent by about two hundred votes. Not long after, she got a call from a Democratic official who opened with an apology, saying that a local sheriff had found eight hundred uncounted ballots in the safe.

Brown was confused by the glum tone of his voice—she had plenty of support in the rural county; she thought surely this would be enough to put her over the top. "So when are y'all going to count them?" she asked. She wasn't prepared for his response. "The race is already certified," she was told. "It's over." Brown felt powerless, as if her victory had been snatched from right under her.

It was, indeed, too late for her to change the outcome of her race. But from then on she dedicated herself to political organizing to influence other elections. By 2017, she and her friend Cliff Albright had founded Black Voters Matter and went to work in the Alabama Senate race, helping Democrat Doug Jones pull off an upset victory. Riding in what they affectionately call the "Blackest Bus in America," the group launched tours across the South, partnering with hundreds of local organizations to motivate African American voters.

With the 2020 races looming, her group's focus shifted to Georgia, where Brown traveled in a bus painted green, black, and red festooned with a banner that proclaimed WE GOT POWER. At stops she asked every voter a variation of the same questions: Are you registered? Is every adult in your house registered? Her crusade kept circling back to her belief in the first three words of the Constitution: "We, the people." To Brown it meant that rank-and-file voters who used their voices at the ballot box should be the center of political power.

On-the-ground legwork wasn't the only way to influence the vote. When she moved to a new county in 2017, Stacey Hopkins almost missed the innocuous postcard stuffed in her mailbox notifying her and her three adult children they were scheduled to be made "inactive" voters, a prelude to their registrations being eventually canceled. Hopkins certainly didn't see herself as "inactive." She had just voted in recent elections, and federal law required that she needed only to update her address with the US Postal Service to remain on the rolls, which she had already done after moving to a new home.

When the American Civil Liberties Union brought a lawsuit challenging the practice of making voters who had moved within their counties "inactive," with Hopkins as the main plaintiff, the complaint noted that one hundred sixty thousand other Georgians received a similar notice, potentially disenfranchising residents like Hopkins. State elections officials settled the case in early 2018 rather than risk a judge's decision, agreeing not to declare voters "inactive" when they fail to confirm their addresses after moving within the same county.

Despite the legal victory, Hopkins was still scarred by the experience. Her voice shook at a congressional hearing in February 2019 as she described how the postcard she'd received seeking confirmation of the new address had seemed "innocent," like something that countless Georgians would throw away without realizing their right to vote was at stake. "I can't really explain all the range of emotions that I felt when I saw this notice," she told federal lawmakers, displaying the postcard she kept as a reminder. "I can only best describe it as an abbreviated version of the stages of grief, except the one thing that I would never do is accept this," she continued. "It put in me a desire and motivation to stand up and fight back against what can only be called as massive and systemic voter disenfranchisement that has gone on virtually unchecked from the days of Reconstruction [and] Jim Crow to the erosion of the Voting Rights Act."

Others, like Nikema Williams, decided to channel their energy into a run for political office. Growing up in rural Alabama, Williams used to ride in the back of a pickup truck as her family dropped off slate cards urging her poor Black neighbors to vote. As a ninth-grade student in rural Alabama, she was surprised when she opened a textbook to find a picture of her aunt, Autherine Lucy, the first Black student admitted to the University of Alabama. When Williams graduated from Talladega College in small-town Alabama in 2000 and moved to Atlanta, her social network and her passion for politics collided, starting with a Young Democrats meeting that bothered her because of the lack of other Black faces.

Williams set out to change that by climbing the rungs of party leadership the old-fashioned way: organizing events at parks around the state, knocking on doors, registering new voters, advocating for other Black women to get involved. She ran for the leadership of Fulton County's Democratic Party, losing by one vote after a supporter got caught in a rainstorm. When the victor didn't serve the full term, she took over the office. She also worked for Planned Parenthood, voting rights groups, and labor organizations, urging anyone who would listen—voters, candidates, activists—to advocate for the voiceless. She met her husband, Leslie Small, who then worked for Congressman John Lewis, on the campaign trail in 2008. They named their firstborn son Carter in honor of the former president.

The turning point in Williams's political life came in November 2018, about a year after she won a hard-fought special election for the state Senate. During a special legislative session in the hushed Senate chambers, she heard shouting and what sounded like shattering glass in the rotunda below. Some of her constituents were attending a planned voting rights protest, so she rushed down the grand staircase hoping to defuse tensions. As she stood in support of the protesters, security officers moved in, detaining Williams and a handful of other demonstrators.

"I was not yelling. I was not chanting. I stood peacefully next to my constituents because they wanted their voices to be heard, and now I'm being arrested," she said, distraught, as two Georgia State Patrol officers restrained her arms behind her back with zip ties. She was brought to the Fulton County Jail, where she rebuffed the security officers who attempted to strip-search her, telling them she was unlawfully detained. After she was released, Williams didn't want to show up at the capitol the next day. Then she thought back to her family's struggle for equality. And she went back to work.

Before the arrest, Williams had been wavering over whether to compete to lead the state Democratic Party. But after she was hauled off to jail, she set her mind to running, winning, and doing everything else in her power to elect Democrats up and down the ballot. When she easily prevailed in the race for chairwoman in January 2019, becoming the first Black woman elected to lead the state party, Williams promised to take the fight to the GOP.

"Sometimes you don't choose the moment," she said. "The moment chooses you."

Chapter 9

"NEVER BACK DOWN"

It was supposed to be a celebration of Atlanta's growing sports scene, and the venue couldn't have been more perfectly picked. On a sunny August 2019 day, Georgia's top politicians and lobbyists were assembled on the club level of SunTrust Park, the new Atlanta Braves stadium that anchored a mixed-use hodgepodge of rowdy bars, upscale restaurants, and sports-themed store-fronts. The billion-dollar complex became home to the baseball franchise in 2017 when the Braves grew disenchanted with Turner Field in downtown Atlanta and rounded toward their new home along sixty acres in Cobb County.

As much as die-hard fans ached at the team's self-imposed exile from the city—and Atlanta leaders worried that the commercial clout of the suburbs was surpassing that of the capital—days like this one made the decision seem providential. A crowded Goldbergs deli just outside the stadium's gates served up warm bagels and iced coffee. Across an outdoor lawn, kitchens of-fered juicy hamburgers on buttered buns and tender brisket sandwiches. In-side the stadium's gates, sweeping vistas beckoned visitors to the club level to admire the skyline of suburban office towers and hotels surrounding the ballpark.

As guests arrived, flat-panel TVs showed off the addictive new multi-player video games that marketing types promised would herald a new era of competitive online sports. Bartenders served up soft drinks and craft beer for the daylong agenda, which featured a lengthy list of local sports executives ready to offer bullish predictions about Georgia's economic climate.

One of those figures was Kelly Loeffler, the co-owner of the city's WNBA franchise, the Atlanta Dream. Loeffler was accustomed to the spotlight as a marketing executive for Intercontinental Exchange, the behemoth financial company founded by her husband, Jeff Sprecher. And since purchasing a major stake in the Dream about a decade earlier, she had been trying to boost interest in the flagging basketball team. As Loeffler walked onstage, she gave glowing introductions to colleagues who ran the business operations of the city's basketball, football, baseball, and soccer franchises. But she couldn't help but notice that hardly a soul was listening; just about every face was staring at a smartphone and taking in the breaking news that Senator Johnny Isakson would retire, a decision that would reshape the nation's politics—and upend Loeffler's life as well.

─────────

If there was an icon of consensus and ethics in Georgia politics, a figure who rose above the partisan disarray, it was Senator Johnny Isakson. In a career of over forty-five years in politics, Isakson had forged a record as both a model conservative and a decision-maker who could find common ground with Democrats, earning him accolades for his skills at the art of compromise—and arousing suspicions from some conservatives who grumbled that he was all too willing to collaborate with political rivals.

The party he'd helped build from tatters also nearly pushed him into permanent exile after he lost a Republican runoff for the US Senate in 1996; Democratic Governor Zell Miller, who defeated the Republican in the 1990 election, brought him back from the wilderness when he made Isakson the chairman of the state board of education. From that platform, Isakson ran for the seat vacated by House Speaker Newt Gingrich, and his victory gave him a launching pad to succeed Miller in 2004 in the US Senate. He became the only Georgian ever to have been elected to the state House, state Senate,

US House, and US Senate. And he had done so from start to finish as a Republican—not as a Democratic convert. He was such a sure bet to win re-election in 2016 that no well-known Democrat bothered to compete against him. So towering was his reputation, none other than Democratic Congressman John Lewis honored him from the US House floor with this glowing praise: "You, senator, led a team that could cross the aisle without compromising your values."

Shortly before winning his third and final term in the US Senate in November 2016, Isakson disclosed that he was suffering from Parkinson's disease. But he insisted it wouldn't stop him from responsibly serving another six years in office. Besides, he and his aides saw his role as more important than ever: an unflinching voice for pragmatism in a party tilting ever more toward political absolutism. He was no fan of President Trump, confiding at the 2016 Republican National Convention in Cleveland that though he had endorsed him, he had grave concerns about his norm-shattering politics. Nor was he afraid to condemn the president when he overstepped; after Trump mocked the late senator John McCain's military service, Isakson called the president's remarks "deplorable."

But as Isakson's health issues worsened in the summer of 2019, it became clear that serving out the remaining years of his term, set to end in January 2023, would be more difficult than he could have imagined. He moved from his longtime Capitol Hill condo, with its balky elevator and cramped staircases, to a handicap-accessible apartment in downtown Washington. On his second night there, he tripped, fracturing four ribs. Two different MRIs showed the seriousness of his condition. One revealed a torn rotator cuff, the other a fast-growing cancerous growth on his kidney. For the first time, Isakson said, he was forced to ask himself if he could continue in office. If he stayed honest with himself, he knew he could not.

Isakson told his wife, Dianne, and a tight circle of three longtime aides that he would step down at year's end. Remaining in office through late 2020 to avoid a messy special election was out of the question. Isakson's confidants tearfully promised to keep the information tight for a few more days.

Around 9:45 on the morning of August 28, 2019, Isakson's aide Trey Kilpatrick called David Dove, the governor's executive counsel, multiple times before he picked up. "The senator needs to talk to the governor—now," Kilpatrick told Dove. Moments later, Isakson was on the line with Kemp to tell him of his plans to retire and pledge to support whomever he picked to replace him. Next, Isakson called Senate GOP Leader Mitch McConnell. Then he broke the news to his emotional staff, many of whom had known Isakson for decades. The email to Kemp's top advisers landed in their in-boxes just before 10:00 a.m.: "Johnny is telling Governor Kemp now that we are announcing today that Johnny will resign his Senate seat." A news release announcing Isakson's retirement hit in-boxes shortly thereafter, just as Loeffler was addressing the ballpark crowd.

None knew then the drama that the senator's decision would trigger. But even in those first moments, it was clear that Isakson's resignation would ensure that Georgia would shape the 2020 election by setting up a second US Senate race in one of the nation's most competitive states. John Watson, a former state GOP chairman who was at the SunTrust Park event that morning, immediately predicted a barrage of attention unlike anything Georgians had ever experienced. "We ain't seen nothing yet," he said shortly after Loeffler left the stage. "This puts Georgia front and center on every political map."

Georgians could blame state law for the onslaught to come. It gave Kemp the responsibility to replace him in the US Senate, one of the most consequential political decisions a governor could make. Whomever Kemp appointed was required to face a special election in November 2020 to serve the remaining two years of Isakson's term. With no party primary to filter out nominees, there was no limit on how many candidates would be on the ballot. And since state law required victorious candidates to win a majority of the vote, the free-for-all to come only increased the likelihood of a runoff between the two top finishers in January 2021, nine weeks after the race.

As much as the quirky system had become a fact of life in Georgia politics, many forgot that it was a remnant of segregation-era efforts. While most states feature plurality voting, Georgia's tiered structure, where the two top vote-getters square off in a second round, had been championed by Denmark Groover, a Democratic House leader and segregationist who readily acknowledged that he wanted to blunt the influence of Black voters. The majority-vote requirement made it harder for a lesser-known candidate to surprise the field by winning a primary election. It also helped segregationists ward off the threat of a popular unifying Black candidate muscling out multiple white contenders who split the vote. As other states abolished or rolled back their runoff systems over the decades, Georgia kept its intact.

———

Kemp knew that an anything-can-happen runoff was a distinct possibility, especially if the GOP couldn't unite behind whomever he picked. He faced immediate pressure to make up his mind quickly. Shortly after Isakson delivered the news to the governor, Kemp called his close aide Ryan Mahoney to brief him: "Start thinking of who needs to replace him." In an instant, Mahoney's phone lit up with texts and calls. Word had traveled fast.

On the Democratic side of the ledger, Jon Ossoff took little time to declare he would stay in the race against David Perdue rather than challenge whichever Republican Kemp picked to fill the seat. Fresh off her long flirtation with Georgia's other Senate race, Stacey Abrams sent word within about ten minutes that she was not interested in entering this one, either. But they were the exceptions. Just about every other major political figure from both parties in Georgia kept at least the door open for a potential run.

Kemp hadn't changed his cell phone number since his years politicking in Georgia's trenches, and his iPhone was full of messages from people dropping suggestions, promoting an ally, or brazenly offering themselves for the job. The false rumors flew so fast that even Kemp had a hard time keeping up with them. Republicans buzzed that the governor would make an immediate decision, that he was considering tapping his former rival Casey Cagle for the seat, and that he had already whittled down a short list. None of that was remotely true. As Kemp and his aides scrolled through the notes, it became clear that they needed to streamline the process before it got out of hand: if someone wanted the job, he or she would have to say so publicly.

Kemp couldn't help but think back to the last time a Georgia governor had such a heady appointment to make. Republican US senator Paul Coverdell had died suddenly in 2000 of a brain aneurysm, and Democratic governor Roy Barnes tapped his predecessor, Zell Miller, to the office. The decision was controversial at the time and even more so in hindsight; Miller, a Democrat, broke with his party to cosponsor GOP tax-cut measures and delivered a keynote speech at the Republican National Convention in 2004 that savaged his party's presidential nominee, John Kerry. ("This is the man who wants to be the commander in chief of the US Armed Forces?" he said to the crowd at Madison Square Garden in New York. "US forces armed with what? Spitballs?")

Turning to South Carolina governor Nikki Haley for inspiration, as she had in 2012 promoted Congressman Tim Scott to an open Senate seat, Kemp's team created an online application portal that was far less rigorous than a typical college admissions process. Those who met the constitutional requirements to serve in the US Senate needed only submit their résumé, address, and contact information. There was no request for a cover letter, references, policy proposals, or even a mission statement.

It might as well have been a blinking HELP WANTED sign. The office was flooded with hundreds of résumés: former US health secretary Tom Price; ex-congressman Jack Kingston; state representative Jan Jones, the second-ranking Republican in the Georgia House; and radio host Martha Zoller were among the wave of applicants. They joined many others who had no chance whatsoever at the gig, like the person who helpfully noted on his application that he was clear of sexually transmitted diseases, or the other who claimed to be "Hillary Clinton." A digital strategist named Matthew Borenstein submitted a one-page résumé on a whim. "I just wanted to see what would happen. I mean, who puts up a job posting for US senator?"

The governor said he hoped it would help "bring something different to the table" beyond the typical office seekers already jockeying for position. But the process drew fire from within the Republican Party and from without. Senator Perdue, nervous about a bitter race dividing the GOP, called Kemp only hours after Isakson's announcement to urge him to seek a change in the state law in how these types of elections were decided. Instead of the melee that pushed all special election contenders onto the same November ballot, Perdue favored a traditional primary election, so that both parties could settle on a favorite pick. It was the right thing to do, he urged the governor.

Kemp and his inner circle powered ahead with their plan, resisting efforts to change the state law, in part to protect whomever he picked from a tough GOP primary challenger. He and his deputies devised a wish list to identify

the most plausible applicants: First, they wanted someone who was unequivocally pro-Trump, no matter what the president said or did next. After all,
who knew better than Kemp how a single tweet from the president could, in
an instant, transform a campaign?

The governor also sought someone who could mesh with his brand as a
business-minded outsider and meld with him on the campaign trail in 2022
when, if all went the GOP's way, both would be up for reelection at the same
time. He needed someone with the fortitude to endure the campaign gaunt-
let, not just for the following year but for the coming decade: run, raise
money, win, run, raise money, and win. And just as significantly, Kemp
wanted to make a statement with his pick—a woman, a person of color, someone who could help broaden the party's appeal.

That last requirement did no favors for the cause of Congressman Doug
Collins, a lanky white lawyer from North Georgia. A fast-talking son of a
state trooper from rural Georgia, Collins got his first glimpse of Washington
politics in the late 1980s while an intern on Capitol Hill, an experience that
inspired daydreams of running for office one day himself. His knack for dad
jokes and silly sentimentality belied a serious side. A Baptist preacher with a
law degree, he served as a US Air Force Reserve chaplain and was deployed
to Iraq in 2008 to minister to battle-scarred veterans. Over three terms in the
Georgia legislature, Collins gained clout as a close ally of then governor Nathan Deal. When a newly redrawn, overwhelmingly Republican congressional district came open in 2012, he narrowly won a nasty runoff against a
popular local talk show host, Martha Zoller, before coasting to victory in the
general election.

Though Collins charted out a reliably conservative voting record in Congress, Donald Trump's election turbocharged his standing in Washington.
As the top Republican on the House Judiciary Committee—and a strident
opponent of the brewing impeachment proceedings targeting Trump—he
became one of the president's most outspoken supporters, a constant presence on Fox News and a favorite of hard-right conservatives. Those also happened to be the exact credentials an up-and-coming Republican needed to
run for premier office in the Trump era.

The day Isakson announced his retirement, Collins made it clear to Kemp and other top Republicans and the media he was interested in the job. But the governor wasn't ready to make a quick decision, and there were plenty of other candidates in the running who better fit his wish list. Over beers at the Governor's Mansion, one well-connected operative urged Kemp to consider BJay Pak, a former state legislator who was the Asian American US attorney in Atlanta. ("I have a great job here," Pak said when word leaked out.) Others pressed him to select Harold Melton, a respected Black conservative who was chief justice of the state Supreme Court, whom Kemp had quietly met to vet his interest. Larry Thompson, a former federal prosecutor and high-powered corporate attorney, turned down overtures from Kemp's senior aides, telling them he was happily retired. Some other Kemp allies pushed the candidacy of Allen Poole, a Black former law enforcement official from rural Georgia who led the state's highway safety agency and who was a blank canvas to most voters.

As Kemp considered the swelling number of applicants, Collins's supporters peppered the governor with appeals and promoted the strength of his candidacy in the media. Soon enough, President Donald Trump added his voice to the chorus by repeatedly encouraging the governor to hand the seat to one of his favorite loyalists. The pressure only seemed to bring out Kemp's stubborn side. An adviser remembers getting word from Kemp to put an end to the chatter about Collins: "I'm not talking to Doug again."

Joel McElhannon couldn't figure out why Kelly Loeffler wasn't calling him back. One of Kemp's earliest and most trusted aides, McElhannon was about to pay his respects at a funeral when word spread about Isakson's retirement. As soon as he saw the news, just before the service, he texted Loeffler urgently to let him know ASAP if she was interested.

Loeffler might not have been a household name to rank-and-file Republicans, but she was a fixture in Atlanta's elite GOP circles. Raised on an Illinois soybean farm, Loeffler moved to Atlanta in 2002 after stints in five cities and rose to become the chief of investor relations at Intercontinental Exchange, a fast-growing energy trading platform. She married the company's chief executive, Jeff Sprecher, in 2004 and helped him woo Wall Street investors to seal the purchase of the New York Stock Exchange, which by 2013 made their company one of the most important financial trading platforms on the planet. At their $10.5 million estate in Buckhead, which was the most expensive residential real estate transaction in Atlanta history when they purchased it in 2009, the couple assiduously courted the city's movers and shakers. In civic circles, Loeffler was best known for her connection to the Atlanta Dream, the WNBA franchise she co-owned with the wife of another powerful Atlanta executive. But a political career was never far from her mind.

Loeffler had prepared to run for the US Senate in 2013, when the retirement of Saxby Chambliss left a wide-open race. She put together an impressive team of operatives that included McElhannon and, over dinner at the Blue Ridge Grill in northwest Atlanta, began to craft the outline of a campaign-in-waiting. She ventured out to a few early events, too. "I bet you've never been in a barn before," one county Republican chieftain quipped to her during a grip-and-grin at a particularly snazzy farmhouse. She laughed, noting her rural upbringing. "I've never been in a barn this *nice* before."

But as their company's negotiations with the New York Stock Exchange heated up, Loeffler and Sprecher worried a Senate bid could jeopardize the deal. She ruled herself out of the 2014 race, ceding the pro-business outsider lane to Perdue. At the time, her campaign team said she was "deferring—for now."

As another open Senate seat beckoned, Loeffler was in another iffy position: she was now chief executive of a newly launched cryptocurrency trading platform owned by her husband's company and had just recruited veteran executives to fill out her leadership team. Even flirting with a bid for office could damage her new company's standing by indicating to investors that she wasn't fully dedicated to the venture. She told friends she didn't want even a whisper about it to surface until she knew for sure that Kemp was genuinely interested in appointing her.

McElhannon thought it was worth a shot. "If you want to be in the mix, let me know. Things are starting to move," he texted a few weeks later. She knew McElhannon well enough to know he would be discreet, so when he didn't receive a response, he assumed she wasn't interested.

He was wrong. As Kemp's search dragged on to October 2019, Loeffler called McElhannon out of the blue. She had received his messages over the last few weeks, she told him, but didn't want her name out as a possibility before she was ready to commit. Now Loeffler told McElhannon she had thought about it and was comfortable with the idea that he could privately float her name to the governor. McElhannon raced for his phone and dialed Kemp seven times before the governor finally picked up. He blurted out two words: "Kelly's interested." The governor was not surprised. By then, he had already heard of Loeffler's interest from another adviser.

Why was McElhannon so sure she'd be a viable candidate? He was convinced Loeffler knew what it took to run after her near candidacy in 2014, and she was willing to turn over the internal research her campaign conducted on her own vulnerabilities. He knew that having a strong woman on the top of the ticket would help broaden the GOP's appeal at a time when suburban women were fleeing the party. She seemed willing to endear herself to the pro-Trump voters she would have to win over. And most important, Loeffler checked all the boxes for Kemp's wish list for the job, someone he could be confident wouldn't buckle under the strain of a campaign. What's more, if any other Republican challenged her, Loeffler could tap into a potentially unlimited bank account. "That's your protection," McElhannon remembered telling Kemp.

The governor had known Loeffler for years, in part through the conservative fundraising circuit, but the two weren't particularly close. When her name first surfaced, one of his biggest fears was that she would come off as an out-of-touch Buckhead elitist. An early-morning meeting was scheduled at the Governor's Mansion—only about a half-mile drive from Loeffler's estate—to allow her to better introduce herself. At the governor's side was his chief of staff, Tim Fleming, a faithful adviser who had worked with Kemp since Fleming was a sophomore at the University of Georgia in 2002 volunteering for his state Senate campaign.

No meetings were scheduled before or after their sit-down, to give them plenty of time to chat—and to ensure no prying eyes happened upon their meeting. As they talked, the governor grew increasingly impressed with Loeffler's rural roots, her humility, her grasp of conservative policy, and her passion for politics. He left the meeting confident she could thrive in a political lane where Republicans were in sore need of a fresh face. Between

Perdue, Trump, and himself, Kemp felt the state GOP had its bases in rural Georgia covered. What the party needed was someone who could stop Democrats from peeling off white college-educated women voters in the suburbs. And Loeffler, a business-minded conservative, seemed to fit the bill.

Next came a thorough vetting with two of his top aides, Ryan Mahoney and Jeremy Brand, who approached the meeting the same way they did for any candidate seeking higher office: they tried to convince Loeffler not to run. Through round after round of questioning, they probed her political stances, her level of support for Trump, and the opposition research file they had already built on her. They knew if she didn't understand the many drawbacks to entering the race—the grueling days on the campaign trail, the sting of constant media scrutiny, the ceaseless political attacks—Kemp's biggest political decision could backfire.

They also wanted to make sure she understood the seamier side of the business: the rounds of fundraising calls, the tireless courtship of local political chieftains, the ability to relentlessly rip into her opponents. "I haven't taken a vacation in fourteen months," she told them. Mahoney laughed, before answering earnestly: "Good, because you won't be taking one for another fourteen."

The governor and his political advisers weren't the only factors in the decision. Loeffler also had to gain the support of Kemp's wife, Marty, who by then had already played a more prominent political role than any other First Lady in modern Georgia history, serving as the chief advocate for a suite of legislation that cracked down on human trafficking. The Kemps' bond was legendary in Georgia's political world, and their relationship dated back to their childhood. Marty's father had represented a slice of northeast Georgia in the state legislature for about a decade, and when he was away on business, Marty would often spend the night with her best friend—Kemp's sister.

Marty and Brian didn't start seeing each other romantically until years later, after she graduated from the University of Georgia, and when they married, she gamely moved six times in three months with her new husband as he started a construction business. A former cheerleader, she liked to compare a bid for political office to a high-stakes athletic competition—one that got her competitive juices flowing. She saw to it that their three teenage daughters were a constant presence during his run for governor; Lucy, the middle child, was often stuck toting a bright yellow plastic diesel canister from stop to stop asking for "gas money" to fuel the campaign bus. (This well-worn shtick usually started with Kemp's mockingly complaining about the high price of fuel before asking the driver, Mike, how the bus was holding up. "It's rattling a lot," he'd invariably say, before Lucy or another aide hauled the diesel can around to amused supporters.)

At another campaign event months later, Senator Lindsey Graham of South Carolina asked Marty and her daughters if they worked for one of the candidates, mistaking them for mere aides. Amy Porter, their youngest, politely told him they were Kemp's family, and Graham awkwardly turned away. When Marty recovered, she laughed. "I should have told that sonofabitch we're the Kemps. And we run this state."

Just about every major decision was made by the family as a group: TV ads, mail pieces, significant policy points in Kemp's speeches. And though the governor was impressed with what he heard from Loeffler, no one close to him doubted that Marty was going to have her say in his selection.

So it was with a bit of trepidation that Kemp's advisers prepared for a dinner at the Governor's Mansion to bring the potential senator together with the First Lady. But the two hit it off, bonding over a shared love of the 4-H Club and common farming heritage. Marty gushed over the important lessons her three girls had learned showing lambs at state fairs, while Loeffler smartly arrived with pictures of herself leading cattle as a teenager on her family farm. Marty appreciated that a high-powered executive who lived in a European-style estate with a secret passageway and a French pool house was "one of us"—a farm girl at heart.

There was, however, another obstacle where the governor's wife was concerned. There was friction between Marty and McElhannon, so much so that Kemp's aides felt the First Lady couldn't find out that it was he who was promoting Loeffler's appointment. The tension dated back almost twenty years, when McElhannon was hired to manage Kemp's campaign for the state legislature. At an introductory dinner in 2001, Marty had asked him what other races he was involved in. He told her he was running a Republican candidate against Tom Murphy, the longtime Democratic leader of the Georgia House. And, he added in colorful language, he was going to whup Murphy's rear end. Wrong move. McElhannon was oblivious to the fact that Murphy was so close to Marty's family that she knew him as "Uncle Tom." She could hardly look at him the rest of the night.

Their strained relationship hit a new low point during a 2017 meeting with Kemp's top advisers at the couple's home in Athens, with Marty and her daughters listening in. His campaign for governor was reeling, with poll numbers on the decline and his fundraising falling behind his top rival's. When a finance operative delivered a plan to turn it around, McElhannon let her know it wasn't up to snuff and demanded that she step it up. Offended by his harsh tone, Marty all but kicked him out of the room.

McElhannon knew his options at that point were to either gingerly apologize for his past transgressions or relegate himself to the background. Just as muleheaded as Kemp could be, McElhannon chose the latter route and, from that point forward, played a much less visible role in the campaign. The tension between McElhannon and Marty, meanwhile, only seemed to grow over the years, which meant McElhannon felt he had to keep quiet about his role in pushing Loeffler. "Marty really liked her and said she was the choice," he later said, "but that's probably in large part because no one—including Kemp—told Marty I was promoting Kelly."

Even with the approval of his wife and his top advisers, the governor took a few more weeks to make up his mind. His aides had grown used to his long deliberations, but this drawn-out process set a frustrating new standard. It wasn't until November that Kemp sealed his decision and phoned Loeffler. "If you're ready to serve," he told her, "we think you'd serve Georgia well." She quickly accepted his appointment, which also came with a promise of a staggering financial commitment of her own. She and her husband committed to spend *at least* $20 million of their own cash to keep the seat in 2020.

Now they just had to break the news to Trump.

———

The governor wasn't on bad terms with the president. But their relationship wasn't particularly close, either, not in the way both men might have expected after their fruitful alliance during the 2018 election. Kemp apparently hadn't consulted regularly enough with Trump about his selection process for the Senate seat, and the irritated president vented to his advisers about feeling left out. He also sniffed that it seemed more like the governor was trying to pick a truck driver than a US senator. (As did Perdue, who grumbled to fellow Republicans that the process was unbefitting the job.) When Trump's advisers updated him on the selection process at marathon White House political meetings, they showed him slideshows of potential candidates gleaned from the *Journal-Constitution*, not from the governor or his closest advisers.

The truth was, like many Republican politicians, Kemp didn't know how to handle Trump. And whether the governor believed it or not, Trump was convinced that he was the reason Kemp was able to defeat Stacey Abrams in 2018—and that he was owed a great debt for his assistance. Trump would tell everyone who would listen—advisers, social media followers, those at campaign rallies—that Kemp had been circling the drain before he'd stepped in to play the hero. In Trump's account, he single-handedly defeated Abrams and her pal Oprah Winfrey by driving up more turnout with his preelection campaign rally in rural Georgia. And Kemp knew he couldn't say anything to the contrary lest he provoke Trump's wrath.

As Kemp inched toward Loeffler's appointment, Collins and his allies boasted to Trump of his popularity in Collins's North Georgia district, home to the state's largest bucket of GOP voters. Even though Georgia insiders knew Kemp had already passed on Collins, a narrative was slowly growing in the national media, as well as among key grassroots activists, that the governor was gravitating toward Collins as the no-risk pick.

During a high-dollar fundraiser for the congressman, Donald Trump Jr. praised Collins as the "fighter" his father needed in the Senate. Fox News personality Sean Hannity called Loeffler a "big mistake," and Florida congressman Matt Gaetz pressed Kemp on Twitter to "do what you *know directly* is the right thing" and tap Collins. After the *Journal-Constitution* published a story reporting that Collins was likely to run even if he was bypassed by Kemp, setting the stage for a nasty GOP feud, Trump phoned the governor to press him to go ahead and anoint the congressman as his selection.

It was not often the two men chatted like that. Throughout his first year in office, some of Kemp's aides urged him to strengthen his relationship with Trump by dialing him up every so often—even if it had nothing to do with politics. Some advised him to look no farther than the state's neighbor to the south, where Florida governor Ron DeSantis appeared to have mastered the complicated dynamic with the president. His 2018 campaign revolved around frequent appearances on Fox News designed to catch Trump's attention and ads promoting his unwavering loyalty to the president. One striking thirty-second spot had DeSantis telling his young daughter to "build the wall"—an homage to one of Trump's base-pleasing slogans—as she played with toy blocks.

But that wasn't the way Kemp wanted to operate. So when it came time to break the news to Trump, they called in a specialist.

Nick Ayers was the thirtysomething operative who understood Georgia Republican politics like few others. The tousle-haired former Perdue aide was both an adviser to Vice President Mike Pence and a confidant of the president. But when Ayers got a call asking him to reveal Kemp's decision to the president, he balked. This wasn't news Trump could hear secondhand; Kemp had to get the president's blessing in person. Ayers was asked to come along to facilitate the meeting.

On a Sunday morning in late November 2019, he, the governor, and Loeffler flew to Washington by private plane for a secretive hour-long meeting unknown even to most of Trump's closest advisers, who were at a retreat at Camp David. The goal was to put the three together in a room and make sure the president was on board before Kemp's decision was finalized.

The problem, of course, was that Kemp's decision *was* already finalized.

The first few minutes went well enough. Trump said he thought Loeffler had the potential to be a star and spoke glowingly of her husband, Sprecher, whom he had known for years. Then he looked toward the governor: "I haven't heard a lot from you—is your mind made up?"

Kemp answered honestly, telling the president that he had, indeed, made his choice. And it was Loeffler.

In an instant, the mood soured.

Somehow or other, Trump was under the impression that the gathering was a get-to-know-you session for a potential pick, not a meeting with an eventual US senator. And Kemp made a tactical error by not giving Trump reason to believe he had any input.

"If you already made the decision," Trump muttered, "then why are you even here?"

What came next was alternately described as a "full-throated confrontation" and a "super-aggressive job interview" by people familiar with the back-and-forth. Trump mentioned a few other names and pointedly asked Kemp why he hadn't chosen Collins. Then he challenged both to explain how she would win the seat. Kemp did his best to answer, but it didn't placate the president. As the meeting closed, Trump said tersely: "Good luck. Good luck, Governor."

Even before they boarded their flight home, the governor and his future appointee were in full-fledged damage control mode. Maybe it was an elaborate plan to test Loeffler, they thought, or maybe the president was genuinely upset. Either way, both knew it was only a matter of days, maybe hours, until the details of the meeting were leaked. More important to Kemp and his aides, they had to salvage Loeffler's image with the party's base before it was too late to redeem her.

McElhannon, back home in Georgia, soon received a phone call from Loeffler.

The meeting with Trump didn't go well, she told him. And they both knew what that could mean. She'd better start ramping up for a primary challenge.

═══════

About a week later, roughly one hundred people gathered in Governor Kemp's ceremonial office at the Georgia capitol, just beyond portraits of his predecessors that lined the building's halls. Behind a massive wood desk framed by royal blue curtains, Loeffler introduced herself for the first time to Georgians as their next US senator in a speech designed to leave no doubt about her conservative credentials. She was "pro–Second Amendment, pro-military, pro-wall, and pro-Trump." She would fight the "socialist gang" in Washington bent on taking down Trump. Most of all, Loeffler wanted to stress, she was no closet liberal.

"I've been called soft-spoken. But I've also been called a lot worse. In Congress I may not be the loudest voice in the room. But you don't have to be shrill to be tough. And when it comes to fighting for Georgia, I will never back down. No one will fight harder for our state, our president, and our conservative values."

Even as she spoke, it was clear Loeffler's political problems were already mounting. Standing just to her left as she spoke was House Speaker David Ralston, one of the most powerful politicians in Georgia. His appearance was not, however, an endorsement; he was a close ally of Collins who wanted the congressman to enter the race. Other Republicans boycotted the event or released terse statements announcing a wait-and-see approach.

Some who backed Loeffler had already paid a political price. Lieutenant Governor Geoff Duncan's quick endorsement cost him the services of his top aide, Chip Lake, a close Collins confidant. Duncan later acknowledged he had taken the advice of a trusted "life coach" to immediately back Loeffler against the wishes of Lake, who wanted him to extract political concessions from Kemp in exchange for his seal of approval. And before Loeffler could finish, an email from Collins landed in the inboxes of reporters with more reason to believe the congressman was inching toward a run.

From the outset, it was obvious that Loeffler was determined not to give Collins even a smidgeon of an opening to run to her right. But it was less clear how her pro-Trump stance would play with moderates and independents—the very constituency Kemp hoped Loeffler could win over. Neither her public embrace of Trump nor her promise to dig deep into her bank account scared off the congressman. In the days since Trump's disastrous meeting with Kemp became public, the pro-Collins crowd had only tried harder to sully the appointee's image before she had time to shape the public's opinion.

Soon, leaked polls touting Collins's popularity with Republicans surfaced in conservative outlets, while activists questioned Loeffler's stance on guns, abortion, and financial policy. On social media, backers of Collins and Loeffler engaged in open, and sometimes hilarious, warfare. In one memorable exchange, Mahoney mocked Florida congressman Matt Gaetz's tight "jorts"—a favorite insult that Georgia Bulldog diehards hurl at their

Florida Gator rivals—and questioned whether they left enough room for childish effects such as Legos and jelly beans. "Oh . . . and mind your own business," Mahoney added. "We don't know you and we don't care what you think." Gaetz, who had previously accused Kemp of betraying the president, fired back in a tweet: "Legos and jellybeans are awesome. Your Senate pick isn't."

Just before Loeffler's rollout, Kemp finally met face-to-face with Collins at a revered site for the two Georgia Bulldogs fans: the annual football grudge match between UGA and Georgia Tech, which that year took place at Tech's aging Atlanta stadium. The two briefly shook hands and exchanged polite greetings, and a few hours later connected by phone. The governor made no apologies about passing over Collins, and the congressman bluntly told him he hadn't ruled out a Senate bid of his own. Indeed, the statement that Collins released in the middle of Loeffler's maiden speech intended to remind reporters he was still considering a run—but that first his "primary focus is defending our president against partisan impeachment attacks."

Collins had time to decide—but not much. He knew Loeffler could stroke a check to blanket the airwaves with ads framing herself as a conservative hero. In mid-January, Collins gathered in his North Georgia home with his family: his wife, Lisa, a retired fifth-grade teacher whom he had met at church, and his three children, Cameron, Copelan, and Jordan. He reminded them of the challenges ahead, of the enormous financial deficit they couldn't possibly overcome, and the physical and mental toll it would take.

Loeffler already had not only Governor Kemp on her side, but the backing of the National Republican Senatorial Committee, the well-financed political arm of Senate Republicans. In the days after her appointment, some sworn critics of Loeffler suddenly started to change their tune, applauding her stances against abortion and tax increases and in support of fewer firearms regulations.

But Collins had a coterie of allies, too, built up over decades of work at the Capitol, in Congress, and at ground-level party gatherings he had frequented throughout his career. During the family meeting, he reminded his loved ones of the hard-earned trust he'd built with fellow conservatives, a reputation he was certain couldn't be undercut no matter how much cash and establishment support Loeffler might have.

The next day, he called Lake to deliver news that came as a surprise to the veteran strategist.

"We are in."

Chapter 10

"REMAIN THE REVEREND"

Reverend Raphael Warnock's address to a crowd of one thousand Georgia Democrats at the party's annual fundraiser in late 2019 was known in political terms as an "everything but" speech. As in, the Atlanta pastor said "everything but" that he was entering the race for US Senate to succeed Johnny Isakson. Nary a soul in the room was surprised that he seemed on the verge of a historic run—they were all just waiting for him to finally announce.

Four years earlier, Warnock had seemed a lock to challenge Isakson, too. Every Sunday, operatives combed his sermons from the pulpit of Ebenezer Baptist Church for any shred of evidence that he would run. He charted out a strategy with party leaders, prepared his church members for the likelihood of a campaign, and gave an electrifying invocation at the party's signature fundraising event in September 2015. Warnock told attendees he was passionate about motivating the seven hundred thousand voters of color in Georgia who "are not disengaged or disinterested. They are disillusioned. They see no connection between the candidates and the people and the politics they serve," he said. Then, he paused to let the message register with the party's elite. "And sadly, in many instances, they are right."

Democrats saw Warnock as the type of preternaturally gifted candidate who could have invigorated Georgia's Black electorate and embraced liberal policies long neglected by the state's mainstream Democrats—basically, as someone who would have waged a Stacey Abrams–style campaign in 2016, two years before she ran for governor. But he faced friction from church leaders concerned he couldn't responsibly fill his day job while also embarking on a rough-and-tumble political campaign.

By October 2015, he was out of the race, telling his flock that "given my current pastoral and personal commitments, this is not a good time." Dispirited Democrats scrambled to Plan B, recruiting an awkward multimillionaire named Jim Barksdale who was perhaps best known for the old-fashioned cap he wanted to make the calling card for his campaign. He lost to Isakson by fourteen points.

Warnock might have counted his blessings that he hadn't run that cycle, but he didn't abandon the idea of seeking public office. Over the next few years the church hired experienced clergy to free him from the important, but time-consuming, day-to-day administrative functions of committee meetings, life-cycle events, and one-on-one visits that filled his schedule. That helped the deacons and other church VIPs become more comfortable with the prospect of their pastor joining a premier political race.

Stacey Abrams, Warnock's ally and confidante, had spoken occasionally with him since 2014 about campaigning for higher office, though in their discussions she served more as a sounding board than another friend pleading with him to run. After ruling out her own bid for Isakson's seat, Abrams told Senate Democratic leader Chuck Schumer that Warnock should be the party's nominee. She quietly pledged her support to the pastor when the time came. For Warnock, the only question was when that would be.

The son of two preachers, Warnock grew up in the Kayton Homes public housing projects in Savannah as the eleventh of twelve children—his parents, he'd often say with a smile, took to heart the Bible's command to be fruitful and multiply. His mother, Verlene, spent summers picking tobacco in Waycross, an agricultural hamlet near the Okefenokee Swamp that Warnock would describe simply as "way across Georgia." His father, Jonathan, spent his weekdays salvaging broken-down cars and his Sundays working on broken-down people as a Pentecostal preacher, a schedule that was so grueling that he'd often chew his food at the dinner table with eyes closed because he was so worn out.

His parents were also progressives: His father supported ordaining his wife as a fellow Pentecostal preacher, a bold decision at the time. Both challenged their congregants to push the boundaries of traditional views of scripture and demand social justice. "We were short on money," Warnock would say, "but long on love and faith."

Nicknamed "the Rev" in high school for his oratory skills, Warnock was inspired by the radio show of a local college professor named Otis Johnson, whose message of Black empowerment through civic engagement stayed with him. He followed Martin Luther King Jr.'s footsteps by attending Morehouse College, and after graduating in 1991 earned his divinity degree from Union Theological Seminary in New York. After stints at churches in Harlem and Baltimore, Warnock landed his dream job in 2005, becoming the youngest senior pastor in Ebenezer's history. He shared the news with his tearful dad on Father's Day.

Once in the legendary pulpit, he put Ebenezer at the intersection of political activism and civil rights, leading voter registration drives, forcefully opposing capital punishment, advocating for criminal justice reforms, and demanding a higher minimum wage. Warnock welcomed visits from Presidents Obama and Clinton to his church over the years, turning it into a hotbed of progressive political activity. He knew how to make an effective political statement, too, getting arrested in 2014 at a Georgia capitol protest of a measure that would ban the expansion of Medicaid. As Warnock was handcuffed and led away by state troopers, a crowd of demonstrators surrounded him and sang "We Shall Not Be Moved."

With Isakson's seat suddenly open, a number of prominent Democrats interested in the vacancy waited for Warnock's word first. At the October 2019 gala, as the potential rivals milled about tables of tipsy donors, the pastor gave the strongest signal yet he would run by calling for partisans to "stand up and fight for the soul of our democracy" while admonishing a president "who is actively courting the support of foreign adversaries."

"That's a scandal and a scar on the soul of America," he said of the growing impeachment investigation into Trump's ties to Russia. The audience buzzed with approval and by the time he finished, texts from attendees shot around the hotel, some silly and some serious, with the hashtag #Warnock2020.

———

The chattering class was right. Warnock's flock was now more prepared for the prolonged absence of its leader, and the pastor was free to chart out the image of a campaign that was inspired by King's vision. In early 2020, he called his close friend Jason Carter and said simply, "I'm doing it." Around that time, he met with strategists Adam Magnus and Elisabeth Pearson at the high-rise offices of a major Atlanta law firm to hone his game plan. The veteran operatives, both visiting from out of town, laid out how one Democrat after another had failed to end the party's losing streak—and impressed upon Warnock that he could succeed only if he embraced his unique moral platform.

To Magnus, an ad maker who built his career on savvy sloganeering, it boiled down to a simple catchphrase.

"You've got to remain the reverend."

The pastor chuckled. "What else am I going to be?"

He probably should have felt less sure of himself, as a first-time candidate edging closer toward a run for office that could define his life. But as he prepared to enter the race there was a quiet confidence about him. "He knew how difficult it would be. He knew what he was getting into," said Lauren Passalacqua of the Democratic Senatorial Campaign Committee. "But he had a sense of peace."

The Sunday before Martin Luther King Jr. Day, Warnock invited Magnus, Passalacqua, and Christie Roberts, a senior adviser to the DSCC, to Ebenezer Baptist Church to see him in his element. They settled into the third row of the packed pews, uncertain of what to expect.

In the middle of his fever-pitch sermon, Warnock suddenly stopped, lowered his voice, and began to talk about an ancient biblical negotiation in modern-day terms. It's like when an impatient cable guy arrives at your house to cut the cord, he said, and you've got to convince him to keep the premium TV shows coming. From the pews, the parishioners hummed in agreement.

When the sermon ended, the three compared notes. Each was struck by that simple aside, which they viewed as proof that Warnock could be relatable while leaning into the moral authority of his pastorship.

Warnock stuck with that approach when he announced his campaign to the public at the end of January, entering the race in tandem with endorsements from Abrams and help from national Senate Democrats. He made clear he would remain in the pulpit, pulling double duty as a candidate and a clergyman. In his mind, it would make sure he would remain a "citizen representative" enmeshed in his community—and not a professional politician enmeshed in Washington.

"This is going to be hard work. And it should be. Anybody running for office knows that it's hard work," he said. "But I've always understood that my service extends far beyond the doors of the church."

For Georgia Democrats, the work convincing party decision-makers that the state was a legitimate battleground was only heating up. Even Abrams struggled to get the message across, penning a memo with top adviser Lauren Groh-Wargo that asserted it would be "malpractice" for national Democrats to snub Georgia in this race. The sixteen-page document was delivered by Groh-Wargo in September 2019 to each of the roughly twenty Democratic presidential campaigns, to every Democratic committee at the national level, to influential financiers, and to many groups Abrams's team never expected to invest in the state.

Among its points: Georgia had by far the highest percentage of Black voters of any battleground state and the youngest overall electorate. Diverse Atlanta suburbs that flipped in 2016 were on pace to turn even bluer in 2020, in contrast with large counties in other competitive states that hemorrhaged Democratic votes in the last midterm. Most of all, Georgia gave national Democrats a three-pronged electoral possibility not available in any other state: a trove of sixteen electoral votes, multiple competitive US House seats, and two US Senate races that could decide control of the chamber. In a *Pod Save America* podcast interview, Abrams described the state as a "cheap date" for national Democratic funders.

The memo was drafted with the help of Seth Bringman, the operative who years earlier rejected pleas from Groh-Wargo to move to Georgia because he doubted Democrats could flip the state. He finally relented and moved to Georgia in late 2018 to help the last stretch of Abrams's campaign, and ditched plans to return to Ohio after Abrams's defeat in the election convinced him that Georgia was on the cusp. He was joined by other former Ohioans—a group that included research specialist Esosa Osa and strategist Jessica Byrd—whose migration to the South reflected how Georgia was on the verge of surpassing the Buckeye State as a premier political battleground.

Now one of Bringman's roles was convincing cynical Beltway reporters of a notion he once soundly rejected: that Democrats could win in Georgia. "Why would national Democrats divert resources from Florida, or the Midwest, to roll the dice in the Peach State?" the journalists wanted to know. "Why would Senate Democrats go big in the pricey Atlanta media market when Iowa, Kansas, Maine, and Montana were cheaper plays?" What grated on him the most, though, were the on-the-record "bless their hearts" jeers from local Republicans who dismissed Democrats as afterthoughts.

Fair Fight, the group Abrams founded, released an analysis to counter that GOP narrative. It noted that an average of 1,250 Georgians were added to the electorate each day—45 percent of whom were under the age of thirty and roughly half of whom were voters of color. Both groups overwhelmingly favored Democrats and bolstered the very line of thinking that drove Abrams's 2018 strategy. (When Abrams was asked by *The Daily Show*'s Trevor Noah why she had chosen to focus on appealing to newer and more diverse voters rather than aiming toward the political center, her answer consisted of one word. "Math.")

Perfecting the sales pitch to state and national figures was one of the reasons that Scott Hogan was hired as executive director of the state Democratic Party. A floppy-haired political savant, Hogan was accustomed to uphill political battles. He had years of experience promoting Democratic causes in his native Indiana, in deep-red Utah, on the beaches of Guam, and in the barrios of Puerto Rico. Most recently he had toiled in South Carolina, where he managed a Democratic gubernatorial candidate who was squashed by a Republican favorite. That red-state experience taught him how to grind, fighting for small victories each day in a place where Democrats were an afterthought.

When Hogan took the job in Georgia in June 2019, the party had about four staffers on the payroll and reams of documents littering its downtown Atlanta headquarters, including an eight-foot-high pile of paperwork crowned by a toppled Christmas tree that obstructed one small office. To relieve stress, Hogan would often roam the building heaving bags of trash into piles.

Hogan and Nikema Williams, the party's chairwoman, knew they needed to line up staffers earlier than ever. And to be able to do that, they needed to beef up fundraising. The word *battleground* was strategically inserted into every piece of literature, every fundraising appeal, in hashtags on just about every social media post put out by the state party. Williams said only half-jokingly she might have uttered "Battleground Georgia" in every conversation she had in those days—even during family dinners with her husband, Leslie, a veteran operative himself.

The duo also committed that 2019 would not be an off year. The party geared up for municipal races, even though candidates in those contests don't run on party affiliation, to make sure Democrats had a robust on-the-ground presence in small communities well before the November 2020 vote. Dozens of staffers were hired to serve as voter protection aides, liaisons to communities of color, and press assistants.

Their mission was to prepare Georgia to *be* a battleground state—even if the national party didn't yet believe it could be.

═══

After he announced, Warnock and other Democrats braced for a blitz of opposition to his candidacy. There were thousands of hours of the pastor's remarks on tape from more than a decade of recorded sermons and speeches, along with statements and stances he staked over the years that Republicans could use to damage him. But the barrage never came. Instead, for Senator Loeffler, the first stages of the campaign had nothing to do with Warnock at all.

Loeffler's opening moves were entirely predicated on preventing Trump from dealing a death blow to her campaign by endorsing Collins. Even the staffers she tapped for key positions were chosen to attract the president's notice. Loeffler hired the top aide of Mark Meadows, a congressman who would soon become Trump's chief of staff, as a key deputy. She brought on staffers with deep ties to Florida governor Ron DeSantis, another Trump favorite. Her media strategy was similar: "Get her on Fox News," one aide was instructed. "And remember: it's an audience of one."

Just as Loeffler ran toward Trump, she sprinted away from Mitt Romney, the former presidential candidate and now Utah senator whom she had befriended years earlier at an Atlanta gathering. They weren't just nominal friends: she and her husband were so close with Romney and his wife, Ann, that they had visited one another on cross-country trips several times over the years, the couple told *Atlanta* magazine. When Romney ran for president in 2012, Loeffler and Sprecher contributed more than $1.5 million to a super PAC supporting his campaign—far more than the two had given to Trump in 2016. Now she was told that "acting like Mitt" would ruin her chances with a Georgia GOP electorate that viewed Romney as a phony. One of her first attention-grabbing acts, in late January, was a tweet that tore into Romney for supporting the impeachment of the president: "The circus is over. It's time to move on." She tagged Trump's handle on Twitter to catch his notice.

The Republican infighting raged over many other fronts. In late 2019, antiabortion activist Marjorie Dannenfelser had declared that Loeffler should be "disqualified" from serving in the US Senate. By February, Dannenfelser pledged to do "everything necessary" to help her win. The senator's allies pushed Trump to float Collins as his next director of national intelligence, urging the president to eliminate the prospect of a nasty Republican-on-Republican feud that could damage his chances, too. Trump mentioned the idea to a plane full of reporters on Air Force One, but Collins shot it down almost as soon as the aircraft could land.

Loeffler and her allies started bursting volleys of ads by late January that boasted of her unshakable support for Trump and, eventually, bludgeoned Collins. His campaign had a name for the pro-Loeffler satellite groups that were launching: Kelly Inc. Among them was a free-spending outside organization called Georgia United Victory that provided Loeffler with backup on the airwaves. It wasn't lost on anyone that the acronym of the group, run by Kemp loyalists, was GUV.

Another was the Georgia Life Alliance, a small antiabortion outfit that in 2018 didn't have to file a detailed federal tax report because it collected less than $50,000. Suddenly, in February 2020, the group announced a $3 million pro-Loeffler ad campaign, a development that was maddening to Collins. The congressman had been one of the group's favorite politicians and, just weeks earlier, had emceed its annual gala. "They've hardly raised $50,000 and then they suddenly announce a $3 million ad buy?" Collins vented to the *Journal-Constitution*. "It's more than fishy." The group's executive director said that it hadn't received any donations from Loeffler, though he refused to disclose who had contributed for fear of compromising the identities of donors who wanted to remain anonymous.

There was no way Collins could match Loeffler's bottomless checkbook, but he thought he could turn her fabulous wealth against her. The congressman's supporters bandied about details of the mega-mansion she owned along exclusive Tuxedo Road, so sprawling it merited its own name: Descante. They weaponized images of Loeffler appearing courtside with Abrams in 2018 at a WNBA playoff game to brand the Republican as a secret bestie of the Georgia GOP's archenemy. (Loeffler countered by noting Abrams was so chummy with Collins she named an annoying yet charming character in a romance novel after him.) And they made sure Georgians took note of her new mode of travel.

In late 2019, Collins aide Chip Lake bought professional-grade camera equipment to take photos of his growing teenagers, though it mostly collected cobwebs. As the campaign got underway, Lake had an epiphany. He had heard that Loeffler had quietly purchased a luxurious private jet to whisk her to small-town campaign events, high-dollar fundraisers, and Washington votes. Soon, he managed to pin down the details. He found a website that tracked the flight tag of her Bombardier CL30 and assigned interns and junior staffers to obsessively monitor her whereabouts.

Lake checked the online site around the clock, too, and one Sunday morning, he noticed the plane was en route from Trump's compound at Mar-a-Lago back to Atlanta. *Jackpot*, he thought as he raced to a tiny executive airport in west Atlanta. He donned a fluorescent safety vest and disguised himself as a maintenance worker, complete with a trash bag and garbage picker, and plopped himself down on one of the runways just in time for Loeffler's landing. Obscured by a tidy row of bushes, Lake snapped a picture of the jet through a barbed-wire fence and then, as Loeffler's SUV roared by, temporarily ditched the camera in a trash bag to avoid notice.

That night, Lake arrived at Collins's first campaign meeting, triumphant that his undercover mission had worked out. The picture of the sleek aircraft would soon be leaked to the *Journal-Constitution*, along with a statement from the Collins campaign disparaging the senator for her extravagant mode of travel—an executive jet that typically lists for at least $7 million but, with upgrades, could surpass four times that—while she posted videos of her purchase of a modest Georgia-made SUV. "Who buys a $30 million jet in secret then posts a picture with their new Kia on Facebook around the same time?" asked Dan McLagan, a Collins deputy known for his abrasive wit. "That's all you need to know about Kelly Loeffler." When Lake arrived at a staff party that night, he was greeted with a roar of applause—and a giant cookie cake plastered with the plane's tail number.

————

Warnock watched the internal GOP bickering with bemused interest. But he couldn't relax. Fellow Democrat Matt Lieberman, the son of former vice presidential nominee Joe Lieberman, had a head start on Warnock after entering the race in October against the wishes of party leaders. And former federal prosecutor Ed Tarver would soon join the contest. Other more notable names might also launch campaigns, too, if Warnock failed to scare them off before a March qualifying deadline. But as he scrambled to ready for his run, his personal problems threatened to undermine his campaign.

On a March 2020 morning, the reverend drove to the home of his estranged wife, Ouleye Ndoye, in south Atlanta to take their two young children to school. The couple had been the toast of Ebenezer a few years earlier when, at the end of a two-hour-long New Year's Eve service, Warnock pulled a small red jewelry box from his pocket, quoted an Indian poet and a favorite line of scripture, and got on bended knee to ask for her hand in marriage.

Hundreds rushed from the pews to surround Warnock as he spoke, hoisting smartphones to film Ouleye as her voice trembled with her answer: "Yes, I will." The explosion of applause that followed was earsplitting. They were wed a few months later at Ebenezer on Valentine's Day and had two children—a boy and a girl—before the relationship fell apart. He filed for divorce in May 2019, and the rift between them only deepened as he prepared his Senate bid.

Moments after Warnock arrived at her townhouse that morning of March 2, the two erupted into an argument over whether he would agree to let Ouleye take the children to Senegal for her grandfather's funeral. He had recently denied his ex-wife's request to allow the children to apply for passports for the international trip, and he told her he didn't have time to rehash the argument that morning. He had a flight to catch. When he tried to leave, Warnock later told police, Ouleye refused to close the Tesla's right rear passenger door. In a hurry to get the kids to school, he slowly drove the car away. That's when Ouleye began to wail and accused him of driving over her left foot.

After police officers arrived, Ouleye tearfully told authorities that her husband wasn't who he made himself out to be. She "tried to keep the way that he acts under wraps for a long time and today he crossed the line," she told the officers, according to bodycam footage. "That is what is going on here. And he's a great actor. He is phenomenal at putting on a really good show."

In a separate interview, Warnock told the officers that Ouleye was exaggerating the incident: "I start to move slowly thinking she's clear. I barely move, and all of a sudden she's screaming that I ran over her foot. I don't believe it." After inspecting her foot, the paramedics and officers on the scene found no visible sign of a traumatic injury, and Warnock was never charged with a crime. The Warnocks' divorce was finalized a few months later.

That Friday, March 6, he showed up to file paperwork to run for US Senate just minutes ahead of the qualifying deadline. Washington, he said, had enough "career politicians and corporate elites." It was time to give a pastor a chance.

Chapter 11

THE PLAGUE

At the very moment that Raphael Warnock was en route to the state capitol to qualify for office, President Donald Trump was preparing to head to Atlanta to address a fast-growing crisis. The outbreak of coronavirus that swept through China and besieged Italy was now threatening the United States. The stock markets tumbled, businesses canceled events, and nervous politicians tried to show they were in command. American public health officials had by now reported more than three hundred cases and at least seventeen deaths linked to the disease, and Governor Brian Kemp had days earlier held a late-night press conference to gravely announce the first two known cases of the outbreak in Georgia.

Trump had initially canceled his March 6 visit on the eve of the trip, when White House officials learned that an employee at the Centers for Disease Control and Prevention in Atlanta might have contracted the disease. But he reversed himself early that morning when her test came back negative, sending his aides and security officials scrambling to piece the trip back together. Before Trump left Washington, he signed an $8.3 billion emergency funding bill to beef up the government's response to the virus. When he landed in Atlanta, his convoy rumbled toward the heavily guarded CDC compound along streets lined with protesters. Public health experts demanded a more aggressive response to the disease, along with expanded testing, and the president's strategy was already under scrutiny. As the motorcade sped toward the security gates surrounding the headquarters, one demonstrator held up a sign in bold black letters reading WE NEED A VACCINE AGAINST TRUMP.

The reporters trailing the president huffed up several flights of stairs and through a series of labyrinthine corridors to a laboratory stocked with scientific equipment where Trump was supposed to hold court for a few minutes. The president wore a red "Keep America Great" cap, an unbuttoned white shirt, and a dark zip-up jacket with the presidential seal, a striking contrast to the suit-clad scientists and politicians surrounding him behind a long black table. To his left was Kemp. Behind him were Kelly Loeffler and Doug Collins, two archrivals who stood on either side of David Perdue.

Instead of short remarks, though, Trump presided over an hour-long press conference that offered an alarming portrait of his strategy to contain the growing outbreak. He falsely claimed that testing for COVID-19, severely limited at the time, was available for anyone who wanted it. He acknowledged that he wanted passengers on a virus-ravaged cruise ship docked in San Francisco to stay aboard rather than disembark because their arrival would raise the number of total coronavirus cases in the United States. He boasted of his "natural ability" to understand medicine. And he tried to tamp down fears about the growing public health crisis with assurances that the disease would naturally disappear. "It will end. People have to remain calm."

His overly optimistic view, of course, was wishful thinking. Within two weeks, vast parts of Georgia, like much of the rest of the nation, were in lockdown in a drastic attempt to contain the spreading pandemic. The economy shuddered, professional sports leagues scuttled their seasons, and healthcare systems were pushed to their limits. The legislative session was abruptly put on hold after lawmakers voted on March 16 to declare a public health emergency, granting Kemp extraordinary powers to suspend state laws, close schools, restrict travel, and limit public gatherings to contain the disease.

It was the first time in modern Georgia history that a governor had been allowed such sweeping powers, and even the daylong vote to approve the declaration underscored the threat of the disease. A state senator who showed up to the capitol sniffling and coughing later revealed he had tested positive for COVID-19, sending the entire legislative branch into self-quarantine. Another state senator who sheltered in his Florida beach house after contracting the disease was berated by the local sheriff for trying to ride out the illness in his vacation home rather than staying put in Georgia.

It didn't take long for Kemp to use his new authority. He banned gatherings of more than ten people, extended school closures, shuttered bars and nightclubs, and imposed restrictions on most businesses. He encouraged the "medically fragile" to shelter in place and dispatched the Georgia National Guard to nursing homes. As hospitals filled with coronavirus patients, Kemp opened a makeshift medical facility at a downtown Atlanta convention center to help relieve the strain.

Suddenly, carefully laid plans to mobilize voters with in-person rallies and door-to-door canvassing had to be abandoned, as traditional campaigning went on hiatus. Candidates quickly shifted to TV ads and digital appeals to reach a newly captive audience stuck on their sofas ahead of a fast-approaching May 19 primary. All contenders had to quickly get accustomed to awkward livestreamed Zoom calls and virtual visits to party gatherings instead of pressing the flesh. An upcoming visit by Joe Biden to Atlanta was postponed and then canceled.

The lockdown was actually a boon to incumbents and well-known figures who could rely on high name recognition and fundraising prowess to pump the airwaves full of ads. Many newer candidates, like Warnock, struggled. Used to the call-and-response of Sunday sermons, Warnock hated not being able to feed off the energy of the crowd. He'd say a surefire applause line and pause, looking bewildered sometimes when it wasn't met with the expected ovation.

By year's end, more than ten thousand Georgians had died of the disease, and hundreds of thousands more had contracted the virus. Jobless rates skyrocketed, businesses went under, and politicians shifted from an initial sense of unity to a sharp division over how to respond to the plague: Democrats argued for mask mandates and sharper economic curbs, while many Republicans aggressively pushed to reopen the economy and objected to face-covering requirements. Governor Kemp found himself caught in the middle,

facing blowback from some conservatives over his decisions to institute restrictions and then more blowback from Democrats and public health scientists when he aggressively rolled them back.

The sharpest fallout came in April, when Kemp allowed close-contact
businesses, like nail salons and barbershops, to reopen as long as they followed a lengthy list of safety precautions. Kemp was expecting a hostile response from horrified Democrats, who blasted him for becoming one of the
first governors to ease economic restrictions and accused him of putting the
health and safety of Georgians at risk. But he was blindsided by Trump, who
used a White House press conference to humiliate the fellow Republican. It
was "just too soon," Trump said, to let tattoo parlors, bowling alleys, and
other businesses reopen. "Would I do that? No," he huffed. "I want to protect
people's lives. But I'm going to let him make his decision. But I told him I
totally disagree."

Indeed, the two men had spoken shortly before Trump's press conference,
and the president had pushed Kemp to reverse his decision. But he also gave
Kemp no indication that he would use his megaphone to thoroughly undermine the governor. Suddenly, Kemp was left explaining why leading Democrats *and* Republicans were condemning his approach. Atlanta mayor Keisha
Lance Bottoms's response was typical of the reaction: "We need to, as government leaders, step up and give people an incentive to stay home. But there's
nothing essential about going to a bowling alley in the middle of a pandemic."

—————

Kemp's most important political ally was also facing repercussions for a
pandemic-related decision of a very different sort.

Even before Kelly Loeffler took office, her potential conflicts of interest
loomed larger than those of anyone else in the US Senate because of her extraordinary wealth—*Forbes* reported that she was likely the richest politician
on Capitol Hill—and because the company her husband ran owned the New
York Stock Exchange. Her every decision was scrutinized for the possibility
that it could help her husband's business; transparency advocates said she
might as well be tiptoeing through an ethical minefield.

The first explosion had taken place in the aftermath of a January 24 senators-only briefing about the growing threat of the coronavirus. At the closed-door meeting, the heads of the CDC and the Department of Health and Human Services briefed the group on the increasing number of cases of the disease, though they were also told it didn't yet pose a serious risk to the country. In Loeffler's mind, she said later, the officials didn't offer any information about the outbreak that you "couldn't have seen on the front page of a newspaper."

In the weeks leading up to her assuming office, Loeffler had insisted she was taking an arm's-length approach to her financial portfolio to avoid ethical conflicts, letting third-party advisers handle her day-to-day transactions. Up until January 24, she hadn't reported a single stock transaction since taking office that year from either her own trading account or the one she owned jointly with her husband. But in the weeks following the meeting, there were more than twenty transactions that off-loaded at least $1 million worth of stocks. Many of the transactions involved companies that had little to do with the pandemic, and some lost money. Others seemed savvy, including an investment of at least $100,000 in the teleworking company Citrix.

Though the stock trades didn't break any laws, they were an embarrassing tactical error for a candidate already struggling against a narrative that she was a wealthy elitist. When the news of the trades broke two months later, first in *The Daily Beast* in March and then followed by blanket coverage in local and national outlets, outrage followed. Democrats called on Loeffler to step down from office. Georgia House Speaker David Ralston said he was worried the fallout would deal debilitating "down-ticket damage" to state legislative candidates. Congressman Doug Collins, Loeffler's GOP rival, said he was aghast that the senator was "profiting off the pandemic."

Loeffler's campaign at first struggled to respond before eventually dismissing the reports as "ridiculous and baseless." Loeffler and her husband had no role in the investment decisions, she said, and her financial filings indicated she hadn't been informed of the transactions until weeks after they had been made. And besides, she pointed out later, some of the trades involved bets on airline and energy firms that got hammered during the pandemic. This was no cabal that got together with a hush-hush mission to make money off the misery of millions of Americans. "There wasn't, like, a group of senators that were told there's going to be a pandemic, but we need to keep it a secret," she later told the *Washington Examiner.*

For her critics, the transactions only reaffirmed the charges that she was profiting from her job. On Fox News, Tucker Carlson called for Loeffler to step down if she knew about the stock trades her advisers had carried out. Sprecher was particularly insulted by media coverage that linked her to Senator Richard Burr of North Carolina, then the chairman of the Senate Intelligence Committee, who had dumped hundreds of thousands of dollars in stocks during the early chaos of the pandemic.

To Sprecher, the idea that the wife of one of the most scrutinized figures on Wall Street would exploit confidential information to make a small profit was laughable. But Loeffler's aides knew it was just the sort of story that could mushroom—and take down her campaign with it. Her advisers were also indignant that Loeffler's attorneys hadn't taken more steps to inoculate her, fuming that any election lawyer worth her salt should have advised Loeffler's portfolio managers to stop trading individual stocks during a heated campaign. "It never should have happened," one of her deputies vented. "She could have avoided the whole thing."

Within days of the revelation, Loeffler's polling numbers nose-dived from a virtual tie with Collins to single-digit territory. Any net positive from the $5 million she had already pumped into her campaign to introduce her to voters had been effectively wiped out. The cacophony grew to the point that Loeffler was forced to state in an interview that she wasn't quitting the race—an ominous sign for any Republican incumbent in a competitive contest, but particularly one who had never been tested by the voters. It grew worse in April when the *Journal-Constitution* reported that more than $18 million worth of her husband's company's stock was sold on her behalf in three separate transactions in late February and early March. Her campaign said the sales were prearranged and exercised as part of the couple's compensation package.

Loeffler was resolved not to quit, but internal discussions were held about scaling back her activity and ad spending, maybe even finding a "way out" in the form of another appointment from Trump to a national post or an ambassadorship. A possible investigation loomed, which Loeffler was certain would lead to her exoneration—but would also draw even more negative coverage of the transactions over the months it would take to complete. Her camp quietly braced for the worst: Loeffler's lawyers briefed some members of her official staff office about what to say if any of them were subpoenaed by investigators.

Had Loeffler had to face a summer primary, as Collins and his allies desperately hoped, she probably would have been sunk. One internal poll conducted by Loeffler's campaign had her trailing the congressman by twenty-three points. But state law held that all candidates in special elections, Republican and Democrat, had to run against each other on the November ballot. And a proposal backed by Collins's allies in the state legislature to require primary elections ahead of the special election went nowhere after Kemp vowed to veto it. The November date gave Loeffler invaluable time to recalibrate.

By now she had only a narrow path back to viability—and almost no room for error. Loeffler's inner circle, led by advisers Taylor Brown and Stephen Lawson, spent the next few weeks in a state of crisis, essentially pounding their fists on the table, insisting that the senator had done nothing wrong, while flooding the media with details about the trades that they hoped would clear her name. Her press shop spent hours with reporters seeking to change the narrative, stressing that Loeffler hadn't been privy to any confidential information and that her financial advisers hadn't been coordinating the transactions with her.

Soon Loeffler and Sprecher announced they would unload the stocks they owned in individual companies and would invest the money in broader exchange-traded and mutual funds. Reports that federal investigators wouldn't charge Loeffler, and that a Senate ethics panel dismissed a scathing complaint from watchdog groups, were hailed as "vindication" of any wrongdoing.

The senator aimed to rebrand herself as a clearinghouse of coronavirus guidance, with a "relief and recovery" website that offered details about the outbreak. She touted every federal allotment of funds to fight the disease in Georgia and wrote checks to purchase meals for first-responders and protective gear for hospital workers. Her campaign broadcast the stories of pandemic "heroes" on its social media pages and showcased her role on Trump's coronavirus task force.

Just as important, her aides fast-tracked $4.5 million worth of additional airtime—money initially earmarked for later in the campaign—for a volley of ads loaded with American flags and uplifting music that labeled the criticism against her "liberal lies" targeting her because she was a "strong conservative woman." "Kelly Loeffler is all about Georgia," intones the narrator in one of the clips. "And it shows. Every day." Collins sniffed at the ad onslaught: "You can't buy love and you can't buy an election." But Loeffler's internal polling numbers started to tick up again and the campaign was beginning to stabilize. Months later, one of her closest advisers marveled that she had survived the fallout. "It was a miracle."

———

Other candidates faced a more imminent reckoning. Georgia's May primary was delayed until June 9 to buy local elections officials time to prepare for socially distanced voting and stock up on personal protective gear and hand sanitizer. After agonizing negotiations over hours of phone calls, Democrats struck a deal with Secretary of State Brad Raffensperger, the Republican top elections official, that would herald a sweeping change in elections policy. For the first time in Georgia history, state officials would mail absentee ballot request forms to Georgia's 6.9 million active voters to encourage them to cast their ballots by mail.

More than 1.1 million mail-in ballots would be submitted by primary day, shattering records and—equally important—familiarizing a swath of the electorate with the ease of casting an absentee vote. Thanks to the rise in mail-in voting, more Democrats cast ballots in the June primary than they had during the previous high-water mark set during the 2008 presidential primary between Hillary Clinton and Barack Obama.

Even with much of the electorate shifting to mail-in ballots, the primary was a disaster. The COVID-19 outbreak hampered efforts to train election workers to use the state's new $104 million multi-computer elections system, which was beset by technical glitches. At times passwords for electronic poll books didn't work, and some overwhelmed staffers couldn't hook up the different components of the system—which involved tablets, touch-screen machines, scanners, and printers—into the proper power sources. Election workers—some hired just a day earlier to replace elderly veteran staffers—threw up their hands in dismay. At scattered polling sites in metro Atlanta, voters waited in line for as long as eight hours.

So broken was the election system that some voters, anticipating monumental delays, arrived with lawn chairs, books, and coolers full of drinks and snacks. Roving advocacy groups delivered slices of pizza and cold drinks outside some of the most problematic voting locations. "This is voter suppression—I'm shaking just talking about this," said Aerialle Klein as she stood, seething, at a metro Atlanta high school in an unmoving line. "But I'm staying. This is my civic duty. Something has to change."

There was no quick tally of the results after the polls closed. Elections staffers in some counties were unprepared for the record number of absentee ballots and took days to total the votes. As the results trickled in, a trend became clear: many better-known candidates thrived thanks partly to high name recognition and partly to a nervous voter base drawn to familiar contenders. No statewide candidate benefited quite as much as Jon Ossoff.

Ossoff had entered the Democratic primary for US Senate as the unquestioned front-runner, even though his rivals had beefier résumés and more experience in public office. From his place atop the polls, he could afford to take aim at Perdue and other Republicans while mostly ignoring the darts from his fellow Democrats. (A rare exception: When former Columbus mayor Teresa Tomlinson brought up a GOP poll during a virtual debate that suggested that Ossoff was struggling outside metro Atlanta, Ossoff laced into her. "Your campaign is so weak they didn't even bother polling your name in that poll.")

He wasn't quite so blasé about challenging the Republican narrative. The National Republican Senatorial Committee had snapped up the jonossoff.com domain name before the campaign got going and turned it into a parody website, complete with a listing for a $13 engagement ring that suggested his marriage to Alisha was a sham. Ossoff replied that the "outrageous and pathetic" attack demonstrated how low his opponents were willing to sink. As polls showed him nearing the 50 percent mark that had eluded him during his congressional run three years earlier, Ossoff pumped in $450,000 of his own funds to finance a final onslaught of ads.

By election night, even Ossoff's die-hard devotees figured he would be dragged into a runoff against Tomlinson, who captured around 16 percent of the vote. Her campaign sent out a boastful press release mocking Ossoff as a "failed repeat candidate" who once again couldn't seal the deal with voters. But as mail-in ballots from populous metro Atlanta counties came in, Tomlinson had to eat her words. Ossoff nudged just over the 50 percent mark—and then kept inching higher. He eventually landed at 53 percent to notch the outright victory that had escaped him in 2017, this time for a statewide contest against multiple well-financed candidates.

Because of the pandemic, there was no lavish Ossoff victory party on the night of the primary, nor would it have been very celebratory even if there had been one. The struggle of counting more than 1 million absentee ballots bogged down the results, and the race wasn't formally called by the networks until a day after the election. Instead, in an online address, Ossoff accused Perdue and other Republicans of leading Americans down a "dark path" and implored Democrats not to grow complacent. "This is not a moment to let up. This is a moment to double down," said Ossoff. "We can no longer go down a path of authoritarianism, of racism, of corruption. We are better than this."

Unlike the other Senate race, an asymmetrical ballot with nearly two dozen candidates, the general election matchup between Ossoff and Perdue was a much cleaner contrast along more conventional lines: on one side, a veteran former corporate chieftain with a direct line to the White House and six years of voting for solidly conservative policies; on the other, a youthful investigative journalist who branded his opponent a "cowardly enabler" embodying all that was wrong in Washington. And Perdue quickly leaned on the playbook he had relied on for his first campaign run to frame Ossoff a "rubber stamp" for liberals.

Perdue had used that phrase to great effect in 2014 when he pilloried Democrat Michelle Nunn as too liberal for Georgia on his way to a comfortable November victory. But despite the rhetoric, Perdue and Nunn had developed a deep personal respect for each other. The family seats of the Nunn and Perdue clans sat just a few miles away from each other in Houston County, a mostly middle-class community in central Georgia where monuments to both families are held in great esteem: an exhibit honoring the accomplishments of Nunn's father, former US senator Sam Nunn, in the center of Perry, and an elementary school named for Perdue's father on the outskirts of nearby Warner Robins.

Though they disagreed sharply on policy, the senator admired Nunn's work as a nonprofit executive who had run former president George H. W. Bush's charitable foundation and later international charities in Atlanta. Perdue's father adored the Nunn family. If he lost to Nunn, Perdue thought, he could rest easy knowing that he had been defeated by a worthy opponent.

Ossoff, on the other hand, he hated with every fiber of his being. Perdue had opened international businesses in Europe and Asia, pushed Dollar General to new levels of profitability, survived the cutthroat world of corporate politics, and was elected to the world's most exclusive club despite great institutional opposition. Now, he told himself, he was about to enter the fight of his political life against a trust fund baby whose greatest accomplishment was an internship with John Lewis.

The strategy he devised with his aides could have been ripped from any other candidate running a close statewide race. He hammered Ossoff as "China bought" because his company's investigative documentary films were rebroadcast by a Hong Kong–based outlet with ties to the Chinese government. He bludgeoned Ossoff as a "radical liberal" who would open the door to socialism. And he leveled a false, but politically damaging, claim that his opponent wanted to "defund the police."

Even so, Perdue knew not to underestimate Ossoff, not least because of the dangers of being considered the favorite to win. In 2014, Perdue had been part of a plucky group of Republicans intent on taking back the Senate. In 2020, he was among a group of GOP incumbents trying to preserve a narrow majority in the chamber—and competing for resources with other Republicans who were thought to be far more vulnerable. Not long after Ossoff secured the nomination, Perdue called a trusted adviser about his predicament.

"Everyone in Washington thinks we'll win," the senator said. "The president thinks we'll win. I know we're in trouble."

Chapter 12

A SOCIAL JUSTICE SUMMER

On cordoned-off streets outside the state capitol in mid-June 2020, thousands of protesters circled Georgia's Gold Dome, demanding social justice reforms. Shirts, signs, and face masks declared in stark, bold letters BLACK LIVES MATTER. Chants of "No justice, no peace!" replaced the cacophony of cars that would have clogged the area before the pandemic. Speakers promised protests, anger, and a "next wave of revolution in America." Somewhere in the middle of the crowd stood Jon Ossoff, fresh off his victory in the Democratic primary for US Senate, wearing a sweat-stained blue shirt while holding a bullhorn aloft on Washington Street in front of the state capitol.

"Where are these politicians who hide in this building and who don't respond to an invitation to address you when they keep talking about our Constitution?" he asked the demonstrators. "I will never know how it feels to have black skin in America. But let me tell you this: I will fight with you and march with you every step of the way."

The death of George Floyd at the hands of Minneapolis police officers in May had incited the largest social justice protests in the nation since the civil rights era, as demonstrators took to the streets in major cities and small towns to oppose racism and police brutality. The peaceful demonstrations in Atlanta had given way to violent clashes in parts of the city days after Floyd's death, as rioters burned police cars and looted stores in downtown and Buckhead despite emotional pleas to stand down from Mayor Keisha Lance Bottoms and legendary civil rights leaders.

In Georgia, the protesters' fury also centered on the death of Ahmaud Arbery, a Black man who was shot and killed while jogging in a neighborhood outside the coastal Georgia town of Brunswick. Authorities initially didn't arrest anyone in the February slaying of the twenty-five-year-old, citing a "citizen's arrest" law dating back to the Civil War to justify the decision not to prosecute. But a graphic video of the shooting surfaced months later, prompting a full-fledged police investigation that led to murder charges against armed white men accused of chasing Arbery with their vehicles then cornering him in the street. The gunman, authorities say, shot Arbery three times with his Remington 870 shotgun and taunted him with a racial slur as he lay dying on the pavement.

The demonstrators who took to the streets each evening made the state capitol a center of protests, demanding the removal of symbols of the state's racist, segregationist past clustered around the statehouse complex. One night, a group of about a hundred chanted "Tear down Gordon!" as officers bristling with body armor formed a protective ring around the focus of their anger: a bronze statue of John Brown Gordon in full Confederate regalia, pointed northward in a gallant pose, astride his trusty steed, Marye.

The homage to the former Georgia governor and US senator, dedicated with great fanfare in 1907, was just one of a collection of sculptures, portraits, and plaques around the seat of state power that commemorated Rebel leaders. Many romanticized the false Lost Cause mythology that the Civil War was premised on a battle for state's rights and not an attempt to prolong the horrors of slavery. As well as being a Confederate war commander, Gordon was also generally acknowledged to have been a leader of the Ku Klux Klan, and civil rights groups were distraught when his statue was left standing as other painful symbols of Georgia's past had been removed, such as the monument to a fist-pumping Tom Watson, another white supremacist leader from a past generation.

The protesters who gathered with Ossoff on this day had a mission beyond uprooting hated symbols of the Old South. They demanded a revival of a hate-crimes law that allowed for stiffer penalties for crimes motivated by race, color, religion, national origin, gender, sexual orientation, or disability. A previous version of the law had been struck down by the Georgia Supreme Court in 2004 as too vague, and a more tailored measure had been regularly blocked by Republican critics for the next sixteen years, leaving Georgia as one of the only states in the nation without these legal protections.

Arbery's death reopened the long-simmering debate over the proposal among state lawmakers, who reconvened in June amid the social justice protests to finish a legislative session that had been interrupted by the pandemic. After a hard-fought legislative compromise, Governor Brian Kemp declared that the hate-crimes measure that passed the legislature was the "silver lining in these difficult and stormy times" as he signed it into law. Calvin Smyre, the dean of the legislature, called it a defining moment in Georgia history: "Ahmaud Arbery's death will not be in vain."

As legislators put one divisive debate behind them, Mayor Bottoms balanced her own outrage over police brutality with the public demand for law and order—and growing tensions with Republican leaders over the unrest in the capital city.

Once a little-known city councilwoman, Bottoms became one of the state's foremost Democratic leaders after narrowly winning a crowded 2017 mayoral race against a rival from the wealthy white neighborhoods on the north side of town. The daughter of R&B legend Major Lance, Bottoms had benefited from the enthusiastic support of her larger-than-life predecessor, Kasim Reed, whose brutal attacks on her opponents, and subsequent endorsement of Bottoms, helped her emerge as the candidate to beat.

Her victory made her the latest symbol of the electoral power of motivated Black women in the Donald Trump era; the local rapper TopNotch composed a song in her honor simply titled "Atlanta's Got a Mayor Named Keisha." Eager to make her name on the national stage, Bottoms was one of Joe Biden's earliest and most prominent supporters in the South, stumping on his behalf to often skeptical audiences across the nation long before he was the Democratic presidential nominee.

During the Iowa caucus, the mayor was dispatched to Davenport, an industrial town on the far eastern edge of the state, more than 150 miles from the searing national political spotlight trained on Des Moines. At a high school just outside the riverfront city's commercial district, Bottoms introduced herself to a predominantly white crowd that had hardly heard of her. When the sound system malfunctioned, the mayor stood on the creaky auditorium stage, abandoned the microphone, and bellowed as loud as she could. "The reason I left 74-degree weather is because I still believe in this country," she said of Atlanta's balmy February climate. "I was reminded of a quote from Kobe Bryant this week. He said, 'The moment you give up is the moment someone else wins.' And I refuse to let someone else win. That's why I'm here on behalf of Joe Biden."

Back home, Bottoms struggled to quell the civic unrest over the summer that had only intensified after another police killing of a Black man, this time in her city's limits. Rayshard Brooks, a twenty-seven-year-old Black father of three young girls, was shot and killed during a June confrontation with police after he had fallen asleep at a Wendy's drive-through near downtown Atlanta. The police officers responding to a complaint about his nap in a parked car gave him a sobriety test, which he failed. When Officer Garrett Rolfe tried to handcuff him, Brooks resisted and grabbed another officer's Taser before fleeing through the parking lot. Rolfe opened fire, and Brooks died from gunshot wounds to the back.

Atlanta's police chief was forced to resign, and Rolfe was initially sacked (he was reinstated in May 2021), but demonstrators demanded more decisive action. The night after Brooks's death, protesters blocked a busy highway and then set afire the Wendy's where the shooting had taken place, as police and firefighters stood at a reserved distance watching flames engulf the building. The parking lot around the burned-out hulk of the restaurant quickly became a rallying point for activists—and a lawless zone that was a glaring embarrassment for the mayor's administration.

Armed demonstrators set up roadblocks surrounding the charred ruins of the Wendy's, creating what *Journal-Constitution* columnist Bill Torpy described as a "ragtag Checkpoint Charlie" with gun-toting sentries stopping and often turning away confused motorists along a forlorn stretch of boarded-up businesses. Police, wary of fanning the flames of the fury in the streets, largely left them alone on orders from city hall.

The hands-off approach proved to be a fatal mistake. A few days later, on the evening of the Fourth of July, an eight-year-old girl named Secoriea Turner was riding in a Jeep with her mother and an adult friend when they were confronted by an armed group of strangers at a barricade. It wasn't exactly clear what happened next, but police have said as many as four people opened fire on the vehicle, killing the child.

Bottoms, overcome with emotion, stood before a bank of TV cameras alongside Turner's family to denounce the violence and plead for the perpetrators to come forward: "You shot and killed a baby," she told the killers, her voice quaking with emotion. "An eight-year-old baby." Two days later, police officers and sanitation crews wielding giant plastic garbage bags methodically dismantled the encampment, discarding wilted flowers, tattered tarps, and windblown hand-drawn signs.

Most Georgia Republicans loudly criticized the demonstrations, even though the overwhelming majority of them had been peaceful marches. Upset at what he saw as Mayor Bottoms's failure to combat the violence, Kemp deployed National Guard troops to protect the state capitol, the Governor's Mansion, and a law enforcement building that had been ransacked the weekend of Turner's death.

For Senator Kelly Loeffler, though, the movement for racial equality was a particularly thorny matter. She was a co-owner of a franchise in the WNBA, the women's basketball league whose players promoted social justice messages, condemned police brutality, and took a knee during the national anthem long before the summer of Black Lives Matter protests. Loeffler knew Doug Collins was certain to tie her to the league's history of racial justice activism. And this was her chance to prove she wasn't the spineless moderate that Collins made her out to be—even if it meant turning her back on the team she once cherished.

She and her friend Mary Brock, the wife of a longtime Atlanta chief executive, had bought the Atlanta Dream in 2011, shortly after the team lost an exhilarating league championship game. She felt the Dream needed to be led by women, and who better than Loeffler? She was wealthy, eager to play a larger role in Atlanta's civic life, and, most important, obsessed with basketball. She wanted to be known as a players' owner and lavished the team with perks such as cars during their summers in Atlanta and apartments clustered in the same luxury complex. From her center-court seat, she analyzed the team's tactics and strategies, groaned at missed penalty calls, and often gave players headed to the locker room after the final buzzer a comforting hug or pat on the back.

But her embrace of Donald Trump put her out of step with the predominantly Black league and threatened her conservative credentials on the campaign trail. George Floyd's killing, and the protests it sparked, only upped the cultural tension over the growing Black Lives Matter movement. Before Collins could deal her another damaging attack, Loeffler penned an open letter to the WNBA's commissioner in July that reverberated across the realms of sport and politics.

The letter objected to the league's plans to honor the Black Lives Matter movement, suggesting instead that American flags be put on every jersey when games resumed that month. And it railed against a "cancel culture" she claimed posed a grave threat to free speech. "The truth is, we need less—not more politics in sports. In a time when polarizing politics is as divisive as ever, sports has the power to be a unifying antidote," wrote Loeffler. "And now more than ever, we should be united in our goal to remove politics from sports."

Condemnations came from all corners of the sports world. Left-leaning activists disparaged her for refusing to back the social justice movement, and Atlanta civic leaders demanded she sell the franchise. Some of her most loyal supporters were stunned by her response, as were the players who once thought they knew her best. "I'm actually shocked by her actions. Sometimes you gotta play the political game, and I get it. But don't mess with us in this political game," Angel McCoughtry, who had been the face of the Dream franchise for about a decade, told the *Journal-Constitution*. "If this is the person that she really is, I know that I don't want to be around someone who just doesn't advocate for what's right."

Loeffler wasn't trying to appeal to Democrats or even moderates. She was in a race to captivate her party's right flank at a time when the questioning of

Loeffler's conservative provenance was coming to dominate the campaign. In fact, it was a feature in just about every campaign speech Collins delivered before crowds big and small across Georgia. In a cramped civic center in the north Georgia town of Resaca, where Republicans reign over local politics, Collins was rewarded with loud applause when he accused Loeffler of trying to "hoodwink" conservatives.

"It's all about smoke and mirrors. It's about trying to make you believe that you're something that you're not," he told a small audience. "You know who I am." In his hometown of Gainesville, where hundreds gathered at a restaurant off the town square, Collins told supporters he was simply defending his honor by questioning Loeffler's true beliefs. "If I'm going to fight for this president, this administration, this country, I'm also not going to sit back when someone attacks me. I'm going to fight back," he said. "You gonna lie about me? I'm going to tell the truth about you."

Now Loeffler was seizing the initiative, tapping into the "stick to sports" battle cry echoing among Trump supporters. Her opposition to the Black Lives Matter movement earned her a blizzard of national attention and became a mainstay of both her fundraising appeals and stump speeches. She wore the bruising criticism from national media and leading Democrats as a point of pride, thrilled to have evidence of her conservative bona fides.

"I want to speak for all Americans who feel like they don't have a voice, who feel like they're going to be canceled if they speak out against a political movement," Loeffler told a gathering at a restaurant in Woodstock, an essential GOP exurb north of Atlanta. "That's not freedom. That's not America."

<hr/>

The uproar over Loeffler's breakup with the WNBA was an opportunity for Warnock, too. At first glance, it seemed Warnock had little to worry about in the early stages of his campaign. He had support from prominent state and national party leaders, an inspiring personal narrative, and no high-profile Democratic rivals.

But the pandemic had knocked his campaign off its stride. He was seldom grabbing headlines after his splashy January debut, even during social justice protests that aligned with a number of his greatest strengths as a candidate.

A few of the party's top donors, even some of his friends, wouldn't return the pastor's calls, leaving Warnock feeling burned and isolated. His advisers would assure him it wasn't personal. Politics was a dirty game, and the pastor needed to learn to play it. Quickly. "He was an imperfect perfect candidate. He'd tell you all the time he wasn't a politician. Keeping him on message was a nonstarter," said Dasheika Ruffin, one of his deputies. "But you could see him just come alive in a crowd."

As his campaign geared up, Warnock insisted on maintaining a semblance of his routine at Ebenezer Baptist Church. The demands of his congregation didn't ease during a pandemic or pause for his Senate bid, and Warnock wanted to give himself part of Tuesdays to attend to his flock by overseeing board meetings, conducting sick calls, and handling other clergy business. It was also on Tuesdays, usually early in the morning, that the pastor would start what was typically the most demanding part of his weekly regimen: a ten-hour process of reading, studying, and then writing and practicing his Sunday sermons. His staff jealously guarded that time for Warnock so he could prepare for the sermon, which was usually recorded on Friday and broadcast remotely to his flock during Sunday services that were forced online by the pandemic.

Though he had long lived a public life, Warnock was by nature intensely private. His aide Terrence Clark drew a glimpse of the pastor's personal side when he drove Warnock from Atlanta to a federal prison in Jesup in June to greet the pastor's brother Keith, a first-time offender who was sentenced to life in prison for a drug-related offense in 1997. Keith's early release from prison was a joyous occasion for his family, and Clark watched teary-eyed as the two men embraced in a parking lot of a southeast Georgia gas station.

It could have been a made-for-campaign spectacle, too, but Warnock wanted to keep the moment out of the public eye. He only let slip the news of his brother's release later that day on a long-planned webinar, by way of explaining to participants the happy reason he was speaking to the group from a moving car. To Clark, that experience epitomized what motivated the candidate he was spending his every waking hour to help win. "He never really lost hope that his brother would be released," Clark said, "and that brought it full circle for me."

He and Warnock's other aides might have been true believers, but polls that still had the pastor in middling territory indicated that many voters thought otherwise. Stacey Abrams nudged Ruffin to start dipping deeper into the campaign's paltry coffers at a time when insiders were concerned that Warnock wasn't doing enough. *"What are you saving it for?"* Abrams asked.

Warnock's strategy in the first months of the campaign relied upon amassing a collection of endorsements to show that he had a groundswell of support. Though the pastor enjoyed solid name recognition in parts of metro Atlanta, he was hardly known elsewhere in the state. Early in the campaign, Warnock held socially distanced gatherings in small towns with local elected officials. Often more people would show up to hear the mayor or county commissioner than the US Senate candidate. At each stop, the speeches were designed to be short—and the time for photos long. Ruffin wanted attendees to post photos and videos of their selfies to create the impression that Warnock had a thunderous choir of supporters across Georgia singing his praises. But his campaign was desperate for a unifying moment to get Democrats in harmony behind him.

Loeffler's stand against Black Lives Matter seemed heaven-sent. Moments after she saw the Republican take a shot at the WNBA, Ruffin texted the first two basketball figures in her list of contacts that came to mind: NBA legend Charles Barkley and three-time Olympic gold medalist Dawn Staley. Within hours, Staley helped line Ruffin up with incensed WNBA leaders who felt betrayed by one of their own—and were venting their anger on social media and in public statements. "E-N-O-U-G-H! O-U-T!" tweeted the Women's National Basketball Players Association. The Dream, in a remarkable rebuke to its owner, issued a statement that concluded: "Black Lives Matter. Vote in November." Some of the of the players wanted to do more. And Warnock gladly courted their support.

Over online meetings, several of the team's standouts told the Democrat they felt betrayed by Loeffler's opposition to a movement so important to a league dominated by Black women. To many of them, it was personal. Loeffler once had been so devoted to the Dream that she built work trips around its schedule, talked strategy with coaches after tough losses, and hosted players for preseason catered meals at the indoor basketball court of her Buckhead mansion. Now she had become the chief antagonist to the very players whose careers she had nurtured.

As angry as the players were at Loeffler, they didn't intend to line up behind Warnock simply because he was running against the Republican. In Zoom calls with the pastor, the players vetted his stances on the issues dearest to them, peppering him with questions about his criminal justice policies and his vision for racial equality. They also consulted with both Abrams and Sue Bird, the WNBA star, who encouraged them to publicly endorse Warnock. Once they agreed to take that position, the players asked the pastor's aides to send over merchandise they could wear to promote his candidacy. The problem, though, was that Warnock's shoestring campaign didn't yet have any. The players came up with their own idea: pitch-black T-shirts with white lettering that read VOTE WARNOCK.

On August 4, a few weeks after Loeffler clashed with the league, social media exploded with images of Dream players and others across the WNBA wearing the pro-Warnock T-shirts ahead of nationally televised games in Florida. "We wanted to make sure we could still keep the focus on our social justice movement, and funny enough, Reverend Warnock is somebody who supports everything that we support and just happens to be running in that seat," Elizabeth Williams, the veteran Dream player, told ESPN that evening. "So it just worked out really well."

Ruffin wept for joy as she saw the images everywhere. And she was just as elated by the first major bump in fundraising all that attention brought—the campaign collected more than $1 million over the next few days, as well as gaining a surge of new social media followers. Though insiders had always viewed Warnock as the odds-on favorite, it was only after the WNBA show of force that he took a convincing lead in public polls over rival Democrats.

"That was the moment we knew we didn't have to worry about other Democrats anymore. We could expand. We could go on TV. We were getting noticed," Ruffin said.

Warnock put it a different way. "It gave fuel to our movement."

Chapter 13

FAREWELL TO A LEGEND

The throngs gathered on the Edmund Pettus Bridge in Selma, Alabama, as they had for decades for the annual march commemorating Bloody Sunday, when brutal police beatings of civil rights activists in 1965 drew the nation's attention to the violent means white authorities used to maintain their grip on power.

In March 2020, the gathering had grown to attract thousands of people paying homage to the crossing that had crystallized the fight for voting rights, where marchers had been trampled, tear-gassed, and assaulted as they crossed the Alabama River. Political icons struggled to be heard over the sound of beating drums and protest chants. Current and former presidential candidates, rising political stars, and aging veterans of the civil rights movement led the masses crossing the bridge. Groups of college students literally followed in their footsteps.

None loomed as large as Congressman John Lewis, the civil rights hero who had been clubbed with nightsticks so badly by Alabama state troopers while leading the peaceful marchers fifty-five years earlier that his skull was fractured. As he was frail now with pancreatic cancer, it had been uncertain whether Lewis would appear at what he reverently called an "almost holy place," a site that had taken on near mythical proportions in the civil rights movement. When the eighty-year-old did arrive at the foot of the bridge, a stir spread throughout the crowd as organizers pleaded for quiet. They left unsaid what many gathered there contemplated, that this could be Lewis's last Bloody Sunday memorial. Hoisted gently onto the shoulders of strong-backed supporters, Lewis was encircled by smartphones recording his every movement as he spoke a few feet from the aging steel arch tagged with the name of Edmund Pettus.

"We were beaten. We were tear-gassed. I thought I was going to die on this bridge. But somehow and someway, God Almighty helped me," Lewis told a crowd that strained to hear him. "We cannot give up now. We cannot give in. We must keep the faith. Speak up. Speak out. Get in the way. Get in good trouble. Necessary trouble. And help redeem the soul of America."

Lewis's central role in the civil rights movement, shaped by his near-death experience, helped steer his course from the pulpit to politics. On the national stage, his commitment to Martin Luther King Jr.'s "beloved community" and nonviolent protest made him the revered conscience of the Congress. Locally he was somehow even more: a link that connected the younger Democratic activists and officials that dominated today's party with the dwindling ranks of civil rights icons, a humble hero who had mentored many of its rising leaders.

When Lewis died on July 17, 2020, *The New York Times* published a brief essay he had penned reminding Americans that "the vote is the most powerful nonviolent change agent you have in a democratic society"—and that it can be put in jeopardy if not protected. His funeral offered his successors a chance to extend a legacy that proved how, in Lewis's words, "ordinary people with extraordinary vision can redeem the soul of America" by getting into "good trouble."

Like so many other seminal events in Atlanta history, Lewis's funeral was held at Ebenezer Baptist Church, part of a weeklong memorial service that symbolized a passing of the torch. Raphael Warnock presided over the ceremony, a poignant final farewell, broadcast on live television. The pews were full of socially distanced dignitaries, and three former presidents spoke, with Barack Obama praising Lewis as a leader who "as much as anyone in our history brought this country a little bit closer to our highest ideals." The memorial was not so much of a tribute as it was a call to action against police brutality, racial discrimination, and efforts to limit voting rights that Lewis had sacrificed so much to fight.

"He loved America," Warnock said, "until America learned to love him back."

———

Lewis's death also forced grieving Democrats to make an abrupt decision forced by the idiosyncrasies of Georgia law. Typically, if a member of congress dies in office or resigns before his or her term is up, a special election is required—as was the case in the ongoing contest to fill the remainder of retired senator Johnny Isakson's term. But since Lewis had died after the June primary, and so close to the November election, the timeline was upended. State law gave party officials until the first business day after Lewis died to determine how to replace him on the ballot.

The awkward process started just hours after news of his death broke on a Friday evening. The state Democratic Party put out a call for applications, and over the weekend more than one hundred hopefuls raised their hands. By Monday, July 20, a Zoom call had been arranged by party leaders to decide Lewis's successor in the US House. The forty-four-member party executive committee singled out five finalists. All eyes, though, shifted to a clear front-runner.

Nikema Williams, the party chair, spent hours preparing for the most important speech of her life and praying she could hold it together without getting too emotional. She was Lewis's protégé, friend, and shopping buddy—they hit the sales rack at Dillard's in Atlanta as often as they could. She met her husband, longtime Lewis aide Leslie Small, when the congressman dispatched him on an errand to a campaign office in 2008 where Williams worked.

She framed herself in her speech as an acolyte of Lewis, right down to their shared Alabama upbringing. And she brought up her 2018 arrest at the state capitol during a voting rights demonstration as proof that she embraced the late congressman's famed brand of "good trouble." As she argued to the committee over a Zoom call, "We need someone who is not afraid to put themselves on the line for their constituents in the same way Congressman Lewis taught us to do."

By day's end, the panel had voted overwhelmingly to select Williams to take Lewis's spot on the ballot. That made her a shoo-in to win the November general election in the decisively Democratic district and, by extension, the heir to a legend.

She had a much easier trip to Congress than other Democrats as the election drew near. Lucy McBath faced a tough rematch against Karen Handel in a contest that mirrored the previous one. McBath still emphasized gun control and health-care expansion on the campaign trail, drawing on the tragic story of her son's shooting death. And Handel highlighted her long-standing ties to the district and her conservative standpoints, as she promoted a "law and order" platform that painted the summer of protests as chaotic, anti-police violence.

In a neighboring swing suburban district, another heated contest was underway. In 2018, Carolyn Bourdeaux had narrowly lost to incumbent Republican Rob Woodall in one of the closest US House races in the nation. Just weeks after his skin-of-the-teeth victory, Woodall decided not to stand for another term. And Bourdeaux barely paused before relaunching her campaign for the diverse suburban seat, which covered much of booming Gwinnett County, confident that a presidential year would draw out even more Democrats. This time, after emerging from a crowded primary, she faced Dr. Rich McCormick, a military veteran and emergency room doctor who had taken a star turn in *American Gladiators* in the late 1980s. "I defeated Saber, Hawk, and Laser," he said, citing the muscled-up combatants of the show. "The frail career politicians in DC will be a breeze."

There were also wide-open contests for newly vacated seats in some of Georgia's most conservative territories, as much a lock for GOP candidates as Williams's Atlanta district was for a Democrat. The first of those two seats was captured by Andrew Clyde, the owner of a gun store in Athens modeled after a medieval fortress, complete with a battlement looming over the building's second floor. Inside, customers could pick from rows of handguns, ammunition, and T-shirts, one of which featured an assault-rifle-wielding George Washington with the caption "I'd like you to meet Martha."

Clyde's political career was motivated by a battle with the IRS that began in 2013 when the agency confiscated nearly $1 million from his bank account, starting a monthslong ordeal that eventually restored most of the money to his coffers. But Clyde didn't stop there, successfully lobbying for federal legislation that made it harder for the IRS to seize assets. The bill, which wound up named in his honor, was an achievement he took to the campaign trail to fill the seat vacated by Doug Collins in northeast Georgia. He easily defeated his runoff opponent, state legislator Matt Gurtler, who was best known for opposing nearly every proposal that came up for a vote in the Georgia House.

By far the most media attention was devoted to a district covering northwest Georgia, where a newcomer named Marjorie Taylor Greene carved out front-runner status even though she had only recently moved to the area. Instead of being dismissed as a carpetbagger, she was embraced for her outspoken support of Trump and unrelenting war against establishment Republicans, the news media, and her hated Democratic rivals. Each revelation about her troubled past only seemed to endear her more to conservatives in the district rather than alienate them: her history of peddling the far-right QAnon conspiracy theory that recklessly claimed Trump was secretly fighting a "deep state" of pedophiles; her insinuation that the 2017 Las Vegas massacre had been orchestrated, and that the September 11 terror attacks were a hoax; her xenophobic rants against Muslims that claimed America was on the verge of an "Islamic invasion"; her repetition of the lie that George Soros, the billionaire Jewish philanthropist, had collaborated with the Nazis; and her warnings that a famed Jewish family directed a secret powerful laser beam to ignite deadly wildfires in California.

Greene's evolution from an apolitical suburban mother into a vessel for raw, pro-Trump anger was proof of the strength of outsider appeal in state Republican politics. The daughter of a wealthy construction executive, Greene had been leading a humdrum life in a five-bedroom house with a movie theater and indoor saltwater pool, spending much of her free time with the energetic CrossFit circles in Atlanta's northern suburbs, *Politico* reported. But as

Trump started his meteoric rise in national politics, she gained fans with hate-filled livestreamed rants that matched her new identity as a hard-right conservative. She began posting attacks on "spineless" Republicans on websites and delved into conspiracy theories that labeled the neo-Nazi rally in Charlottesville, Virginia, as another "inside job." During a visit to the Capitol, she harangued David Hogg, the survivor of the Parkland, Florida, mass shooting and a leading gun control activist. "Coward," she yelled at him, questioning how he got "major press coverage" on the massacre while she "had zero" on her protest of new gun restrictions.

When she announced a run for Congress in Atlanta's close-in suburbs in May 2019, it hardly registered with anyone. She was unknown to local Republican movers and shakers, and her promise to rein in federal spending sounded like most every other GOP campaign message. At the Alon's Bakery in Dunwoody, Greene boasted to me that she could win over suburban moderates by framing herself as a generic outsider who would pummel her main Republican rival, former congresswoman Karen Handel, for her votes on spending measures. But she offered a glimpse at her bare-knuckled strategy, calling Handel a "professional campaigner—but she loses."

Greene loaned herself about $500,000 that month and corralled a group of high-powered consultants to steer her campaign, even though most Republicans wrote her off as an also-ran. That changed after incumbent Tom Graves announced in December 2019 that he would not stand for another term in rural northwest Georgia, and members of the conservative House Freedom Caucus encouraged Greene to switch to his district and run in far friendlier territory.

Within a week, she launched a new campaign to prevent "a tax-hiking career politician or Never Trump activist" from winning the district—and imported her ready-made operation to northwest Georgia, where caught-off-guard local Republicans scrambled to catch up. With a blitz of radio ads across north Georgia that criticized feminists and proclaimed her allegiance to Trump, Greene steadily built support among local Republicans against a field of little-known rivals.

When she easily overcame local neurosurgeon John Cowan, who called himself "conservative without the crazy," in an August 2020 runoff, she became known nationally as the first QAnon adherent on the verge of winning a congressional seat. (She would later walk back her support of the outlandish Internet-born conspiracy.) Locally, Democrats branded Greene the new face of the state GOP—prompting hand-wringing from Republican leaders who worried about the lasting consequences of the monster they'd helped create. Still, few dared speak against her, worried she'd turn her antiestablishment fervor on them.

At her victory party in a riverside hotel in Rome, packed with exuberant supporters not wearing masks despite the raging pandemic, Greene kicked off the celebration by promising that she wasn't afraid of ticking off the powerful. To prove her point, she called Nancy Pelosi a "bitch," giving her future constituents a taste of what was to come. While the national outrage over her racist and xenophobic past made her a punch line to much of America, her take-no-prisoners stature skyrocketed her reputation in conservative circles and drew the president's adulation. By dawn, Trump had labeled her a "future Republican star."

True, Greene still had to win a November election to solidify her victory. But the district was so solidly red that the only Democratic challenger was Kevin Van Ausdal, an IT specialist with no political experience. At first, Van Ausdal hoped to capitalize on Greene's growing list of incendiary comments, including the assertion that wearing masks to prevent the spread of coronavirus emasculates boys, and a photo montage posted on Facebook that showed her posing with an assault rifle next to pictures of three freshman Democratic congresswomen.

But Van Ausdal's own campaign consultant warned him of the "horrifying hellhole" that awaited by going up against Greene and her poisonous attacks, *The Washington Post* reported. He was quickly proved right. Greene called him a "communist" and made fun of his appearance on social media, and her online rants targeting Van Ausdal pushed him to his limits. He once locked himself in his spare bedroom, confiding to his wife through a text message he was "breaking down," according to *The Post*. Death threats piled up on his social media too quickly for Van Ausdal's campaign staff to delete them, asserting the "only good Democrat is a dead Democrat." By early September, his campaign issued a statement announcing that for "family and personal reasons" he was abandoning his race for Congress. Van Ausdal was in his Honda en route to his parents' place in Indiana when the message went out.

=====

Assured a November victory, Greene became one of the most sought-after endorsements in the race for US Senate. Internal polls showed the biggest pool of undecided GOP voters lived in the territory she would soon represent, and both Collins and Loeffler figured that the short-term gain of earning Greene's approval outweighed any long-term damage of her toxic brand in a general election. Loeffler and her aides were particularly aggressive in appealing for Greene's support.

By then the senator had proven time and again that she had no problem shifting her ideological boundaries. In late September, Loeffler aired a thirty-second ad that boasted she was "more conservative than Attila the Hun" and then displayed a mock image of the gruesome despot. It was, to many, the most concrete sign of the total transformation of a candidate who was initially recruited to help woo on-the-fence moderate women but was now comfortable tying herself to a murderous warlord from the 400s.

Along with her vast wealth and encouraging recent polls, Loeffler leveraged another distinct advantage in the race for Greene's support: she and Greene had found a kinship as two conservative women upset at what they felt were unfair portrayals in the media. Greene regularly blasted reporters who brought up her hateful comments and her embrace of the QAnon ideology, arguing that they mischaracterized her beliefs. And Loeffler was still shell-shocked by the blistering coverage earlier in the year of her stock transactions. When Collins learned that Greene had decided to endorse his opponent, the congressman could offer only begrudging praise. His campaign called it "a good endorsement for Kelly."

Ecstatic aides to Loeffler planned a "major announcement" to break the news on a foggy October morning at a serene park crisscrossed by a web of jogging trails in the small Georgia town of Dallas. About ten minutes after reporters arrived at a pavilion adorned with Loeffler's campaign signs, a faint rumbling was heard in the distance: a tan Humvee soon approached, with a

Trump campaign sign affixed to the front, a large Greene placard in the bed, and an American flag flapping in the wind behind. When the vehicle stormed onto the grass just outside the pavilion, Greene checked her hair in the side mirror and hopped out of the driver's seat with a growing grin on her face. Loeffler, wearing an American flag trucker hat, followed out of the passenger side and waved to reporters and a handful of supporters who were waiting at picnic tables.

Standing beside each other before a bank of cameras, Greene praised the senator's outspoken criticism of the Black Lives Matter movement. And Loeffler paid the future congresswoman the ultimate compliment by comparing her upstart campaign with President Trump's rise to the White House. "He's a great patriot. He's like us: a businessperson, a political outsider."

When the two finished talking, there was a rapid-fire burst of questions from the reporters assembled. Asked about Greene's history of racist remarks and embrace of conspiracy theories, Loeffler blamed the media for twisting her words and called the future congresswoman the embodiment of the "American dream." "No one in Georgia cares about this QAnon business. It's something that fake news is going to continue to bring up and ignore antifa and the violence promoted across this country," said Loeffler, adding: "That's not going to distract us. It never has distracted her."

A few other questions followed, as reporters pressed both Republicans on Greene's controversial history. Greene dodged each question, accusing them of abetting a "hoax" against Trump. Before the press conference descended into chaotic shouting and the two roared into the horizon in the Humvee, Greene offered the senator one more resounding affirmation. "What impressed me with Kelly is I found out that she believes a lot of the same things that I believe."

Chapter 14

A CARTER CONNECTION

Over half his lifetime in Georgia Democratic politics, TJ Copeland had grown distressingly accustomed to the familiar cycle of statewide campaigns: the delighted optimism at the start, the discomforting polls, the defensive maneuvering, the depressing defeats. As a rookie operative, he had worked on Governor Roy Barnes's losing campaign for a second term in 2002 and was side by side with Mark Taylor during his failed bid for governor four years later. After that, he watched his party's hopes dashed time and again from the front rows, including the crowded hotel ballroom where Jason Carter's gubernatorial campaign was derailed in 2014. Losing political battles was basically all he ever knew.

When Copeland was hired in early summer 2020 as one of the first Joe Biden campaign advisers in Georgia, he joined the former vice president's skeleton staff with mixed feelings: a deep belief that Democrats could flip the state for the first time since 1992 was matched by a deep skepticism that the campaign would do what it took to win. In his long history as a state operative, he'd grown used to hearing no when making requests of national campaigns. But he was mildly surprised, and even a bit baffled, when Biden's brain trust actually followed through on minor requests for extra field staffers and additional funding for early initiatives in Georgia. *Maybe they know something we don't*, he thought.

It wasn't just a feeling. Deadlocked polls and reams of internal data showed Biden had a legitimate chance, giving even the jaded veterans of failed Georgia campaigns a glimmer of hope. At the request of a Biden senior adviser, the Georgia team assembled a wish list of requests for the homestretch. A few days later, Copeland and others got a note back: *Be more ambitious.* Their next request sought even more money, more staff, and more spending on ads. Again, to Copeland's surprise, the Georgia operation got much of what it wanted.

Still, despite the cries of "Battleground Georgia" and the sense of momentum after the Democratic National Convention in August 2020, Georgia was relegated by Biden's inner circle to a "tier two" state. That meant it would be getting some investment and attention, but not nearly as much as the six key states at the center of his election strategy: Arizona, Florida, Michigan, North Carolina, Pennsylvania, and Wisconsin. Georgia Democrats were envious. Scott Hogan, the state party's director, leaned on many of the top-level advisers he knew from his work on the 2012 Obama-Biden campaign, insisting that Georgia was up for grabs. Still, at the end of the day, Georgia was getting just a fraction of what the other battlegrounds received.

Stacey Abrams had seen this play out before. It confirmed to her a valuable lesson learned during the 2016 presidential race: never put your hopes in the decision-making of national campaigns. Back then, she and other Georgia leaders begged Hillary Clinton's campaign to take the state seriously. Abrams raised about $300,000 for Clinton's state efforts, which helped pave the way for a $1.5 million cash infusion from the national campaign. The token investment helped finance a campaign office that opened near downtown Atlanta in the final months of the campaign with the help of actor Tony Goldwyn, the star of the then hit TV show *Scandal*. Clinton came closer to flipping Georgia than she did the battlegrounds of Iowa and Ohio, a fact that became a key part of the state's 2020 argument. And Abrams, who had cultivated a solid relationship with Biden and his inner circle, was in a key position to help make the state's case.

Shortly after Abrams met with Biden in March 2019, as she was publicly weighing a Senate bid, one of the former vice president's allies leaked word that he might consider launching his campaign for the White House with Abrams as his out-of-the-gate choice for running mate. Though both camps quickly shot down the idea, it helped establish Abrams as a legitimate vice presidential contender—a notion that she played up after Biden clinched the nomination.

Though potential veeps usually don't openly maneuver for the job, Abrams defied political convention by publicly campaigning to be picked. She framed her pursuit of the job as a sacred responsibility she must wholeheartedly embrace as one of the few Black women with a viable shot at the position. And she maximized the attention surrounding her bid to be Biden's running mate to promote her most prized causes.

When pressed by former senator Chris Dodd, one of the chief vetters on Biden's vice presidential selection committee, on how she would make the most of a generational "crisis" in the opening days of the presidency, Abrams hardly hesitated. "Democracy," she said of the ongoing effort to expand voting rights. Then, she added, she would push for a more effective response to the COVID-19 crisis and rebuild the nation's international stature.

Though she was eventually passed over as a running mate when Biden selected Kamala Harris, Abrams and her aides maintained their ties to his senior staffers and the national party, refusing to let high-level decisions about Georgia be made by Washington operatives without the benefit of her honest local input. And one point she made relentlessly was to dispel the "mythology" that Black people in Georgia were already energized and didn't need new resources directed toward turning them out to vote.

The pressure campaign—and increasingly friendly polls—was starting to work. In September, Biden's team announced the hires of about a dozen new staffers to crunch data, mobilize voters, and streamline messaging over the crucial final stretch. Republicans already had scores of staffers on the ground in Georgia. Democrats were beginning to catch up.

Among the new recruits was Jaclyn Rothenberg, whose return to Georgia to work as Biden's top communications specialist in the state was both a homecoming and a continuation of her family's legacy. Rothenberg had been New York mayor Bill de Blasio's national press secretary during his ill-fated run for president. Desperate to stay involved in the White House race after de Blasio flamed out, she couldn't think of a better fit than helping Democrats flip her home state.

Rothenberg was the granddaughter of Gerald Rafshoon, the TV adsmith who had helped Jimmy Carter mold his image as a humble peanut farmer turned presidential hopeful and later became his White House communications director. Inspired by tales of his adventures in Washington and beyond— he spent his post–Carter administration career producing TV dramas and movies—Rothenberg plunged into a life of politics. Growing up, she'd pick through a bag of the mementos her mom kept of her grandfather's adventures: decaying advance schedules, dusty bumper stickers, yellowing press clippings. "I fell in love with the idea," she said. "It was a complete romance."

On long drives around rural Pennsylvania in 2016 while working as a junior press aide to Clinton's campaign, Rothenberg would phone her grandfather for advice and feedback. Rafshoon lived vicariously through his granddaughter—both the good and the bad. At the 2016 Democratic National Convention in Philadelphia, the joy in her voice made him beam with pride. When Clinton fell to Trump, they shared sobering stories about dealing with loss, born out of Carter's 1980 defeat to Ronald Reagan.

When Rothenberg arrived in Atlanta, she set to work amplifying Biden's message. She expected at most one or two campaign trips from some top surrogates—and planned a daylong blitz of media attention when Jill Biden, the nominee's wife, traveled to a parking lot in the liberal hub of Decatur to deliver a pep talk to local Democrats standing in socially distanced Hula Hoops. But Rothenberg's expectations were about to be shattered.

As the election neared, Georgia Republicans found it increasingly impossible to explain away one public poll after another that showed the race within the margin of error.

During the 2016 race, Trump hadn't bothered campaigning in Georgia after he secured the GOP nomination. But in 2020, his Georgia advisers warned him that an embarrassing defeat was growing ever more likely if he didn't squeeze in more visits and allocate resources to the state.

There were already growing concerns on the ground that the campaign wasn't taking Georgia seriously enough. Republicans enjoyed a larger field operation than their Democratic counterparts, boasting more than a hundred staffers in the summer, and the campaign launched its first round of radio ads in June. But veteran operatives worried that too much money was being spent on frivolous extras and not enough on effective TV and mail advertising. The national campaign opened an office in downtown Decatur, designed to resemble an Apple Store with sleek iPad stands and comfortable furniture, as a "community center" to appeal to Black voters. But after Trump campaign manager Brad Parscale was replaced by Bill Stepien, the outpost was turned into a more traditional field office, with the expensive couches and chairs shoved aside.

Each week, Georgia Republican campaign officials would hold an update call with Stepien, during which several would warn how close Georgia would be. Stepien pointed to Trump's easy victory in 2016, confident that the only reason to spend heavily in Georgia would be to help other contenders like Senator David Perdue. "There are other candidates on the ballot in Georgia, and we want to make sure we bring them across the finish line with us," Stepien said in one conference call with reporters, before adding a taunt to Biden's campaign: "I invite the Democrats to spend—and spend heavily—in Georgia."

In late September, Trump trekked to suburban Atlanta to try to put Democrats on the defensive with the party's most reliable bloc of supporters. At a rally in Cobb County aimed at Black voters, he proposed a "Platinum Plan" to create a federal Juneteenth holiday commemorating the end of slavery and to overhaul financial rules to help more minority-owned businesses. But he spent more time ripping Biden and Georgia Democrats than delving into the specifics of his initiative. Before he left, Trump reprised his polarizing 2016 appeal to Black voters, asking the crowd of hundreds at a convention center to ditch Democrats once and for all. "What the hell do you have to lose?"

The president was back a few weeks later, this time at an airport outside the midsized city of Macon, the heart of a rural territory where Republicans were trying to wring out every vote they could to counter Democratic gains in Atlanta's suburbs. Party leaders acknowledged that losing handily in dense urban and suburban areas while dominating rural Georgia was no formula for long-term success. But they hoped their strategy was enough to squeak by in 2020. The president, of course, was more confident, promising at the mid-October rally that a "red wave" would wipe out Democrats. Before Trump arrived, however, Senator Perdue overshadowed his appearance by intentionally mangling the pronunciation of Kamala Harris's name. Democrats called it a "racist tactic," and within two days Ossoff's campaign said it raised more than $2 million from donors outraged by the insult to Biden's running mate.

Democrats responded to the GOP visits by deploying Harris to Atlanta for a full day in mid-October, where she faced a tough line of questioning at what she'd hoped would be a friendly chat with students of historically Black colleges. At an eatery tucked inside the Gathering Spot, a members-only club in Atlanta that was a favorite stop for Democratic candidates and elite entrepreneurs, Harris was ushered into a room with a few of Atlanta's best-known hip-hop stars.

One was Jermaine Dupri, the music mogul who confronted her with a question that had been gnawing at many Black Democrats. How could Harris calm voters concerned about her background as a prosecutor who "put a lot of Black brothers away" when she was a district attorney in California? Harris responded by listing the ways she thought Trump had hurt the Black community and empowered white supremacists.

"Yes, I was a prosecutor," she said. "I decided to go in a system that I knew was flawed to reform it. Yes, I decided to go up the rough side of the mountain, as we say in church. And I didn't fix the entire system."

It was tough timing. Some recent national and statewide polls suggested that Black men could vote for Trump at a higher rate this cycle than they did four years ago. Polls of Georgia voters, too, showed a relatively high number of undecided Black male voters, as compared with other blocs of voters. With Trump trying to sow doubts among Black voters by bringing up Biden's past votes for tough-on-crime measures—he said at a debate days earlier that Black men "remember that you treated them very, very badly"—Democrats needed a bigger boost to get them across the November finish line in Georgia.

Chapter 15

"TRANSMISSION DEAD"

As Joe Biden and Donald Trump hurtled toward their final showdown, the rivals in Georgia's two US Senate races girded for a longer battle. The twenty-candidate special election for Senator Kelly Loeffler's seat had already split into two separate contests: a race pitting Loeffler against Doug Collins for one spot in the runoff, and a test of how effectively Raphael Warnock could consolidate Democratic support.

The pastor had made it through most of the year relatively unscathed, and the fact that he was rising in the polls without significant pushback from Republicans baffled both local conservatives and Warnock's campaign. Even though Warnock was runoff-bound regardless, as one Perdue operative vented, why was "no one considering taking him down a few pegs earlier"—even with a comparably meager amount of spending—so that he didn't enter the next round with high favorability ratings?

In Washington there was sharp disagreement among national Republicans over how to respond to the pastor's candidacy. There were plenty of chances to confront him early, say, by invoking his defense of the Reverend Jeremiah Wright, a controversial Chicago clergyman who had also caused President Barack Obama headaches. A team of opposition researchers spent weeks poring through thousands of hours of footage of his sermons, his public stances, and his published works to build a thick file of possible attacks to unleash during the campaign. But they were put on hold.

The National Republican Senatorial Committee, which pledged to support Loeffler, was distracted by the more immediate threat from Collins. Strategists were confident there was enough in the stockpile to bludgeon Warnock in November or December when Georgians were focused on the runoffs rather than trying to grab a share of the spotlight in the teeth of an all-out presidential blitz. "We knew we had a chance to disqualify Warnock when everyone is paying attention," said one senior national GOP official. "If we had dropped some of that stuff in September, it would have competed with thirty other stories."

Each day that went by without a broadside by Republican groups, Warnock's advisers marveled to one another that he remained relatively untouched. After a particularly vicious round of Republican infighting in October, one senior Democrat shared her astonishment at the "completely crazy malpractice" of giving Warnock a free pass until the runoffs. Adam Magnus, one of Warnock's chief advisers, wondered whether it was naivete or overconfidence. *Why aren't they trying to define us?* "It wouldn't take a lot for them to try to be a hindrance to us," he observed at the time.

At an October campaign stop at the Busy Bee, a soul food café in downtown Atlanta, the pastor wondered aloud when the Republicans were going to grind him. Later that week, after another day gone with Warnock untouched, a Democratic aide was astonished by how "laughably shortsighted" it was for Republicans to hold their fire in a race that could decide control of the US Senate—and, if the election went their way, Biden's agenda. "If we pull this off, there will be trillions of dollars decided, maybe Supreme Court justices. And it's all because we're not getting attacked."

—————

The full-scale warfare between the two Republican rivals only escalated as they one-upped one another with appeals to the party's most conservative voters. After US Supreme Court Justice Ruth Bader Ginsburg died in late September, Collins won the first skirmish for attention with a tweet mourning not the legendary jurist's passing but the millions of "murdered" babies he said were the victims of her support for abortion rights. Loeffler countered by becoming one of the first US senators to call for Trump to speedily nominate her successor, ensuring that another conservative appointee would take the bench before the election.

The congressman hoped a string of important endorsements could earn him free media attention to neutralize the millions Loeffler was spending. One of his biggest backers was House Speaker David Ralston, a north Georgia maverick and master manipulator of the gears of statehouse power. Not only was Ralston an old friend of Collins, but he was also engaged in open warfare with Governor Kemp, Loeffler's patron. In a pointed critique of the incumbent in September, Ralston praised Collins as someone who "didn't come to his views in the middle of a political campaign." Collins also had the support of former governor Nathan Deal, who said he was drawn to the congressman's "authenticity."

But nowhere was the gamesmanship as aggressive as when it came to the exhausting courtship of Trump, who stayed on the sidelines but reveled in the competition for his affection. "Well, I sort of like it. You know why? They're going to be in there fighting, fighting, fighting. Don't anybody get out," Trump said during one visit to Georgia. "And everybody's going to come with them. And the only thing I know for sure, they're all going to vote for me."

Whenever Trump traveled to Georgia, his trips played like a flashback to high school theatrics, with both candidates trying to outdo each other for even the most meager shout-out from the big man on campus. During the president's briefly delayed visit to the CDC in March, Loeffler earned a coveted invitation to fly to town with the president on Air Force One from Trump's chief of staff, Mark Meadows. When Collins caught word, he raced to the airport to await their arrival on the official receiving line—and to ensure that he was also in the camera frame when Trump and Loeffler descended to the runway.

After Loeffler disembarked from Air Force One, she almost immediately came face-to-face with Collins. They grasped hands and chitchatted for a few seconds until Collins asked: "Kelly, do you have any pets?" She appeared surprised for a moment, and then talked about her cat. Later, Collins shrugged that he didn't know what else to do in such an awkward moment. "What else are you supposed to say?"

In May, when Vice President Mike Pence flew to Atlanta, Loeffler was once again invited by Meadows to board the plane. Eager to avoid the appearance of playing favorites, Pence's aides asked Collins to join the greeting party and ride back with the vice president to the airport on the return trip, ensuring that both got roughly the same amount of face time with the veep.

———

Loeffler's wealth continued to be a constant source of tension. By October, she and Sprecher had spent more than $31 million on her election bid, which made her the third-largest self-funding candidate in the nation, behind only billionaires Michael Bloomberg and Tom Steyer, who by then had both abandoned failed campaigns for the presidency. While much of that sum was allocated directly to her campaign, Loeffler and Sprecher also donated to other GOP senators, to state Republican organizations, to the Republican National Committee, and to pro-Trump super PACs.

They also stroked checks for more than $10.5 million to finance an outside group called Georgia United Victory that had also received donations from Home Depot cofounder Bernie Marcus, Citadel hedge fund titan Ken Griffin, and other ultra-rich patrons of the couple. The group purchased TV ads, hired strategists, and pushed get-out-the-vote messaging. It also sent thousands of glossy magazines called *Red Clay* to likely Republican voters with a cover image of Loeffler and Trump and glowing stories about the incumbent senator—along with a mock ad picturing Collins with Stacey Abrams.

While Loeffler crisscrossed Georgia in her private jet, Collins campaigned across the state in his family's navy Suburban SUV, a creaky 2012 vehicle that had logged 158,000 miles by the campaign's homestretch. It broke down on the side of I-95 in southeast Georgia in October, leaving Collins and former Trump adviser Carter Page, in Georgia to help Collins spice up rallies, stranded on the side of the road. A rescue from the local sheriff got them back on the campaign trail, but the Suburban didn't fare as well: it was declared "transmission dead" at a coastal mechanic shop before noon. Loeffler could afford to spend nights at the Trump hotel in Washington on her own dime, while Collins slept on a cot in his Capitol Hill office or, while on the campaign trail, at budget hotels with staff cramming two or three to a room. "That's an advantage that she has that we don't," Collins adviser Chip Lake said at the time, "so we have to do it the old-fashioned way."

One of their most bizarre tangles over wealth was on display in an October 19 debate hosted by the Atlanta Press Club, an hourlong affair held virtually with the top five candidates in the race. Framed by three American flags against a blue-curtained backdrop, Collins used his head-to-head question to quiz Loeffler on a heretofore-unmentioned controversy: Did she, he asked, still have "the $56,000 portrait of Chairman Mao hanging in your foyer, as was seen on social media? It seems a little hypocritical. Or maybe it's just enlightening."

Loeffler expected a swipe on the stock trading scandal or her past support for Mitt Romney; she seemed mystified that her archrival spent his question bringing up a 2018 Facebook photo. The picture from a gathering at her mansion was taken in front of what looked like an Andy Warhol painting or print of Mao Zedong that was inspired by President Richard Nixon's landmark visit to China in 1972. After momentarily hesitating, Loeffler accused Collins of lying and called herself the "true conservative" in the race.

Off-screen, her campaign scrambled to make sure the photo was taken down moments after Collins mentioned it. Over the next few days, Collins talked more of the portrait than he did about Loeffler's stock transactions. His supporters even began showing up at her events with oversized images of the Mao painting and Chinese Communist flags, invariably leading to confused questions from attendees.

Some of the younger staffers on Loeffler's campaign were eager for payback. When a Collins backer tried to recruit people on Facebook to hold the Mao sign outside Loeffler's upcoming events, the senator's digital director created a fake Gmail account with the alias that football coach Lane Kiffin was rumored to use at college bars to conceal his identity: Joey Freshwater. Soon "Joey" connected with a Collins aide who invited him to meet outside a 4:00 p.m. event that Loeffler was expected to headline. Bringing an intern with him, the Loeffler aide grabbed the Mao posters and raced back to Loeffler headquarters, where they hung on the wall throughout the rest of her campaign. They stood as a reminder and a warning, Loeffler staffer Chris Allen said, of "all the weird stuff that can happen in the homestretch."

A runoff in Loeffler's race was always assured. But as November neared, polls started to also show the possibility of overtime in the contest between Senator David Perdue and Jon Ossoff. The two opponents were engaged in a more traditional matchup: a slugfest to the finish, with a long-shot Libertarian candidate who seemed poised to draw just enough of the vote to force a runoff. Just as Loeffler had been under fire for her stock trades, Ossoff pummeled Perdue with claims that he'd orchestrated well-timed financial transactions to profit from his perch in the Senate. One *New York Times* analysis revealed that Perdue was by far the Senate's most prolific stock trader, sometimes logging more than twenty transactions in a single day. Ossoff hoped to draw a line between Perdue's trades and his role on powerful Senate committees, as the senator's internal polls showed the perception of corruption was his biggest vulnerability.

Perdue hit back with the same ominous message he had promoted all along, branding Democrats as revolutionaries bent on bringing "socialist" change to a fundamentally conservative state—and Ossoff as all too willing to cave to China's demands. Six years earlier, Perdue's soft-focus ads had highlighted his work in Hong Kong for Sara Lee and featured a picture of him and his wife, Bonnie, on the Great Wall of China to accentuate his worldliness. Now his ads omitted any sort of connection to China as he falsely claimed that Ossoff was a bona fide communist. His justification? Ossoff's company had received around $1,000 through a British distributor for two investigative films it made on international war crimes that were rebroadcast in Hong Kong by a media giant with connections to the Chinese government. As conservative outlets amplified Perdue's falsehoods, the Republican's operatives expressed amazement they were able to get traction out of a claim so convoluted because, as a senior Perdue hand admitted, "there wasn't much meat on the bone to go after."

Privately, Perdue was growing more frustrated with his struggle to break out against a Democrat who was proving hard to pin down—and harder, even, to knock off message. But Perdue also wasn't taking to the campaign trail with the same vigor he had shown six years earlier. "He doesn't want to lose," said a close friend, "but I don't know if he wants to win." His venom toward Ossoff was one of Perdue's main motivating factors. Still, as much as Perdue's closest advisers also abhorred the Democrat, they also admired his chutzpah. "He's the type of guy who looks in the mirror in the morning and says, 'I want to fly an F-16.' And then he goes out and does it," one aide said at the time.

Perdue had been in a mental funk before and had managed to spring himself out. During the 2014 campaign, after he had struggled in one of his first debates against Michelle Nunn, Perdue seemed exhausted and disgusted with the entire political process, eager to dismiss the long list of dos and don'ts in the final days of the race.

His chief adviser, Derrick Dickey, sat him down for hours to help him snap out of his foul mood, drilling into his mind, over and over, that debates were a game of sound bites. He needed only hammer home one message to survive their next scrap: Nunn was a rubber stamp for President Barack Obama. Perdue didn't favor the idea—in part because of his personal admiration for Nunn—but he followed the strategy anyway. Sure enough, his Obama-centric message dominated the news coverage in the closing days of the race as he coasted to an eight-point victory.

This time around, Dickey wasn't on hand to pull him out of the doldrums. The veteran consultant, who had subsequently served as Perdue's chief of staff, had amicably parted ways with his former boss a few months earlier. Some veterans of Perdue's first run viewed his reelection campaign as a mechanical, poll-driven process that failed to capitalize on the personality and charisma that had turned him from a straitlaced CEO into a Republican star.

During an early debate with Ossoff, Perdue took on the role of the underdog, coarsely challenging both his Democratic opponent and the debate's moderator throughout the session. Afterward, a few of the Republican's staffers coined a phrase for his hyperaggressive performance: "Godzilla fire breath." As Perdue prepared for a second hourlong debate, held six days before the election, polls suggested that he return to one particular attack, no matter that the foundation it was built upon was so flimsy: China, China, China.

With the cameras rolling at the Savannah studios of a local TV station, Perdue dramatically reached into the pocket of his suit jacket during the debate and unfurled what he claimed to be a damning document that Ossoff needed to "own up to"—proof, he said, that Ossoff was trying to hide business ties with the firm he had long maligned. "Sooner or later," Perdue said gravely, "we need somebody in the United States Senate that will stand up to Communist China." Everyone involved in the campaigns had seen it coming—Ossoff included. After the theatrics, the Democrat was prepared to level a devastating counterpunch that brought up past attempts to "other" him.

"First, you were lengthening my nose in attack ads to remind everybody that I'm Jewish," he said of a digital ad that had brought embarrassment and scorn on Perdue's campaign. "Then, when that didn't work, you started calling me some kind of Islamic terrorist," Ossoff continued, referring to past criticism over his firm's connection to the Al Jazeera English news outlet. "Then, when that didn't work, you started calling me a Chinese Communist."

Perdue tried to steady himself by declaring that Ossoff would "say and do anything to hide this radical socialist agenda." And the senator described himself to the viewers as another outsider fed up with the "swamp in Washington." But as the debate wound down, Ossoff got the last word with a blistering monologue.

"It's not just that you're a crook, Senator. It's that you're attacking the health of the people that you represent. You did say COVID-19 was no deadlier than the flu. You did say there would be no significant uptick in cases. All the while, you were looking after your own assets, and your own portfolio. And you did vote four times to end protections for preexisting conditions. Four times."

Afterward, Perdue retreated to a local Waffle House—one of his favorite restaurants—to review a performance that his advisers initially thought was a solid, if not outstanding, defense of his record. While he and Bonnie feasted on waffles and bacon in their booth, the clip of Ossoff's teardown went viral, ultimately logging more than 15 million views. Texts and fundraising appeals linking to the takedown were sent to tens of thousands of donors in Georgia and across the nation. Within days, Perdue canceled a final debate against Ossoff as word spread that Trump could make a last-minute visit the same night as the showdown.

On the heels of his viral debate moment, Ossoff tried out a new attack line going into the final days of a razor-tight race—one that played off the famous poultry company that shared the senator's name.

He labeled Perdue a "chicken" every chance he got.

Chapter 16

POETIC JUSTICE

Even some of the state's most senior Democrats were caught off guard by Joe Biden's plan to visit Georgia a week before the election. But they were even more surprised by his choice of venues.

Before a drive-in rally at an Atlanta parking lot, complete with honking horns and tailgating crowds that had become a pandemic standard for Democrats in Georgia, Biden paid a visit to the rural hills of west Georgia, in a field that overlooked the majestic panorama of rolling forests and blue skies of Warm Springs.

This wasn't just any mountain resort: Warm Springs, a town of roughly four hundred people seventy-two miles southwest of Atlanta, was the home of former president Franklin Delano Roosevelt's private retreat, the "Little White House" where he sought treatment for his polio for decades, drew inspiration for New Deal programs, and took his final breaths in 1945.

The setting awaiting Biden looked like it had hardly changed since FDR's days. About three dozen white folding chairs were spaced out in socially distanced circles along the freshly mowed lawn. A well-worn firepit, the site of many s'mores tastings and spooky ghost stories, was a few steps from a set of hewn-wood stairs. Fresh-baked pecan pies were carefully placed on a table under a pavilion for hungry staffers and a stage surrounded by American flags was set up against the backdrop of a mountain vista. Only a handful of staffers and guests were invited to the event, and each stood as Biden navigated the winding staircase early in the afternoon.

This was no fireside chat. There was no time left for that. Biden's argument was for the "restoration" of America during the most serious public health emergency it had faced in a century. He called the Little White House a "reminder that though broken, each of us can be healed. That as a people and a country, we can overcome this devastating virus. That we can heal a suffering world. And yes, we can restore our soul and save our country." He called on Americans to summon the same spirit that prevailed during past generational crises, like the Great Depression and World War II, to defeat the pandemic. And he insisted the fears that partisanship has "passed the point of no return" were unfounded. "Has the heart of this nation turned to stone?" Biden said. "I don't think so. I refuse to believe it. I know this country. I know our people. And I know we can unite and heal this nation."

Biden's appearance that day sent a message to skeptics in both parties that the tight polls in Georgia were not just hype. After all, if Biden planned to spend much of the day in Georgia so close to the election—the Democratic nominee also headlined a drive-in rally in Atlanta that evening—it couldn't just be a head fake to force Trump and other Republicans even more onto the defensive. "They're playing for keeps," a senior GOP official conceded.

Indeed, Biden's off-the-beaten-path trip to Warm Springs—a place that gubernatorial candidates, let alone White House hopefuls, rarely visit—was meant to secure an important building block in the Democratic coalition. By then, Biden advisers concluded the vice president likely had a better chance of winning Georgia than her two hard-fought neighbors, North Carolina and Florida. His campaign felt he could win if he assembled liberal Democrats, Black voters, and suburbanites. But he also needed to siphon off just enough white voters in rural areas to give him the edge over President Trump.

"That type of campaigning is more than just a campaign marketing ploy," said Keith Mason, the Democratic strategist who helped persuade Biden to visit Warm Springs. "You're never going to carry some of these counties. But you can cut the margins."

Seth Clark, an amateur historian and Democratic operative who scored a ticket to the Warm Springs event, predicted that if the visit could goose Democratic performance in rural west Georgia even a few percentage points—from 20 to 22 percent—it could be a difference maker. "The reason you saw people like my grandfather vote Democratic down the ticket was because Georgia was saved by Roosevelt's New Deal," he said. "And Roosevelt pushed the most progressive policies the party has ever pushed from little old Warm Springs."

Internally, it was a morale builder for the campaign. Tharon Johnson, a Biden adviser who was President Obama's southern regional director in 2012, called it a "game changer" that showed Biden could compete anywhere. "It was the boost we needed," he said. "And we saw the media began treating us differently, starting to believe what we were saying about flipping the state."

At his stop in Atlanta that evening, Biden gave a more conventional speech, one punctuated with reminders of Georgia's importance in the November race. There was "no state more consequential" than Georgia in the Democratic fight to win control of the US Senate, he said, nodding to the novelty of his visit. "There aren't a lot of pundits who would have guessed four years ago that the Democratic candidate for president in 2020 would be campaigning in Georgia on the final week of the election."

Republicans went on an even more elevated sense of alert. In 2016, the GOP practically begged Democrats to funnel money into Georgia, hoping to bog their rivals down in a hopeless battle. But Biden's visit put to rest any thought that Democrats were merely flirting with a flip. Some of the state's top Republicans gathered in front of a shuttered textile mill in the downtrodden nearby city of Manchester, urging the hundred or so supporters who arrived on short notice to send pictures of the forlorn building to their friends and neighbors as a sign of what could happen to the economy in a Biden presidency.

"Maybe he wants some good barbecue and southern hospitality, or maybe he needed to get out of his basement and taste some freedom," Governor Kemp said. "But if Biden is down in Georgia looking for electoral votes, he's come to the wrong place."

Biden's visit wasn't the only reason Georgia Republicans had begun to panic. For months, Trump had been denigrating the mail-in voting system that more Americans than ever were relying upon during the pandemic, especially the elderly. He falsely asserted that counting ballots after Election Day was evidence of a "rigged" vote and predicted wide-scale fraud with the surge of absentee votes, even as bipartisan elections officials, and members of his own administration, refuted his conspiratorial claims.

Even Kemp, forced to quarantine after he was exposed to someone with a coronavirus infection during the Manchester event, struggled to assure conservatives that ballot drop boxes and other ways to cast votes by mail were secure. He posted a video on Twitter of himself returning his ballot at a drop box near his home in Athens to show the process was trustworthy. Democrats, meanwhile, raced to maximize the expanded vote-by-mail programs. While polls showed just 10 percent of Republicans planned to cast their ballots by mail, nearly half of Democrats said they would do so.

Despite pleas for help, many in Trump's inner circle remained convinced he would easily capture the state. A key state Republican official was informed by Trump headquarters that the campaign projections showed the president was on track to win the state by three hundred thousand votes—a margin that far exceeded his edge over Clinton in Georgia four years earlier. An initial list of Trump's final campaign rallies planned for stops in Michigan, North Carolina, and Pennsylvania—and, to the horror of local Republicans, did not include Georgia. One campaign deputy was told that another visit to the state was a "waste of time."

Senator Perdue had been hounding Trump chief of staff Mark Meadows and other advisers to the president to step up their game in Georgia, only to get repeated reassurances that he would easily win, and that Perdue was overthinking his situation. Trump campaign manager Bill Stepien was convinced the president was in good standing in the state, up by at least four points in their polling. If Trump loses Georgia, anxious state Republicans were told, then he's in trouble everywhere else.

But the local Republican concern proved to be not just a case of paranoia;

by late October, Perdue's campaign had hard numbers from early and absentee data that showed the senator was in peril, specifically in parts of deep-red rural Georgia where early turnout numbers were abysmal. Frustrated by the lack of alarm, Perdue appealed directly to the president to ignore his campaign's assurances about Georgia and to believe him: *"You and I have a tough race in Georgia,"* Perdue told him, *"and the polls show it's even."* The president was caught off guard; Perdue had hardly ever asked him for a favor. He told the senator he'd make one last pit stop in Georgia, even though his advisers repeated that it was a waste of time.

On November 1, two nights before the vote, Trump squeezed in a late-night visit to an airport on the outskirts of Rome, a northwest Georgia town in the foothills of the Appalachian Mountains. His campaign initially wanted to travel to Atlanta's suburbs or return to the central swath of the state, but Perdue's operatives insisted on a trip to the part of the state where early voting was lagging.

The backdrop might have been a fantasy come true for the legions of Trump supporters who lined the one-lane roads hours before the event. As Air Force One whooshed down the runway behind the stage, the roaring crowd craned their necks to see Trump emerge from the plane. Lee Greenwood's "God Bless the U.S.A." blasted from loudspeakers as thousands of smartphones captured the president's walk down the airstairs to the stage. The ovation reached a crescendo as Trump, wearing a dark overcoat and bright red power tie that matched his MAGA cap, crowed that his advisers hadn't wanted him to come.

"I shouldn't even be here. They say I have Georgia made. But you know what? I said, 'I promised we have to be here,'" Trump said as a whipping wind raked the airfield. "'No,' they said, 'sir, you don't have to come to Georgia. We have it made. It's won.' By the way, just go out and vote. OK? Just go out and vote."

The supporters interrupted him with deafening chants of "Four more years!" Trump raised a hand to quiet the crowd: "No, they said this morning, 'Sir, honestly, we can skip Georgia.' You know, I've done four of these. I'm going to Florida for another one, you believe this? Wonderful! Oh, and I had such an easy life before this."

═══

Democrats landed one last big name of their own: an election-eve visit by former President Barack Obama. The party was desperate to drive up Black turnout, and Obama promised that Georgia could be the "place where we put this country back on track" if voters showed up for Biden and the two Senate candidates. He took a special interest in urging progressives upset with the more mainstream appeal of the Democratic ticket to turn out, too: "The fact that we don't get one hundred percent of what we want is not a good reason not to vote."

Obama attracted more applause, though, for scathing attacks that tore into the two Republicans for their stock transactions during the pandemic, calling them "Batman and Robin gone bad." "They're like the dynamic duo of doing wrong," Obama said from a stage set up near a towering cauldron in downtown Atlanta commemorating the 1996 Olympic Games. "I don't know what they were thinking, but Georgia, I promise you: Georgia was definitely not on their minds."

Before the rally's end, Senate candidates Jon Ossoff and Raphael Warnock joined Obama onstage as their supporters sounded their car horns in approval. Obama took in the spectacle, telling the crowd he couldn't pass up the chance to help his old running mate flip a state that "could be the place where we put this country back on track."

"I said, 'Well, I got to go. I got to come.' I told Michelle, 'I'm sorry, babe. I got to go to Georgia. This is a big deal.'"

═══

As the candidates crisscrossed the state, county elections officials were madly trying to keep pace with the amazing quantity of mail-in ballots. During the 2018 general election, about 220,000 ballots had been cast by mail, accounting for about 6 percent of the nearly 4 million overall votes. Ahead of the November race, more than 1.3 million absentee votes were tallied, either mailed remotely or deposited in ballot drop boxes approved under emergency circumstances by state elections officials. That accounted for more than one quarter of all the general election votes in Georgia. The surge was particularly pronounced in important Democratic counties like Athens-Clarke, DeKalb, and Augusta-Richmond, where Biden would capture more than 60 percent of the vote.

In a final conference call on November 2, state election director Chris Harvey warned dozens of local administrators to get ready for intense scrutiny. "I'll see you guys on the other side of history," he added.

But the increase of mail-in ballots also meant it would take days, not hours, to finish the tallies—leaving campaigns and voters on tenterhooks long after election night. Dan Coats, who headed Trump's Georgia operation, remained somewhat optimistic that Trump would squeak by with about fifteen thousand votes to spare before the tallying began. But hours after the polls closed, elections data from around the state that streamed into sophisticated campaign spreadsheets showed Trump's chances beginning to fade.

Coats's outlook dimmed that night when an aide called to update him with the news that there were seventeen thousand ballots outstanding in Chatham County, a Democratic-leaning enclave surrounding Savannah—not the fifteen hundred the campaign had wrongly heard from a local official were still waiting to be tallied. He knew that if there were still significant numbers of votes remaining to be counted in Chatham, the same must be happening in the heavily populated Democratic strongholds of metro Atlanta.

By early Wednesday, the returns showed Trump with a roughly one-hundred-thousand-vote lead over Biden. But the bulk of the outstanding ballots would be coming from counties dominated by Democrats. The Democratic data gurus who briefed Stacey Abrams on election night had told her as much. She had gone to sleep that night confident of victory. Seth Bringman, one of her closest advisers, delivered a tart message on Facebook hours later: "Good morning, world! We told you so!"

Indeed, as each trove of ballots was counted, Biden cut bit by bit into Trump's advantage. Even the late-counted mail ballots from GOP strongholds Houston and Forsyth Counties tilted to Biden because of the strong Democratic push for voting by mail—surprising cable news number crunchers who struggled to correctly pronounce the names of the counties.

As Wednesday dawned, Perdue's chances of avoiding a runoff were narrowing, too. He had a more robust lead over Ossoff than Trump held over Biden on election night, but each tally dragged him lower toward the 50 percent mark he needed to surpass to win the election outright.

At the campaign's war room on the second floor of the InterContinental Buckhead hotel in Atlanta, some aides were prematurely cheering a GOP victory. Senior operatives who were flooded with congratulatory texts quickly tried to tamp down the celebratory buzz. One ventured to Perdue's upstairs suite to deliver the bad news to the senator, who was also getting elated calls from friends praising him for a hard-fought win. Ignore the chatter, he and his wife, Bonnie, were told, and get ready for a potential runoff.

Hundreds of Republicans still packed the ballroom at the InterContinental past midnight into Wednesday morning to hear what was supposed to be a victory speech from Perdue. They left, gloomy, by 1:00 a.m. after the senator sent word he wasn't about to announce anything. Perdue's aides knew there was no doubt the senator would finish ahead of Ossoff. But as hotel staffers swept up decorations from the aborted celebration, the aides were also certain that he couldn't notch an outright win. The Libertarian candidate, Shane Hazel, was on track to garner about one hundred fifteen thousand votes— enough for about a 2 percent share, neutralizing any hope Republicans had for a clean Senate victory.

The other race had a more clear-cut finish: at around 10:30 p.m., Doug Collins called Kelly Loeffler to concede, as projections put her on pace for a second-place finish and a spot in the runoff. At Collins's campaign party on the banks of Lake Lanier, the music abruptly cut off and aides told the press he wouldn't deliver remarks. An hour later, Loeffler told a cheering crowd that Collins had called her to pledge his support. "He's a strong conservative, he supports our president, he supported our country, loves his family," she said of Collins. "He's a man of faith, and I am honored to have him on our team."

There were many reasons for Loeffler's six-point advantage over Collins: her rebound from the stock-trading scandal, her success in metro Atlanta and the crucial exurban ribbon stretching across the city's northern reaches, and a late endorsement by legendary University of Georgia running back Herschel Walker that aired during the team's prime-time game against Alabama. Collins's camp pointed to one factor above all else: the $31 million that Loeffler and her husband had poured into the campaign, along with all the advantages their fortune afforded.

At around the same time Collins conceded, Warnock stood on a stage in Atlanta flanked by overjoyed members of his family, who held signs that read SEE YOU ON 1/5/21. The Democrat declared that "something special and transformational is happening right here in Georgia" and then warned of what was to come: while he would be "busy trying to lift the families of Georgia up," he told his supporters, Loeffler would "try to tear me down."

He was set to notch about a third of the vote, enough for a first-place finish ahead of Loeffler and Collins. But many were surprised how the other Democrats on the twenty-candidate ballot had fared. Matt Lieberman and Ed Tarver, the pastor's best-known Democratic rivals, hardly registered with voters. Instead, it was former Lithonia mayor Deborah Jackson who posed the most significant threat; she wound up in fourth place with more than three hundred twenty thousand votes.

Democrats scored significant victories down the ballot. US Congresswoman Lucy McBath fended off the comeback attempt by Republican Karen Handel with a solid win that would send her rival into political retirement. And Carolyn Bourdeaux became the only Democrat to flip a Republican-held US House seat that cycle, aside from two North Carolina districts redrawn after court-ordered redistricting, when she won a seat centered in Atlanta's northeastern suburbs. For the first time in decades, the bedroom communities stretching across metro Atlanta's north side, so long a fortress for Republicans, were now to be represented in the US House by Democrats.

———

Though the networks hadn't called the presidential race, the trend lines were clear the day after the election. Trump dominated the state's deep-red rural strongholds, capturing 85 percent of the vote in some smaller counties. But Biden loosened the president's grip in the exurbs and capitalized on high turnout in metro Atlanta's suburbs, handily winning the former GOP bastions of Cobb, Gwinnett, and Henry in convincing fashion. In fact, an analysis by the TargetSmart data firm showed no county in the nation had a larger swing to the Democrats over the last four years than Henry. Hillary Clinton won the county south of Atlanta by four percentage points, while Biden carried it by about twenty.

Just as important, exit polls showed Biden had strong backing from the cornerstones of the party: he won roughly 90 percent of Black voters, almost two thirds of Hispanic voters, and more than half of people under thirty. Biden also carried 53 percent of the state's independent voters—a bloc of voters that once reliably backed Republicans—and made marginal improvements with evangelical Christians, netting double-digit support.

As the vote-counting dragged on deeper into the week, even senior Republicans privately conceded Biden would eventually overtake the president—it was only a question of how quickly that would happen. As Friday, November 6, dawned, the moment seemed only a heartbeat away. And Georgians' gaze was fixed on the slow and steady counting of absentee ballots being tallied in a cramped Clayton County administrative office on Atlanta's south side.

A few weeks earlier, Democrats had raised concern about an early voting lag in Clayton, Georgia's bluest county. Ossoff and Warnock were both dispatched to the Slutty Vegan, a popular vegetarian restaurant in the county, to plead with residents to show up. "The world is watching," Ossoff, voice sounding hoarse, pressed the crowd. The message got through: Biden captured the county with 85 percent of the vote, and in the early hours of Friday morning the last batches of Clayton's uncounted ballots were being processed.

As Georgia politicos—and countless others—watched on social media, the gap between Trump and Biden was whittled down from 2,497 to 1,902 to 1,797 votes. Then 665. A few minutes later, it had dwindled to 466.

Then, at around 4:20 a.m., one of the largest batches of absentee ballots was reported. Biden had nudged just ahead of Trump, enough to give him the enduring lead in Georgia's election.

The formal call by the networks wouldn't come for a few more days, but that was a mere afterthought. Most of the other outstanding ballots came from Democratic-leaning counties. Biden's advantage with absentee ballots would pay off: he would ultimately tally roughly four hundred thousand more mail-in votes than Trump.

As voting data surfaced, another trend became even clearer: a surge in

Black voter participation was decisive. More than 60 percent of Georgia's Black registered voters cast ballots, state election data showed, compared with 56 percent in 2016. That made for a net increase of two hundred twenty-one thousand votes, according to a *Washington Post* analysis, far greater than Biden's thin margin of victory of roughly twelve thousand ballots.

That Clayton County delivered the final blow—and not more populous Fulton or DeKalb Counties—made the victory even sweeter for local Democrats. John Lewis had represented a swath of the majority-Black county just south of Atlanta for years in Congress. And President Trump, in a pique of rage shortly before taking office nearly four years earlier, had called his district "crime-infested" and "horrible." TJ Copeland, a local Democratic leader who was a friend of Lewis, remembered all the times he watched the congressman connect with voters in Clayton—and the deep sense of anger they felt when Trump insulted their county.

"I can't think of a way to capture it other than this," Copeland said at the time. "This is poetic justice."

<hr />

Jaclyn Rothenberg was hunkered down in a subterranean hotel conference center stocked with candy bars, grocery-store snacks, and copious Coca-Cola products, surrounded by sleep-deprived aides. Democrats called it the "boiler room," a windowless stretch complete with socially distanced tables, a cot, and a bottle of tequila in case of, well, emergency.

The night before the vote, Rothenberg confronted Scott Hogan, the state Democratic Party's enigmatic executive director, with a point-blank question: "Can we do this? I need to know." Without a pause, he responded. "Absolutely."

As early returns showed Trump with a wide lead, she and other Democratic operatives in the bunker began to down the emergency tequila shots to ward off the lurking fear of "Clinton PTSD"—the sense of humiliating defeat being snatched from the jaws of victory. But by Wednesday her dread had given way to a sense of joyous inevitability. Biden had the votes—it was just a matter of when.

She was in the middle of a minor spat with a colleague early Friday when she glanced up at the TV screen and saw that Biden had taken the lead in Georgia. She dropped the glass of red wine she was nursing and forgot all about the silly argument. Suddenly, the boiler room was alive with celebration. In a few hours, her grandfather, the longtime Jimmy Carter aide Gerald Rafshoon, would be awake, and she wanted to be the first to tell him the news.

Just about every day over the last few months, they'd talked about the ins and outs of the campaign, pored over the latest internal polls, and traded stories about triumphs and setbacks. He lived vicariously through her, and she knew the joy he got from their daily updates. On this Friday morning, she called him at his home in Washington's Dupont Circle, knowing he'd be surrounded by the Carter posters and pins arrayed on his walls. She greeted him with eight simple words.

"Grandpa, we did it. We won Georgia back!"

PART 3

A BATTLE FOR
THE SENATE

Chapter 17

"NONSENSE"

Two nights after the election, President Trump took the White House podium to declare that he had won Georgia "by a lot." Back in Atlanta, his son Donald Jr. and a coterie of pro-Trump figures scraped together a rally in a darkened parking lot not far from the Governor's Mansion to advance that fraudulent claim.

As the TV cameras set up their shots, an enormous Trump flag was draped along a section of the pavement where a crowd of about one hundred supporters gathered, some who were compelled to show up by last-minute text messages and the promise of pizza. While the speakers assembled, the crowd formed a semicircle around a giant campaign RV plastered with Trump's image and the words KEEP AMERICA GREAT!

This was no fringe group. Standing with Trump Jr. were some of Georgia's foremost supporters of his father: state representative Vernon Jones, the Black Democrat and former chief executive of DeKalb County who had defected to Trump earlier that year but still hadn't formally switched parties; Georgia GOP chair David Shafer, a party operative and former state senator who won the job to lead the state GOP organization after narrowly losing the 2018 runoff for lieutenant governor; and Doug Collins, fresh off his losing Senate challenge to Kelly Loeffler.

It was Collins who introduced Trump Jr. by listing a litany of claims of fraud—but no proof of a single ballot illegally cast. Then came Trump Jr., who promised that his father's coalition of supporters would seek revenge on anyone—Loeffler and David Perdue included—who contradicted the president's claims that he won Georgia's election and dared acknowledge Joe Biden would be the next president.

"I think the Democrats are used to this from a Republican Party that hasn't had a backbone. You're not going to see that this time around. That party is gone," Trump Jr. said, adding that his father should "fight each and every one of these battles to the death" in the name of election transparency.

"You're going to have another election here in about two months that could decide the fate of the United States Senate," Trump Jr. said. "So, we're going to be watching this nonsense. Because everyone knows what's going on."

As he finished speaking, his father's backers broke into a chant that would reverberate throughout the runoffs. "Stop the steal!"

———

Trump Jr. was wrong about election fraud. But he was right about the enormous stakes of the Senate runoffs. The always remote possibility that Georgia's runoffs could decide the fate of the Senate became a stunning reality overnight. Though Democrats had flipped Senate contests in Arizona and Colorado, Republicans had held off challengers in Iowa, Maine, Montana, North Carolina, and South Carolina, along with defeating a Democratic incumbent in Alabama. That left disappointed Democrats with a net gain of just one Senate seat, far short of what senior party leaders had envisioned. Neither party emerged with a majority of the chamber's seats, leaving a 50–48 edge in favor of Republicans.

That meant if either of the Georgia Republican incumbents won in January, the GOP would maintain control of the Senate. But if Jon Ossoff and Raphael Warnock managed to sweep both runoff races, Democrats would flip the chamber, thanks to the tie-breaking vote from incoming vice president Kamala Harris. Even the slimmest Democratic majority made possible the ambitious items on the Biden administration's long wish list: initiatives to combat climate change, rebuild the nation's infrastructure, tighten gun control restrictions, and expand the social safety net. But the top-of-the-agenda item was a more robust coronavirus relief package.

As ecstatic as state Democrats were about flipping Georgia in the presidential race, adding sixteen votes to Biden's already winning Electoral College tally, it was Jon Ossoff's surprising finish that might have been the most important outcome of the November election in Georgia. Ossoff ended the race trailing Senator David Perdue by about eighty-eight thousand votes—just enough to drag the Republican slightly under the 50 percent mark he needed to notch an outright victory. That close call kept alive Democratic hopes of taking back the US Senate.

As the four runoff campaigns prepared to resolve the extended cliffhanger contests, they each came to a similar conclusion. These races were not to be scrambles for small segments of undecided voters. They hinged on persuading the same fragile political coalitions that cast ballots in November to return to the polls once again, this time after a supercharged nine-week runoff period that would end with a January 5 vote. And the task ahead for all four candidates was monumental. They needed to motivate voters during the worst public health crisis in a century to return to the polls following an exhausting November election that had already tested the patience of millions of Georgians.

Republicans entered the contest with the odds in their favor. No Democrat had won a statewide post in Georgia since 2006. And runoffs tended to attract an older, whiter, and more conservative electorate. In fact, the GOP had won all seven partisan general election runoffs held in Georgia since 1992, when Democratic senator Wyche Fowler was defeated in overtime by Republican Paul Coverdell, even though he led the general election by roughly thirty-five thousand votes. While overall turnout invariably plummeted between the general and the runoff, voter participation from Black Georgians fell even more precipitously.

Jim Martin, the Democratic nominee in Georgia's last US Senate runoff, decisively lost the 2008 campaign to Republican Saxby Chambliss largely because he couldn't motivate Black voters to return to the polls weeks after

Barack Obama's election victory. In his downcast concession speech, after the strains of Carly Simon's 1980s hit "Let the River Run" faded, the defeated Democrat summed up his loss by quoting Abraham Lincoln's tale of stubbing his toe as a boy: "I was too old to cry, but it hurt too much to laugh."

With Martin's defeat a warning to all four candidates about the necessity of motivating their bases, both parties began pouring unprecedented amounts of money and resources into Georgia. Small armies of canvassers prepared to march to doorsteps in cities, subdivisions, and farm towns all across the state. After a general election campaign in which Democrats mostly relied on online mobilization efforts while Republicans only briefly paused their in-person campaigning, the rival tickets were now on equal footing. Democrats and their allies resurrected their door-to-door appeals and outdoor in-person rallies, following a set of safety guidelines such as social distancing and mask requirements.

None of the four candidates had to fret about mustering all the resources on their own for the showdown. Back in October, South Carolina Democrat Jaime Harrison had reported raising a colossal $57 million in one fundrais-ing quarter, shattering records for a US Senate race as he prepared for his ultimately unsuccessful showdown with Senator Lindsey Graham. Ossoff and Warnock each collected more than $100 million in the span of just two months. More than $500 million was spent on TV ads alone by the quartet of candidates and their allies through the end of the year, fueled by a surge in contributions from outside Georgia.

The out-of-state interest reached a fever pitch so early that strategist Karl Rove was recruited by Republicans to help marshal a fifty-state fundraising effort. "This is the last line of defense to conservative values," Rove said on Fox News, charting out his plan on his trademark whiteboard. "This is the last line of defense to conservative values. If we don't have a Republican ma-jority in the US Senate, they're going to have a clear path to this nutty agenda." Former Democratic presidential candidate Andrew Yang helped sound the alarm for his party, too, taking it a step further by announcing he would move to Georgia to help the two challengers—and he encouraged members of his social media #YangGang following to join him.

Already wary of the Republican narrative of "outsiders" rushing to Georgia, Stacey Abrams pleaded with Yang and other Democrats from other states to stay put—and to find other ways to help the two challengers from afar.

Yang wasn't the only out-of-state Democrat who threatened the party's chances with overheated rhetoric. An overjoyed Chuck Schumer, who stood to become the Senate majority leader if the two seats flipped, made the first major gaffe of the runoff cycle as he celebrated Joe Biden's victory before a rowdy crowd at the Grand Army Plaza in Brooklyn. "Now we take Georgia, then we change America," he bellowed, unknowingly playing into attacks that Georgia conservatives had used for years to pummel local Democrats as extremists. Almost as soon as the clip popped up on social media on November 7, overjoyed Republicans turned it into a digital ad, one of the first in a wave warning of "radicals" bent on changing America.

———

With stakes this high, it made sense for Republicans to forge a united front. State GOP leaders quickly discovered how challenging that would be.

A few days after the election, a small group of senior staffers and officials gathered at the GOP headquarters off East Paces Ferry Road in Buckhead to chart out the opening strategy and make sure everyone was reading from the same playbook. It was clear from the start they all were not.

As some of the state's most trusted Republican figures gathered in a suite of offices, organizers asked the faces in the crowds to identify themselves. Agriculture secretary Sonny Perdue and senior GOP strategist Nick Ayers needed no introduction. But eyebrows shot up when one man stood up and declared, "I'm here to represent the deplorables. I represent the president." None of the leaders in the room had ever seen him before, and he began spouting nonsense about legions of dead people who voted in the November election.

Perdue had a habit of fiddling with his ear when he grew irritated, and he began tugging at his earlobe as the man spoke. Ayers, a veteran White House aide, let the man rattle off conspiracy theories for about a minute before interjecting. "Stop talking," Ayers said. "I have no idea who you are." When the man insisted Trump sent him, Ayers pulled out his phone, went to a neighboring room, and dialed up the president. Trump promptly told Ayers that he, too, had never heard of the guy.

Suddenly, Ayers heard the White House operator chime in. Trump's chief of staff, Mark Meadows, wanted to join the call. He explained the man was sent on his behalf and was linked to Cleta Mitchell, the lawyer involved with the pro-Trump attempts to challenge the election results in court. Ayers, frustrated, told the group the confusion about who was leading the GOP runoff effort only made it more difficult to mount a coordinated campaign. "We need to be on the same page," Ayers said, "and decide who's running the show."

When the call ended, Ayers returned to the conference room and informed the operatives and politicians that Perdue would lead the GOP runoff effort with the president's blessing. But even then, it was clear to the participants that each competing GOP faction had its own designs on how to steer the runoff campaigns, and that getting them to pull in the same direction would be nearly impossible. As one attendee put it, that meeting signaled that any notion of a united Republican front was already "disintegrating." It would be one of the last attempts to get the various GOP powers in the same room—and unified behind the same plan—through the rest of the runoff.

The GOP's competing priorities would fast become apparent in other ways. Shortly after the election, senior Republicans decided on a bifurcated strategy to address Trump's efforts to overturn the Georgia election while also preparing for the January 5 showdown. Brian Barrett, a regional director for Trump's campaign, had recently been put in charge of leading the GOP's recount effort, while Dan Coats, the president's state director in Georgia, was tasked with organizing the machinery of the runoff campaigns.

After getting his directive, Coats headed to the fifth floor of the GOP headquarters, where a handful of staffers were busy at work on the recount effort. There he encountered Mitchell, a former Oklahoma state legislator who was a partner in a major law firm. She fussed to him about the need to shift staffers back toward supporting Trump's election-related claims. "Your priorities are in the wrong place," she told Coats, a low-key, well-respected Georgia operative. All he could do was shrug. "We have a job to do," he responded, according to multiple witnesses, turning back to his work.

For the state's GOP elders, it was another portent of the distractions to come from Trump and his allies—and a recognition that the president wasn't about to accept his defeat.

═════

Democrats had come to the same reckoning.

Biden campaign aide Jaclyn Rothenberg was supposed to return to New York and pick up where she had left off with Mayor Bill de Blasio's office, but she canceled her one-way ticket back to her studio apartment in Lower Manhattan to help fight the barrage of bogus claims being made about the election. She and her dog, Clinton, a chihuahua-poodle mix, moved out of her mom's condo and into a Hyatt in midtown Atlanta with other Democratic operatives, holing up in the "boiler room" for a few weeks longer. The exhilaration of having tipped Georgia turned to exhaustion as the next chapter began: a constant fight against Trump's disinformation.

Every morning she woke up feeling as if she were trapped in the movie *Groundhog Day*, replaying the same drama again and again. Rothenberg memorized menus and befriended hotel staffers—and realized she needed to restock her wardrobe, since she'd brought clothes for only a few days. Her fellow operatives became members of a fractious, fatigued family. Attorneys hopped on planes from New York and Washington to help the campaign's Georgia team respond to the legal onslaught, and reinforcements arrived from Biden's losing operations in Florida and North Carolina. The next few weeks became a constant battle against lies. "It's not even defense," Rothenberg told her staffers. "Our job, at this point, is just to communicate facts."

At the same time, Rothenberg and other campaign veterans had to rev up for the runoffs. The November victory had given Democrats a sense of momentum that had eluded them for decades. During campaigns, strategists and candidates repeat the same tired lines: *This is the most important election ever. This is the election where everything changes.*

In Georgia, that pep talk rang hollow—until November. For the first time in decades, state Democrats could walk confidently into meetings and point directly to the results and say, unequivocally, that they had won. And that the runoffs could, indeed, change *everything.*

As party executive director Scott Hogan asked donors to dig into their wallets to spend even more on TV and digital ads, on door-knocking and beefing up the voter protection system, he didn't need to remind them that he was asking them to recommit to a strategy that had succeeded oh-so-narrowly a few weeks earlier.

"I could look at them in the eye and tell them just two words: it worked."

Chapter 18

THE TSUNAMI

The first GOP runoff rally was held about six days after the election in the strip mall headquarters of the Cobb County GOP, a low-slung building sandwiched between a taqueria and a Mexican-owned grocery store. A cardboard cutout of Donald Trump welcomed visitors, a visceral reminder of the president's outsized influence even after his defeat. In a room so crowded that visitors were pressed against the walls—several television crews wouldn't enter over fears the event would turn into a pandemic super-spreader occasion—Senator Marco Rubio of Florida stepped up to a small platform in the back. The mostly unmasked crowd cheered wildly, with some almost inadvertently knocking over a portrait featuring highlights of Ronald Reagan's life, as they welcomed Rubio to the last remaining battleground of the 2020 election cycle.

Not once mentioning Trump's name, Rubio urged Republicans to return to the polls to prevent the nation from careening in a "radical" direction. "Normal people that want to own a home and raise their family in a safe community and retire with dignity and have a country that's safe and stable and give their children a chance at a better life, they're going to vote against people that are crazy and want to undermine all of that," he said. "That's what's at stake in this election. And if we don't control the US Senate, that is the agenda that's going to be pushed. It doesn't even matter if the majority of the Democrats, if you polled them and gave them truth serum, are not in favor of it."

It was no accident that the campaigns of Kelly Loeffler and David Perdue chose Cobb to display the combined might of their newly launched joint ticket. While the former GOP stronghold was now a solidly Democratic bastion, which Joe Biden had just carried with 56 percent of the vote, it was also still an epicenter of the state's traditional GOP establishment, and one of four Georgia counties that Rubio had carried in the 2016 presidential primary when he was competing against Trump. If Republicans hoped to reclaim control of the Senate in a little more than two months, they would have to chip away at the Democratic support in Cobb.

Loeffler and Perdue made for a unique duo despite largely having avoided each other during the general election campaign. Perdue had been reluctant to appear alongside Loeffler through the November vote, worried that even the smallest hint of support for his Senate colleague would alienate backers of Doug Collins. Nor was Perdue as aggressive on the campaign trail as Loeffler in the run-up to November. In fact, he was largely absent from public events on the trail during the first days of the runoff campaign as he recovered from knee surgery and, in one aide's words, "got his mind right" for the tough road ahead. At the Cobb event, Perdue's introverted wife, Bonnie, spoke in his stead, telling the crowd her husband's "entire life has prepared him for this moment."

The two senators were confronted with distinctly different challenges. Perdue needed no help selling himself to the Republican base, and his opponent, well-defined in the media for years, was already a villain to many GOP voters. Loeffler, on the other hand, limped into the runoff in more perilous straits: she was resolved to shore up her standing with fellow conservatives skeptical of her record, and faced a Democrat with high approval ratings after going mostly unharmed by Republicans for the last year.

Still, despite their differences, the candidates and their aides realized they had no other option but to unite. Since runoffs are turnout elections, Republicans saw banding together to woo as many supporters as they could as the best way to combat voter apathy after Trump's defeat. One of the first signs of the all-hands-on-deck GOP approach came even before it was clear Trump lost, when the Senate election results showed Collins trailing Loeffler badly on election night. Loeffler's staffers were ready for a repeat of the drawn-out drama that had followed the 2018 race for governor, perhaps with a refusal by Collins to concede the race. But the congressman and his advisers had acknowledged there was no path to victory and accepted his new "team player" role. Soon after, aides to both of the rivals met with senior Republican officials to work out a reconciliation plan that Jay Williams, a veteran GOP consultant, called a "surprising" sign of how quickly the former enemies put aside their internal conflicts.

By the end of the month, Collins campaigned with Loeffler outside a gun range in Pickens County, near the southernmost stretch of the Appalachian Mountains, where they made peace in person. As Collins put it, they united to help "Republicans rising up again from the ashes" to maintain control of the US Senate. "This was not a defeat—this was a victory. Because come January 5, the nation and the world is gonna see Georgia stand up."

———

Even as Collins spoke on that late November Saturday, Republicans were dealt a sharp reminder of the aftershocks of Trump's lies about a "rigged" election. A pep rally featuring Republican National Committee chairwoman Ronna Romney McDaniel at the Cobb GOP headquarters turned into angst-ridden fretting from Republican activists as she fielded complaint after complaint from Trump backers wondering why they should vote. One asked an exasperated McDaniel why voters should bother with investing more "money and work when it's already decided." McDaniel pleaded with the crowd to understand that the runoff vote was not predetermined, no matter the president's claims that the fix was in. "It's not decided. This is the key—it's not decided," she said. "So, if you lose your faith and you don't vote and people walk away, that will decide it."

Instead of unity and bonhomie, a full-blown civil war had begun raging within the Georgia GOP at a moment when Republicans could least afford it. And with the Senate on the line, Georgia had suddenly become not just ground zero for the nation's political attention, but also the foremost battleground over disinformation—much of it originating directly from Trump.

Long before the election, he had leveled unfounded claims of voter fraud involving mail-in ballots. With the margin in Georgia so close, he steadily began pressuring his allies in the state—first privately, then publicly—to interfere with the vote count on his behalf.

The candidates and their aides—not to mention the entire Republican establishment—knew how important Trump's unequivocal support was to their runoff chances. Even the slightest misstep, such as a tacit acknowledgment of his defeat or a refusal to buy into his claims of fraud, could give rise to one of Trump's notorious tweetstorms—and risk spurring the president's legion of loyalists to boycott the election. GOP incumbents and many of their allies instead trumpeted their loyalty to the president while scrupulously avoiding issues that could put any distance between them and the White House.

That deprived them of one of their strongest runoff messages: the argument that a Republican victory would be the strongest check on total Democratic control of Washington, because that would mean acknowledging Trump's defeat. Instead, they talked of a "potential President Biden" and urged Republicans to "hold the line" in the GOP-controlled Senate. "It could go either way. There are a lot of voters who are Trump voters in Georgia who are disheartened. They're angry because they think that the president didn't get a fair shake in Georgia," Perdue said in a Fox News interview, adding: "We've got to convince people their vote is going to be counted and counted accurately."

The conspiracy-riddled Atlanta rally helmed by Donald Trump Jr. two days after his father's defeat was just a taste of what was to come. Trump hectored anyone he could in search of a way to block the certification of Georgia's election results. Several of his aides convinced him that a "signature audit" of Georgia's mail-in ballots would be the breakthrough he needed to reverse his defeat, an issue he fixated on for weeks despite the fact that signatures on absentee ballot envelopes had already been verified by county officials when voters returned absentee ballot application forms and again on ballot envelopes. And there was no way to trace the signatures back to individual ballots; they had been separated to preserve the right to a secret vote enshrined in the Georgia Constitution.

Regardless of the facts, Trump's rage about Georgia's election eventually focused on Secretary of State Brad Raffensperger, the official presiding over the most scrutinized state election since Florida's hanging-chads debacle in 2000.

Tall and thin with wire-rimmed glasses and salt-and-pepper hair, Raffensperger was a backbench conservative legislator from Atlanta's northern suburbs inevitably described by his colleagues as "unassuming" when he ran for higher office. He emerged from a competitive Republican primary thanks to a burst of late TV ads financed by a hefty bank account built through Raffensperger's successful career as a civil engineer and an entrepreneur. In an election cycle overshadowed by Kemp's brawl with Stacey Abrams, Raffensperger eked out a slim 2018 runoff victory over former congressman John Barrow, a moderate Democrat who followed the party's more conventional strategy, appealing to middle-of-the-road voters by highlighting his knack for bipartisanship, reverence for Georgia's gun culture, and votes for slashing taxes. "Yeah, I'm a Democrat," Barrow said in a thirty-second TV ad filmed on a scenic farm, "but I won't bite ya!"

For Raffensperger, his election victory was also tinged with sorrow. His oldest son died after years of struggling with addiction, a tragedy that gave him and his wife, Tricia, a sort of armor for the trials to come. "They can call me all the names they want. They can do whatever they want," Tricia later told the *Journal-Constitution*. "But they can never hurt me like that."

The job Raffensperger had fought so hard to win involved a grab bag of state duties: licensing nurses, regulating massage therapists, credentialing businesses. But the most important assignment was overseeing electoral activity, from voter registration to state and local elections. Over the years, the secretary of state position had also become a stepping-stone for politicians seeking higher office. Max Cleland launched a successful run for US Senate while he was in the job; Cathy Cox and Karen Handel both used it as a springboard to seek statewide positions; Kemp served in the role for much of the 2010s, and refused to resign from the post while running, and winning, his 2018 bid for governor.

Not many saw that sort of political ambition in Raffensperger. But the November election transformed him from a state official whose name most Georgians could hardly pronounce—let alone recognize—to a walking litmus test on Trump-era politics. With his aggressive response to the attacks launched against him, Raffensperger would become to some an icon of integrity for defending a vote in the face of the president's unrelenting pressure. To others who believed the lies about widespread fraud, or were just frustrated with Trump's November struggles, he became the subject of derision, the scapegoat easily blamed by the president and his allies for Biden's victory in Georgia.

Raffensperger had already managed to peeve conservatives earlier in the year, in the opening months of the pandemic, by deciding to mail absentee ballot request forms to nearly 6.9 million Georgians ahead of the June primary, paving the way for record Democratic turnout. GOP leaders like Georgia House Speaker David Ralston worried that a dramatic shift to mail-in voting would give their rivals an impregnable long-term edge. In a slip of the tongue, Ralston admitted as much, saying such a change in policy would be "extremely devastating to Republicans and conservatives" before walking back his remarks amid outrage from voting rights advocates.

Ralston might have been a little too on the nose. About 1.5 million Georgians had been added to the voting rolls since late 2016, when the state adopted automatic voter registration for everyone getting their driver's licenses. Under the change, implemented by Kemp while he was secretary of state, those who filled out a driver's license form were registered to vote unless they specifically checked a box to opt out. Sophisticated voter modeling used by both parties showed the newly registered voters who didn't normally cast ballots tended to lean Democratic. Republicans fretted that encouraging them to vote by mail could swing the election.

Raffensperger understood the objections from conservatives to expanding mail-in balloting but felt he had no other option. Scores of poll workers, many of them elderly, quit rather than risk an interaction during the pandemic with voters who could potentially put their lives at risk. And even after a monthslong delay in the primary to hash out safety protocols and update training, many voters who cast their ballots in person had still been forced to wait for hours in close quarters.

To gauge the mood before the June primary, Raffensperger's top aide, Jordan Fuchs, polled Georgia voters and found that 80 percent of Republicans supported his idea to mail out the ballot request forms. Even if they hadn't, Raffensperger was still committed to the idea. "Election workers weren't going to come in," he said. "That's the only way voters were able to vote."

On election night in November, Raffensperger holed up in a state command center reviewing election reports and balancing the returns with how many absentee ballots were still outstanding. Shortly after midnight, he knew Trump was going to lose—and that he would get the blame. *The tsunami is out there,* he thought. *And it will be here in a few days.*

He was right. Raffensperger was the only Republican to oversee elections in one of the battleground states where Trump's campaign was vigorously contesting the results. And in the days after his defeat, the president unleashed a seemingly ceaseless barrage that labeled Raffensperger an "enemy of the people" for denying his lies about the election outcome. Raffensperger and his aides held twice-daily press conferences at points during the postelection frenzy to try to beat back the tumult of falsehoods. They noted that the two subsequent recounts of the nearly 5 million votes confirmed the results, and a December audit of absentee ballot signatures in an Atlanta suburb showed no evidence of fraudulent votes.

That investigation found that ten absentee ballots were accepted despite mismatched or missing voting signatures. But agents with the Georgia Bureau of Investigation contacted the voters and found they had submitted them. It blew another hole in the leaky pro-Trump narrative about election fraud, though the president responded by complaining about the process and questioning why other counties weren't included in the probe. Every time elections officials rebutted a false claim, Trump and his allies moved the goalposts to raise another objection.

Rather than stand by Raffensperger, many Georgia Republicans remained silent, while others amplified Trump's call for the official to resign in disgrace. In a last-ditch attempt to stay on the president's good side, both of Georgia's Republican US senators followed his lead, demanding six days after the election that Raffensperger step down over vague charges of "failures."

Even some of Loeffler's most trusted advisers were caught off guard when she took the drastic step, which they later framed as a way to both placate the president and stay ahead of his increasing demands. "We've shot the prisoner.

Enough is enough. Now let's move on—we can't keep getting jerked around on this nonsense," one Loeffler adviser confided at the time. What they later realized was that it was just the start of the scramble to keep Trump in their corner, a "damned if you do, damned if you don't" mentality that shaped the length of the runoffs.

Publicly, Raffensperger charged that the senators had "folded like a cheap suit." He directly accused the president of "throwing him under the bus" and authoring his own defeat by sowing doubts about mail-in votes. His evidence? About twenty-four thousand voters had cast mail-in ballots during the Republican primary but sat out the November vote—roughly twice Biden's margin of victory.

The secretary of state paid a tremendous price for his defiance, one that went far beyond the standard rough-and-tumble of political clashes. The night the two US senators called for Raffensperger's resignation, his phone lit up with obscene and violent threats. His wife was targeted, too. No longer did they feel safe having their two grandchildren, both under the age of five, visit their home. Parades of people waving Trump flags descended on a quiet suburban neighborhood where they thought Raffensperger lived—though many wound up in the wrong subdivision—and some posted selfies at the end of his driveway to their social media accounts.

Some of the threats were terrifying. Someone took a video of Raffensperger's widowed daughter-in-law while she was out shopping. When she returned to her home a few hours later, she discovered someone had broken in, apparently trying to frighten her: the lights were on, the garage door was open, and her dog's kennel had been moved. The same night, suspected members of a far-right militia group known as the Oath Keepers were spotted outside the Raffenspergers' home, claiming they were in the area to deter Black Lives Matter demonstrators. The couple went into hiding for nearly a week, Reuters reported, concerned for their safety even with round-the-clock security.

"I voted Republican and voted for President Trump. I support Republican policies. I like when our team wins," Raffensperger later said. "But we're just doing our job. We're following the law. And everything we're doing went above and beyond the call of duty to make sure it's transparent."

Chapter 19

THE BROMANCE IS BORN

On her second day on the job, Jonae Wartel was summoned to a Zoom call by Raphael Warnock and asked point-blank a question that was at once the simplest and most complex she may have ever had to answer.

What do we have to do to win?

Without hesitating, Wartel rattled through the most pressing points: Democrats needed to revive the coalition that had powered their November victory, to introduce Warnock and Jon Ossoff as a joint ticket, and to slash through the misinformation that continued to plague some voters about the runoff. But her main challenge was also the most complicated. "We've got to organize. We can't let this moment outpace our organizational capacity. We need to invest in the field operation."

That task took Wartel back to her roots as a young operative. She cut her teeth running Georgia House races in the early 2010s, a time when Democrats were scrambling to tread water just to avoid a GOP tidal wave. Later in her career, as she hopscotched between Georgia and Washington, Wartel earned a reputation as a savvy strategist who could come late into campaigns to give Democrats a burst of needed energy—like a bench player pressed into action in the pivotal final minutes of a basketball game.

All that hustle had worn Wartel out. She was plotting an exit from campaign politics when Georgia's two Senate races landed in overtime—and once again she was summoned from the sidelines to help, this time as the director of the Democratic runoffs. But never had she—or anyone else—faced a campaign quite like this one.

Democrats had no time to waste. First up was quickly hiring scores of local activists, particularly in some of the rural communities where the party couldn't afford to let Republicans widen their advantage. But right alongside that mission, she told Warnock, was transforming the campaigns of two very different rising-star candidates into a true tag team.

"We had to birth a bromance," Wartel said.

Warnock and Ossoff had run independently in the early days of their campaigns, though they were always friendly when their paths crossed on the trail. And they both grasped the math: one win would amount to little more than a symbolic victory; Democrats needed to flip both Senate seats to take control of the chamber. Over the course of their campaigns, though, the two forged a genuine friendship and kept aligned in tone and message, texting each other a steady stream of updates and stray thoughts as they crisscrossed the state in giant luxury buses. "If we had seen them going in different policy directions on the campaign trail, that would have been the story," said Wartel. "But instead they brought a unified message to every corner of the state."

The two also had similar strategies to put their Republican foes on the defensive. Much of Georgia had already heard about scrutiny of Loeffler's stock transactions at the start of the pandemic. Perdue faced growing backlash, too, over his financial history. In November, *The New York Times* reported that Perdue dumped more than $1 million worth of stock in the financial company on whose board he had once served, then bought back a major portion and earned a windfall. Though both Perdue and Loeffler were investigated by the Justice Department and never charged with any wrongdoing for their separate stock-related transactions, they were forced to address the issues on the airwaves. "When you're spending money saying you're exonerated, you're losing," sighed a Perdue campaign official.

It was part of a unified strategy that Ossoff and Warnock, along with their top advisers, helped devise during a meeting following the November election. Ossoff suggested that their policy themes would revolve around three issues to energize liberals: health, jobs, and justice. Skilled at stagecraft, Ossoff grasped the need for a good narrative that went beyond just the drama of the dual runoff cliffhangers. The best way to tell the story was as a "buddy movie," he told his team, to save the country from the "Bonnie and Clyde of corruption."

"Think about how far we've come in the American South. Georgia is the most competitive battleground state in the United States," Ossoff said at one stop. "Your standard-bearers are the young Jewish son of an immigrant and a Black pastor who holds Dr. King's pulpit at Ebenezer Baptist Church."

———

Republicans once preoccupied with battling each other for a spot in the runoff were now free to pummel Warnock. And almost as soon as his matchup with Senator Kelly Loeffler was set, the pastor knew they would unleash the enormous book of opposition that researchers had painstakingly compiled since even before he entered the race, a torrent of attacks unearthing his past sermons and stances. Of course, his own operatives had also mined hundreds of hours of footage and thousands of pages of his writings and sermons to find the most potentially damaging material—and strategize ways to counter it.

As he gathered with his aides to map out the runoff, Warnock's strategists urged him to remember over the next nine weeks the same phrase that had powered him through November: "Remain the reverend." That meant sharing his life story, explaining to voters what guides his moral compass, detailing his background as an activist, and promoting his personality to make Georgians feel as if they knew him.

But it also required launching an aggressive ad campaign to introduce a Democrat whom many voters had still never heard of—and prepare them for the bitter, and often racialized, criticisms that were to come. Adam Magnus, the campaign's lead adsmith, huddled with his campaign team to develop an initial thirty-second spot that reassured supporters and skeptics alike that Warnock was about to be brutalized by a wave of attacks—"so don't be fooled by it."

His first TV spot of the runoff, airing two days after the November election but filmed in early October, set the tone with an ominous voice-over mockingly warning of Warnock's cardinal sins: he scarfed down pizza with a fork and a knife, stepped on a crack on the sidewalk. But the star of the ad was Alvin the beagle, whom Warnock lovingly cradled in the final frame of the ad after the narrator threateningly claimed the Democrat "even hates puppies." "And by the way," Warnock says as the image fades out, "I love puppies."

Alvin wasn't really Warnock's dog; he belonged to a supporter who lived in exactly the type of north Atlanta suburb where the Democrat needed voters to return to the polls. Warnock jokingly referred to the puppy as a "volunteer," though he insisted his connection with the cuddly canine was legit. Instantly, Alvin became a hit online and a mascot for Warnock's campaign. Supporters brought their own puppies and other pets to campaign rallies to pose for pictures with the Democrat. The campaign sold dog-themed merchandise, like "Puppies 4 Warnock"–branded coffee mugs, and printed yard signs catering to the canines. Just as important, some political scientists said, was the implicit message the ads sent to voters with imagery tailor-made to appeal to white suburbia: along with the cute beagle, the American flags and white picket fences and puffy vests that seemed carefully calibrated to deracialize the pastor.

In total, Warnock's campaign aired sixty-four ads during the runoff, many of them featuring the pastor speaking directly to the camera and many with defense in mind. When Republican commercials brought up Warnock's past remarks about the Reverend Jeremiah Wright, whose sermons became a flash point in Barack Obama's 2008 presidential bid, his campaign responded with an ad highlighting his work against hate crimes. After Republicans unearthed a clip of Warnock sounding critical of the military, his campaign swiftly rolled out a thirty-second spot that showed the candidate with his father, a proud veteran. And to counter volleys claiming that he was a "radical liberal," pro-Warnock TV spots featured footage of Loeffler's visit to his church on Martin Luther King Jr. Day earlier that year.

Amid the onslaught, it seemed only a matter of time until Alvin would make a return appearance. Biking on the outskirts of Washington, Magnus had an epiphany, pulled to the side of the road to email himself before he could forget, and then went straight home for a gut check with his eight-year-old daughter to make sure it worked. Some seventy-two hours later, Magnus was on the streets of Decatur, just east of Atlanta, filming the idea his daughter had signed off on: The reverend, wearing a puffy vest and sneakers, is walking Alvin in a slice of suburbia. As he ticks through fact-checks of Loeffler's negative attacks, Warnock pauses by a trash can. "I think Georgians will see her ads for what they are," he says, dumping Alvin's poop in the garbage. "Don't you?" The camera cuts to Alvin, who barks in approval.

Once again, Alvin's ad went viral online, garnering five million views. Warnock's campaign reserved airtime to feature the ad in strategic slots, including the National Dog Show. As strategists from both parties praised the effectiveness of the ads, Magnus touted the "power of puppies—they were the period at the end of the sentence of the campaign."

"It was purposeful. People formed a relationship with him," said Magnus. "We knew that the negative ads were coming, and we needed enough people to feel like they knew him and would stay with him to win."

———

Of all the four candidates, Ossoff might have been best prepared for the attention, given his experience in what was then the most expensive US House contest in history in 2017. Not long after the November vote, Ossoff gathered his brain trust to remind them of the most pressing challenges ahead.

For starters, the same playbook he used to force a nine-week runoff against Perdue wouldn't win the overtime contest. Far more needed to be done to energize voters of color, who had historically turned out in lower numbers for runoff elections in Georgia. The campaign would soon have more cash than they knew how to spend and had to start planning *now* how to allocate it. "Let's do something huge," Ossoff told his advisers.

Within days, Ossoff instructed his team, led by campaign manager Ellen Foster, to build an unprecedented network of field staffers they called "community mobilizers." Text messages were sent to tens of thousands of young unlikely voters, largely from minority communities, inviting them to apply, though many learned about the program through old-fashioned ways: flyers posted on telephone poles or word-of-mouth chatter.

A team of twenty-five staffers raced through the more than twenty thousand applications that came pouring into the campaign and wound up interviewing roughly three hundred to four hundred people a day. Of those, they hired nearly three thousand people who represented each of Georgia's 159 counties and then built out custom software to channel that energy into higher turnout. Each of the new organizers, overwhelmingly young and Black, mined his or her social networks and phone contacts for eligible voters who might support Ossoff. Then they pleaded with them to vote in the runoffs, promoting fine-tuned messages that keyed on social justice or public health themes.

Over the next few weeks, Ossoff held private town halls with some of the most active organizers, always encouraging them to reach out to even more voters. His promise to "raise a grassroots army unlike any this state has ever seen" at the outset of the campaign was coming to fruition.

He also played a hands-on role in developing his runoff ads, coauthoring in some form or fashion every one of them. Each was directly aimed at winning over Black voters, with emotional spots featuring young men voicing concerns about police brutality, business owners struggling with the economic slowdown during the pandemic, and women excited by the prospect of dramatic change in Washington. Ossoff's advisers saw it as the most unconventional TV campaign in Georgia, though it drew skeptical responses. Senate Democratic leader Chuck Schumer phoned Ossoff about a month into the runoff to politely let him know some Washington operatives were "concerned" about the ad campaign. One senior DC consultant used harsher words, calling the strategy of a white candidate singularly targeting voters of color "insane." Ossoff told the senator, and anyone else who asked, that he would stay the course.

Behind the scenes, the campaign polled white voters each week to ensure that his support with them wasn't eroding, in case he needed to pivot. Some on his team were surprised to see the social justice messages, which highlighted his support for demonstrations demanding racial equality, working better than they expected with white voters.

Ossoff also was the first to hit the campaign trail with an aggressive travel schedule. His team, which included communications director Miryam Lipper, press secretary Jake Best, and political director Steven Parker, recognized the importance of immediately getting their candidate on the road to harness the Democratic energy. Before a wave of joint rallies with Warnock, he went out on his own for a four-day, seven-stop tour of Georgia that featured prominent local figures and was accompanied by a heart-thumping soundtrack from the likes of Bruce Springsteen and Big Boi. The implicit message of the tour was that Ossoff, facing a more popular opponent than his fellow Democrat, had more work to do to win.

On a dreary afternoon about a week after the November election, he arrived at the coastal town of Savannah, where he went to a historic railroad museum to share his vision of a Biden presidency with Democrats in control of Washington. "Maybe you felt these last few days what I have in my heart for the first time in a while, y'all. It's hope," Ossoff said as a misty rain fell and outside a small group of Republicans waving communist flags tried to heckle Ossoff and his allies. "Change has come to Georgia."

Chapter 20

"IT'S UN-AMERICAN"

The rampant misinformation spreading across Georgia didn't threaten only high-ranking public officials. A thirty-second video of a county elections staffer named Lawrence Sloan went viral among conspiracy theorists, who alleged he was complicit in a ballot-rigging scandal. Sloan had taken a job as a temporary worker in the Fulton County elections department operating "cutter" machines, which opened the envelopes with mail-in ballots inside. On the video, a narrator portentously claims Sloan crumpled up a ballot in a fit of anger as the footage shows him flinching at the machine, flipping it the middle finger before tossing the paper aside.

Within hours, the video had been retweeted thousands of times by pro-Trump conspiracists hungry for any sign of proof of a "stolen" election, some of whom hurled racist slurs at Sloan. Donald Trump Jr. and Eric Trump both amplified the video, which soon drew more than five million views. Sloan deleted his social media accounts and went into hiding as information about him and his relatives, including license plate numbers and other personal details, proliferated online. He told WSB, a local TV station, that he had to ask friends to pick him up from a local restaurant and whisk him away after he felt threatened by Trump supporters. "And as a Black man in the South, I know when pickup trucks start pulling up and honking their horns, it's time to go."

He later shared the story with local media outlet WABE of what had really happened with the machine: the cutter hadn't sliced open an envelope properly, and when he reached to check it, the conveyor belt nipped his hand. The paper he crumpled wasn't a ballot of some cheated Trump supporter. It was instructions for how to cast a vote by mail.

In another incident, selectively edited video showed a Fulton County worker moving a ballot container from beneath a table while counting votes at State Farm Arena on election night, footage that was promoted by Trump attorney Rudy Giuliani as proof that election staffers were secretly tabulating phony votes.

In reality, the footage showed that workers had packed the boxes with valid, uncounted ballots as they prepared to quit for the evening. When they were told they had to keep counting, the staffers took the boxes out and went back to tallying the votes. There were no suitcases full of phony ballots, as Giuliani and other Trump supporters contended at state legislative hearings.

Sometimes, otherwise anonymous county elections staffers came under fire. An email was sent to elections officials in nearly a dozen counties threatening to blow up polling sites "unless and until Trump is guaranteed to be POTUS again." A veteran Fulton County elections staffer named Ralph Jones received calls bombarding him with racial slurs, vowing to shoot him or drag his body through the streets tied to a truck. After the county's election chief, Rick Barron, received a chilling call in December promising to execute him by firing squad, police were posted outside his home. All Barron could do was lament the descent into what he told Reuters was a "third-world mentality."

State elections officials and fact-checkers couldn't keep up, playing a constant game of whack-a-mole to debunk one conspiracy theory before another would quickly arise. The tidal wave of lies gained purchase with some Republican elected officials, who joined lawsuits trying to overturn the elections and called for sweeping changes to the election system, like getting rid of "at will" absentee voting and automatic voter registration.

The irony was that Republicans had turned on the very systems they had championed over the years. State Republicans backed the passage of no-excuse absentee voting rules in the mid-2000s, back when the mail-in system seemed to favor older, more conservative voters. After Joe Biden trounced Trump with two thirds of the mail-in vote in Georgia, voting by mail had suddenly become unpalatable to Republicans. The same was true of the computerized voting machines that Trump supporters were now vilifying: the process had been adopted by the Republican-controlled legislature in 2019.

Officials also struggled to cast aside other falsehoods that seeped deeply into pro-Trump media. Democratic state representative Bee Nguyen found three familiar names on a list of voters who Trump's campaign claimed cast illegal ballots. One was Nguyen's constituent, and two were her friends. She vetted the Trump list personally, finding that dozens of the voters were, in fact, legal voters. Nguyen, who succeeded Stacey Abrams in the legislature, detailed her findings over the course of twelve minutes during a Georgia House hearing arranged by Trump's allies in December. By the end, Matt Braynard, whose research underpinned many of the rejected lawsuits filed by Trump's backers, stammered a note of thanks for "helping to raise issues to help better validate data."

No debunker of the false Trump mythology drew as much attention, in Georgia and perhaps the nation, as the state voting implementation manager, Gabriel Sterling. A bushy-haired Republican former council member in the suburban Atlanta city of Sandy Springs, Sterling was at heart a policy geek and a no-nonsense enforcer who had been hired by Raffensperger after helping to organize his victory party in 2018. Sterling had earlier established a name for himself in GOP circles, having run the campaign of the late US representative Charlie Norwood in 1994 when the Augusta Republican flipped the seat in a stunning upset. After a stint in Washington, Sterling returned to Atlanta to work as a Republican strategist and played a part in helping Sandy Springs become the first new city in Georgia in decades.

His job during much of the 2020 campaign had involved diving into the granular details of the state's new multi-computer voting system, which added a paper ballot to elections for the first time in eighteen years. After the vote, Sterling's role morphed into conducting a daily clinic in thoroughly squashing pro-Trump conspiracy theories, such as lies that machines mysteriously "flipped" votes or that Raffensperger was compromised because his brother

"Ron" worked for a Chinese technology company. (Raffensperger, Sterling wryly noted, has no brother named Ron.) There was such a torrent that Sterling proclaimed one particularly rough morning as "Anti-Disinformation Monday."

His role in dismissing unfounded claims earned him acclaim—and, as with so many others, unwelcome attention. One person urged Sterling to kill himself; another sent him a text containing Sterling's home address, a not-so-veiled threat. A website showed his face in the crosshairs of a rifle, along with Kemp and Raffensperger, and a security detail was eventually posted outside his home.

An affable policy wonk at heart whose social media accounts show off his amateur chef skills, Sterling managed to take most of those threats in stride. But that changed one day in December, when a young technician working on the recount in Gwinnett County was threatened by someone who displayed a noose and said the staffer should be "hung for treason" for doing a routine part of his job. Sterling, enraged, stalked to a capitol podium and delivered an impassioned speech directed squarely at the president.

"Someone's going to get hurt. Someone's going to get shot. Someone's going to get killed," Sterling said, his voice quaking with anger, adding that Trump and others who have "not said a damn word are complicit in this.

"It's time to look forward. If you want to run for reelection in four years, fine, do it," he said. "But everything we're seeing right now, there's not a path. Be the bigger man here and step in. Tell your supporters, 'Don't be violent. Don't intimidate.' All that's wrong. It's un-American."

———

That did little to stop the cycle of disinformation abetted by a small circle of Georgians whose popularity exploded in 2020. Vernon Jones had begun the year as a backbench Democratic state legislator loathed by his own colleagues. He ended it as a newly minted member of the president's Georgia elite, with a coveted speaking slot at the Republican National Convention as one of Trump's top Black supporters, hundreds of thousands of Twitter followers, and viral photos of him crowd-surfing without a mask on the outstretched arms of throngs of Trump fans in Macon.

The Guardian called it "arguably the most ill-advised and dangerous crowdsurf since the electro dance legend Steve Aoki broke a concertgoer's neck in a dinghy." On *Saturday Night Live*, Colin Jost jested that Jones crested atop "the second wave of COVID."

But for Jones, the attention transformed him from a Democratic has-been to a budding pro-Trump star, and the runoff cycle offered him an even greater platform. At an early November "Stop the Steal" rally he warned that if Biden won, "there's going to be some payback—not violence, but half this country will believe that they cheated us out of this election."

Thirteen-year-old CJ Pearson had drawn millions of YouTube viewers with videos slamming then president Obama as "ignorant" and "incompetent" from his grandparents' kitchen in the suburbs of Augusta. His grandmother, a loyal Democrat, regularly confiscated his arsenal of electronic equipment when he misbehaved, but he still found ways to log back on. He once conducted a radio interview from his room during a time-out.

Now an eighteen-year-old student at the University of Alabama, Pearson's more polished Twitter feed and regular podcast show were sources of inspiration for Trump loyalists who believed in the fantasy that the president had won reelection. And Pearson was one of the lead plaintiffs on an error-riddled election lawsuit—quickly tossed by the courts—challenging Biden's win.

The most infamous member of the Georgia peddlers of disinformation, however, was Lin Wood, the celebrity attorney who had represented a list of famous clients including Richard Jewell, the security guard falsely accused of the 1996 Olympic Park bombing, and Nicholas Sandmann, the pro-Trump high school student who was maligned after a viral encounter with a Native American protester in Washington. After stepping back from his lucrative law practice, Wood had transformed himself into a pro-Trump figure with a massive following on social media, propagating sham theories while urging his allies to do everything they could to prevent Biden from taking office. His baseless claims spread like a contagion on social media, including a tweet amplified by the president falsely asserting that Governor Kemp and Secretary Raffensperger, both wearing photoshopped Communist China face masks, were "going to jail."

One of Wood's most notorious moments in the runoff occurred at a pro-Trump rally at an equestrian rink in the wealthy north Atlanta suburb of Alpharetta on December 2, which might as well have served as a study of the conflicts running wild in the Republican Party. It was advertised on social media as a chance for Trump loyalists to learn about the conspiracy theories the former president's campaign and its allies were promoting in its flailing legal challenges. But rather than a gathering with just a few dozen curious onlookers, the park was so jammed with visitors that cars parked on grassy embankments and blocked paved walkways. One attendee even carried a pitchfork.

The throngs of people funneled into a covered outdoor equestrian arena, trying to find space in an area usually reserved for Cub Scout horse camps and elite show-jumping competitions. Nearly two thousand people eventually surrounded a small stage illuminated by towering lights as a bank of TV cameras captured Wood publicly discouraging people from voting for the Republican runoff candidates, since the elections were "rigged."

Then he aimed his attacks directly at the Senate incumbents: "If Kelly Loeffler wants your vote, if David Perdue wants your vote, they've got to earn it," he said. "Brian Kemp, call a special session of the Georgia legislature; if Kelly Loeffler and David Perdue do not do it, they have not earned your vote."

Rather than willing them to the ballot boxes to help fellow Republicans, Wood was pleading with them to boycott the election. And many in the crowd believed he spoke with Trump's blessing. As Wood continued, ear-splitting chants of "Lock him up!" aimed at Kemp reverberated throughout the open-air arena, a theme Wood returned to when he wrongly claimed the governor would soon be headed to prison. Asked for advice by one voter on what to tell friends who thought conspiracy theorists were "crazy" for insisting that Trump won, Wood deadpanned: "Tell them they said the same thing about Jesus."

Georgia Democrats welcomed the Republican civil war, and some amplified the chatter from pro-Trump figures promising to skip the vote or write in the president's name (which would automatically disqualify their vote). Liberal groups financed billboards in conservative parts of the state that read PERDUE/LOEFFLER DIDN'T DELIVER FOR TRUMP—DON'T DELIVER FOR THEM. The Democratic candidates themselves mostly steered clear of the topic, instead focusing on the coronavirus crisis.

Such fanaticism had already struck fear in the hearts of Republican leaders, who had watched the lies and misinformation extend their reach ever deeper into the base of dedicated Trump loyalists they relied on most to turn out in the runoffs. If they had attended Wood's rally, they would have had even more cause for panic. Interviews with more than a dozen people in the audience revealed deep misgivings about whether they would back the Republicans when early voting started in just a few weeks. On her way out, a voter named Tammy Converse confided that she was considering skipping the vote to send a message to Kemp because he had refused to overturn the election results.

"I don't think we should vote until we fix the systems. We need to let them know that it's not acceptable. It's tough. But I don't think any voting is acceptable until they prove it's safe."

Even if that meant, she was asked, ceding control of the US Senate to Democrats?

"I'm torn. I don't know. I'll be watching to see what they can do before then," she answered, sounding genuinely conflicted. "I'm really angry."

———

At his home in Atlanta's northern exurbs in early December, Lieutenant Governor Geoff Duncan watched Trump's latest rant play out with his three sons. Duncan, who liked to tart up his remarks with references to his days as a former Miami Marlins minor league pitching prospect, hadn't generated much controversy during his first years in office, backing Governor Kemp on most major issues and establishing himself as a solid conservative with a friendly disposition.

The biggest scandal he had faced was the resignation of his top aide, who bolted in 2019 because he believed Duncan spent too much time seeking advice from a "life coach" and not enough trusting his paid political advisers. But as Duncan and his children watched Trump thunder about a "stolen" election for yet another day, one of his sons asked him a question that took his breath away. "Dad, why aren't you speaking up?"

He couldn't answer it with a straight face. Duncan had been charmed by Trump during a 2019 visit when he rode with the president in the famed

Beast, the heavily armored Cadillac limo that ferried around Trump and his most trusted guests. Over a short drive, they talked about roughly thirteen different issues in twenty minutes, starting with a boast from the president that they were riding in the most expensive vehicle in the world. Duncan knocked on the windows, which to him felt nine feet thick.

"You can shoot that window with an AK-47 seventy-two times and nothing will happen," Trump told the lieutenant governor.

"What happens on the seventy-third shot?"

Trump nodded to the Secret Service agents sitting nearby.

"Don't worry, they'll have us covered up on the ground then."

Trump didn't stop talking the entire ride, singling out a lone supporter who waved a blue pro-Trump flag in a sea of protesters. "Look, Melania," he told his wife. "They love us in Georgia."

Duncan later wrote in *GOP 2.0*, a memoir of his 2020 experience, that he was convinced Trump meant it. "He only saw one person in the crowd."

Before they parted ways, Trump told Duncan he had a "bright political future" that could land him in the Governor's Mansion one day. Duncan knew that it was just a well-practiced line from the president, and that Trump likely forgot his name minutes later. But he was nonetheless impressed by his grasp of policy and his magnetic persona. He left with a thought: *If everybody could meet* that *Trump, he'd win every election he ever ran for.*

As the campaign heated up, Duncan often talked to his skeptical sons about how Republicans could support Trump without embracing his hateful rhetoric. But navigating that balance became more difficult as the president and his allies injected partisanship into just about every election debate. Two nights before the November election, his middle son, Bayler, then fifteen, fretted about how his father would handle delivering one of several introductory speeches at Trump's rally in Rome. "Dad, how are you going to thread this needle?"

Duncan thought he had figured out a way to pull off that balancing act. Over the course of his five-minute speech, Duncan spoke about slashing regulations and supporting the military. And each time he mentioned how Republican principles can benefit "everyone," the applause from the restless crowd dimmed and the boos grew louder.

As he stood onstage, looking at thousands of Georgians who had probably voted for him two years earlier, he felt more distanced than ever from his party's base. Shortly after leaving the stage, he asked himself: *Why do I feel like a stranger?*

On the uncertain morning after the November election, Duncan called his top aide, John Porter, and predicted that Trump would somehow manage to win. Porter, a youthful-looking thirtysomething, was pumping gas at a RaceTrac station when he told his boss he'd better prepare for a different outcome. "You need to start thinking about what Georgia will look like in a Biden administration." Soon Duncan resolved to push back on some of the vitriol about Georgia's election coming from Trump and his allies that he was convinced would weaken the Republican Party in the long run.

Using the same media contacts he had cultivated from summer stints on cable TV, Duncan landed appearances on CNN and Fox News, where he defended the state's election process and invited Georgians who had evidence of legitimate voter fraud to come forward. None could do so. As his TV hits mounted, Duncan grew more outspoken in his criticism, saying that Trump's "mountains of misinformation" undermined the cornerstone of American democracy. He started calling Joe Biden the "president-elect." Then, on December 6, he told a national CNN audience that he wished he could spend five minutes with every Georgian who doubted the election results to "win their hearts over" and convince them there was no secret plot to rig the election. "On January 20, Joe Biden is going to be sworn in as the forty-sixth president. And the Constitution is still in place. This is still America."

Bayler didn't often go on Twitter, but a few hours after his dad's cable news appearance, he went to his room and found a coaster he and Duncan had made at a father-son retreat. Inspired by his father's stand, Bayler tweeted out the inspirational quote that Duncan had written around the edges: "Doing the right thing will never be the wrong thing," he wrote in a December 7 social media post.

By nightfall, Trump had been alerted to Duncan's latest round on TV. He called the lieutenant governor a "puppet" and a "RINO"—Republican in name only—who was "too dumb or too corrupt" to remain in office. The attention drew Trump supporters to Bayler's tweet, which Duncan had amplified through his own Twitter account. Soon Bayler was being hounded with criticism. "Scum," one Trump supporter wrote the teenager. "RESIGN!" wrote another.

Duncan's wife, Brooke, got a glimpse of the invective hurled at her son. Furious, she wanted to delete the tweet or restrict Bayler's account to protect him from the toxic attacks that her husband, a public figure, was facing. Duncan knew better than to argue with her. Just as they were talking it over in the family's kitchen, Bayler rounded the corner and interrupted his parents. He threw his dad's words back at him.

"Doing the right thing is never the wrong thing," he said. "Leave it up."

———

It seemed as if everywhere Duncan went, people were talking about Trump's tirade against him—at church, at sporting events, on errands—either thanking him for standing up to the president or condemning him for not backing the party's leader. Some would bait him with a conversation about his kids or the weather, then barrage him with far-fetched conspiracy theories. Duncan was struck by how deeply the lies had infiltrated even his wealthy, well-educated corner of Georgia.

Every so often, Duncan would click on the profile of one of the malcontents targeting him on social media and be saddened to find that many times they were civic leaders, proud grandparents, and church volunteers—the folks who form the backbone of a strong community. Like other state officials, he and his wife also faced death threats, requiring extra security at their house, an armed presence that hovered near him even as he tossed a baseball in his backyard with his kids. Investigators found a website with his image, along with Kemp's, centered on crosshairs. He was later informed by law enforcement officials, he wrote, that the architects of the site were Iranian terrorists "trying to destabilize the country."

By early December, the pro-Trump forces rallied behind a call for a special legislative session to reverse the election outcome, or at least cast doubts about the results through an investigation. The main sponsors, a handful of GOP state senators, drafted a petition claiming "systemic failures" necessitated emergency action from state leaders to nullify Biden's victory in Georgia.

Though many rank-and-file Republicans were ambivalent or outright opposed to the effort, Duncan knew the scattered calls for a special session
could turn into a stampede if he didn't use his platform to halt the effort in
its tracks. At a Hyatt Place hotel on the edge of downtown Athens, the college
oasis where the entire legislative branch gathered for a postelection training
session, Duncan and his aide Porter summoned key lawmakers for individual meetings. Each was warned that a special session was unconstitutional,
potentially dangerous, and wouldn't help Trump or the Senate incumbents.

That night, Duncan was eating a slice of pizza while seated on a high-
top chair at a Mellow Mushroom restaurant in downtown Athens when
Trump tweeted yet another insult at him. Duncan figured word had gotten
back to the president about his behind-the-scenes attempt to squelch the
special session and he impulsively wanted to fire back with his own retort:
"Mr. President, you're fired." Porter begged him to sleep on it. The next morning, Duncan took a more measured tack, thanking Trump for appointing conservatives to the US Supreme Court. "Let's agree that re-electing @kloeffler &
@sendavidperdue should be your top priority."

Later, Duncan wrote in his book of the calamity that could have followed
if Republican leaders had caved and allowed lawmakers to debate invalidat-
ing the election results.

"Can you imagine how the millions of Georgians who voted for Joe Biden
would have responded? The marches and protests would have made the 2020
racial justice protests look like picnics and July 4 parades. Counterprotesters
would have countermarched," he wrote in *GOP 2.0*, adding: "Someone would
have pushed too far. People would have been hurt and almost certainly killed.
We would have opened Pandora's box. Georgia would have burned."

Of all the Georgia Republican officials on Trump's wrong side, though, none
was as much a target of the president's fury as Governor Kemp.

The two had a long and complicated relationship, dating to the president's
surprise decision to endorse Kemp in the teeth of a heated runoff back in 2018.
At a rally three days before the November election that year, Trump paid Kemp
his ultimate compliment, telling a crowd of thousands thronged at a middle

Georgia airport that a vote for Kemp was the same as a vote for him. Ever since that endorsement, Trump had claimed credit for Kemp's victory over Casey Cagle in the runoff—even though polls indicated he would have won regardless—as well as for Stacey Abrams's narrow defeat in the general election.

Now, Trump told aides, the governor owed him payback. He urged Kemp to use "emergency powers" to block the certification of the results and demanded that the governor call a special session to overturn the election results and name a slate of Republican electors to award him the state's sixteen electoral votes. Each time he was rebuffed, Trump leveled a new wave of vicious attacks at Kemp, ultimately calling for the governor to resign. And each time Trump's advisers cautioned him to tone it down, he kept going back to the November 2018 rally that he headlined for Kemp.

"They were there for me, not for him. They didn't know who he was," Trump later said in a radio interview. "And then when I ask him for help on a special session for election integrity, 'Sir, I won't be able to do that.' I say, you've got to be kidding. One thing has nothing to do with the other. He's a disaster."

Each time Trump blasted him, Kemp refrained from returning fire, careful not to antagonize the president. He was determined to soak up the president's rage, hoping it would prevent Trump from punishing Loeffler, who couldn't win without the president's full-fledged support.

When asked directly how he dealt with the misinformation efforts, Kemp would speak only in broad brushstrokes, saying he told deniers, "Look, I'm telling you the truth, I'm being honest with you, but I can't make you believe me," before acknowledging that "some people are not at the point where they can believe that yet."

The fact that Trump was very clearly one of them made the runoff a nightmare for the governor. Kemp formally signed off on Georgia's results on November 20, just as Vice President Mike Pence was wrapping up a campaign stop for the two Senate incumbents in North Georgia. The veep's motorcade had gone in the wrong direction on I-285, heading eastbound on the busy highway instead of westbound to Dobbins Air Reserve Base, snarling traffic as far as the eye could see.

As the cars trailing Pence sputtered along, Kemp told me in a phone interview he had no other choice but to uphold the law. "I understand why he's frustrated. He's a fighter. But at the end of the day, I've got to follow the laws of the constitution of this state and that's exactly what I'm doing."

A former state election official, Kemp knew he lacked the legal power to overturn Trump's defeat and he didn't want to leave any wiggle room for the president and his allies to think otherwise. Some of Trump's aides urged the governor to "grow up" and accede to the president's demands. But Kemp knew that if he were to summon lawmakers back to the capitol for a special legislative session, it would turn the statehouse into a made-for-TV media circus with the potential for violent demonstrations.

Just a week after the election, the governor issued a joint statement with Duncan and House Speaker David Ralston that any effort to reverse the election results through the legislature would lead to "endless litigation." Kemp and his aides had been told that both Loeffler and Perdue were on board, but as the pressure on the senators intensified to "fight for Trump," Perdue pushed Kemp to reverse course, in part because he hoped it would fire up the base.

Ahead of a December 3 fundraiser at Truist Park—the new name for the Atlanta Braves stadium where Loeffler had learned of the Senate vacancy about fifteen months earlier—Kemp called a meeting with the two senators and three of their top aides to hash the matter out. His office had been communicating with the senators' campaigns on a daily basis about the legal problems with a special session. Perdue said his deputies didn't always speak for him. He wanted to meet in person and talk it over face to face.

They gathered into a cramped room on the fringe of the stadium, a windowless event space with a few couches and a small bathroom. Like so many other instances in the runoff, the Republicans in the room felt that Trump had put them in an impossible bind.

After some idle chatter, Perdue made his position clear. The campaign aides who indicated he didn't want to summon legislators back to the Capitol didn't represent his stance on this issue, Perdue said. Looking Kemp directly in the eye, the senator told the governor that he wanted a special session to prove to the party's base that their elected officials would go to the mat for the president. Trump could say whatever he wanted since he didn't have a runoff to worry about, but Perdue still had a campaign to wage. He viewed a special session as a way to prove his worthiness to the GOP base without joining the ranks of the conspiracy theorists.

Kemp took it all in, then presented his own view. State lawmakers can't retroactively change election law after a vote to help a candidate, he said. Not only was it constitutionally problematic to call a special session, he told them, but it would also put tremendous pressure on the state's 236 lawmakers—and shift attention away from the Senate incumbents already struggling enough with internal party divisions.

"I have no problem being the bad guy," he told the two senators. "I'll take the arrows to make sure y'all win."

Three days later, the governor delivered a similar message to a room full of state lawmakers at a training session in Athens, making a point to let his words to the gathered Republicans sink in. "This is not an option under state or federal law," Kemp said. "The statute is clear. The legislature can only direct an alternative method for choosing presidential electors if the election was not able to be held on the date set by federal law."

Some Republican legislators welcomed the attempt to shield them from fallout. Ralston, the House speaker, told fellow legislators that same day he understood why they might be "very suspicious" of the election process. "I would remind people if we overturn this one, there could be one overturned on us some day."

Others were incensed. At a closed-door caucus meeting, Republican State Senator Brandon Beach demanded that his colleagues try to call a special session themselves, a gambit that was sure to fail because it would require the approval of three fifths of the legislature. As well as seeking to invalidate Trump's defeat, Beach wanted lawmakers to get rid of drop boxes and impose stricter absentee requirements for the runoff—restrictions that would have triggered an immediate court challenge. "If we don't make a change," he told his colleagues, "we're going to have the same result and we're going to lose two US Senate seats."

———

The governor's straightforward approach only pushed his relationship with Trump to a new breaking point. If loyalty is paramount to earning Trump's trust, then disloyalty is the original sin. And people close to Trump kept tell-ing the president that "Kemp is ungrateful." Some senior Republicans tried to get the two men in a room together to work out their differences, but the logistics never worked out.

There was talk of a compromise: maybe Kemp would embrace Trump's nar-rative that there was a rash of fraudulent mail-in votes without endorsing his broader conspiracy theories. One Republican close to Trump urged the gover-nor to phone the president daily. "I sound like a broken record," he told Kemp one day, "but this thing is going to go from bad to worse unless you do that."

There was nothing to indicate that Trump would be placated by half mea-sures, though, and when Kemp didn't comply with his demands to reverse his defeat, the name-calling ramped up. He called the governor a "moron" in a phone call and "hapless" in a Twitter attack, along with declaring himself in a Fox News interview "ashamed" that he had ever supported Kemp. He also fumed about Kemp to the two senators, pondering in a call with Perdue the idea of recruiting a Republican challenger to run against Kemp in 2022, when the governor would be up for a second term. "He would be nothing without me," he told the senator, according to a GOP official. Perdue relayed the president's fury to Kemp, urging him to find some way to appease Trump.

Even as Georgia Republicans fretted about Trump, the two Senate incum-bents sorely needed a late push by the president in heavily conservative parts of the state. Each day it was becoming clearer to Republicans that their prob-lem wasn't converting voters in the suburbs, it was turning out voters in rural Georgia.

Perdue spoke with the president daily, patiently listening as he vented about how angry he was at the governor and Raffensperger, before making his own ask. Just before Thanksgiving, Perdue pleaded with Trump to sched-ule another visit to Georgia, his first campaign rally since his election defeat. So did Republican National Committee chairwoman Ronna McDaniel, who floated the idea that he could claim credit for the Senate runoff victories in January if he visited in December.

As Trump prepared to fly to the town of Valdosta in the southern part of the state, friendly conservative territory just north of the Florida state line, Georgia Republicans faced a moment fraught with promise and peril. Would he vouch for the two senators? Or would he continue to harp on his own grievances? A group of Georgia GOP elders, including former governor Nathan Deal and former senators Saxby Chambliss and Johnny Isakson, issued a statement days before the event calling on Trump to avoid a tirade about his defeat. "If he wants his legacy to remain," Chambliss told CNN at the time, "then he needs to ensure that we win both these seats—and he needs to say that in no uncertain terms."

The president offered a hint of his direction the morning of his Saturday visit with a phone call to Kemp, opening the conversation by asking the governor how he was doing. Answering honestly, Kemp told the president it had been a "rough twenty-four hours."

So, Trump bitingly suggested, Kemp had seen his latest poll numbers?

"No," the governor sighed in reply. "We lost a close friend of the family."

The day before, Loeffler aide Harrison Deal had died in a traffic accident while on his way to a Savannah airport to prepare for the Mike Pence visit, and Kemp and his family were in the throes of mourning. The lanky twenty-year-old with an easy smile and humble upbringing was the longtime boyfriend of the governor's middle daughter, Lucy.

Not long before the accident, Deal had posted on Facebook how proud he was to stand by Kemp; after his death, the governor abruptly canceled his appearance with Pence and rushed to console Deal's parents at their home in Statesboro about an hour west of Savannah. Unfortunately, Deal's death also quickly became fodder for malicious Trump supporters, so much so that even Stacey Abrams's aides, standing on watch for threats against the Democrat, were alerted to the high level of poisonous conspiracy theories surrounding the auto accident.

The president briefly offered his condolences to Kemp—and then launched into a series of familiar demands, ranging from a special session to a statewide audit of all signatures on mail-in ballots. To each point, Kemp countered politely but firmly that he couldn't help. He repeated to Trump what he'd said days earlier—that any attempt to change the election laws before the runoffs would result in "endless litigation." The president's tone grew more acrimonious. He warned that Kemp would lose a reelection bid if he didn't comply. The governor bluntly told him no again without any equivocation. If there had been any sliver of hope of repairing the relationship, it was dashed when the call abruptly ended.

As Air Force One pointed south, Kemp decided not to be anywhere near Trump's rally. The tragedy of Deal's death had put in perspective for the governor what mattered most—his family, his duties, and his loved ones—and what did not. He told friends that he paid no mind to Trump's tongue-lashing that morning.

"I didn't give a shit about what he had to say," Kemp told them.

Chapter 21

"ASHAMED"

A town of about fifty-six thousand just north of the state line with Florida, Valdosta was first settled in the early 1800s as Troupville. When a major rail line bypassed the town by about four miles, many of its resourceful citizens pulled up stakes and moved to be closer to the train tracks—and renamed it Valdosta, in honor of a former Georgia governor. And when cotton crops were devastated by the boll weevil in the early 1900s, the area's farmers pivoted to growing pecans, tobacco, and peanuts to stay afloat.

Like those of many other small Georgia cities, Valdosta's residents were politically adaptable, too. Over the course of generations, they had gradually abandoned a conservative brand of Democratic politics; by 2016, Trump carried the surrounding Lowndes County with 58 percent of the vote, and the president drew more than seventy-five hundred people to a February rally at the local college, Valdosta State University. His popularity had dipped slightly in November 2020, when he won 55 percent of the vote, an alarming sign to local Republicans, who knew they would need to rev up the region's Trump loyalists to win the Senate runoffs in January.

The fact that the president referred to his December 5 visit there as a "Trump rally" and not a Senate event only heightened the concerns of state

GOP leaders worried that the Republicans on the ballot in January would play second fiddle.

What's worse, state Republicans feared that Congressman Louie Gohmert, the Texas firebrand who egged on Trump's efforts to subvert the election, would only inflame tensions by joining the president on the flight south. After a year of jockeying for position on Air Force One with Doug Collins, Loeffler's campaign aides took some solace in the fact that her former rival would also be on the journey, confident the congressman would keep the president at least partly focused on the runoffs.

Trump and his entourage arrived at a full-blown festival. Thousands of the president's followers had arrived well before the event, many parking miles away at a local middle school to shuttle to the Valdosta Regional Airport. Food trucks sold tacos, barbecue, and ice cream to winding lines of red-capped fans draped in oversized TRUMP 2020 flags.

Anchors for pro-Trump outlets such as Right Side Broadcasting and One America News were greeted like celebrities, along with Trump surrogates who boasted that Biden's victory would be overturned. A soundtrack that mixed Backstreet Boys with Andrea Bocelli blared over loudspeakers, and Senators David Perdue and Kelly Loeffler warmed up the crowd by trash-talking Democrats. "If we win Georgia, we save America," Perdue declared. By the time Trump triumphantly took the stage, the audience was at full tilt.

The president briefly praised the two Senate Republicans before spinning lies about votes in Georgia coming out of ceilings and leather bags, pausing while a video full of spurious accusations played on an enormous screen. As he falsely proclaimed he had won the election, the multitudes cheered, "Four more years!" By the time he paused to introduce Loeffler, the chanting had morphed to a repetition of "Stop the steal!" When Perdue took the stage, Trump loyalists began repeating "Fight for Trump!" so loudly that the words echoed off the tarmac into an unintelligible roar.

The two senators could only shorten their already brief remarks. Perdue, who tried to personally thank Trump for his support, was almost entirely drowned out. "We're not ready to give up Georgia, y'all," he said, voice straining against the din.

While Trump spent most of his time airing his own baseless grievances, Republicans took solace he at least attempted to talk his supporters back into voting in a "stolen" election.

"You say, 'Well, we're not going to do it.' We can't do that. We have to actually do just the opposite," Trump told the crowd. "If you don't vote, the socialists and the communists win, they win. Georgia patriots must show up and vote for these two incredible people."

Whatever help Trump did offer the Senate incumbents, though, was tempered by his determination to stoke the growing civil war within the Georgia GOP. In a barbed message to Kemp, who skipped the event to grieve the death of the young aide, Trump said his former ally "should be ashamed of himself." He scanned the crowd for Collins, a hero to many Trump fans for leading his Georgia recount effort.

"Doug, you want to run for governor in two years?"

———

The following afternoon, Jon Ossoff, Loeffler, and Raphael Warnock arrived at the midtown Atlanta studios of Georgia Public Broadcasting to participate in the sole debate of the runoff cycle. Each seemed anxious about their appearance, hosted by the Atlanta Press Club but broadcast live nationwide on CNN, Fox News, and C-SPAN, as well as livestreamed on dozens of online outlets and local Georgia stations. There was one glaring omission in the runoff foursome: David Perdue ducked the event, determined not to make a gaffe or hand his opponent another viral moment.

A few weeks before the debate, Perdue had huddled with two of his top advisers to decide whether he'd take part. From Perdue's vantage, he had already participated in two debates against Ossoff, though both had taken place in October. Neither had gone particularly well for the Republican, particularly the second showdown, remembered mostly for the extended Ossoff attack that had gone viral. The senator and his advisers concluded he had little to gain, and plenty more to lose, from another tangle with the Democrat, which this time would be watched by a national audience of millions. They surmised that his taking part would only bring "bad things" in this type of election—a race to maximize GOP turnout and not to win over undecided voters—and urged Loeffler to forgo taking part as well.

As he stood alongside an empty lectern, Ossoff relished the singular focus on his campaign. With radio host Lisa Rayam and me serving as panelists, the Democrat took questions about coronavirus relief and health-care policy and turned them into attacks on his "coward" opponent whose no-show reflected his record on the pandemic.

"The reason that we are losing thousands of people per day to this virus is because of the arrogance of politicians like David Perdue," Ossoff charged, motioning to the vacant lectern to his right where Perdue would have stood. "So arrogant that he disregarded public health expertise and so arrogant that he's not with us here today to answer questions. It shows an astonishing arrogance and sense of entitlement for Georgia's senior US senator to believe he shouldn't have to debate at a moment like this in our history."

After the thirty-minute sequence was up, Ossoff walked briskly to an upstairs lobby to take questions from dozens of reporters from around the nation who had assembled to cover the debate. After watching Ossoff's performance, Perdue and his aides sounded confident that skipping the showdown had been the right decision, and whatever bump the Democrat got from his solo turn in the spotlight wouldn't outweigh the damage a poor performance might have exacted on the Republican's campaign. Instead, Perdue's operatives spent the evening tearing down Ossoff on social media, which included a quip from campaign manager Ben Fry that the Democrat "lost a debate against himself."

Other loyalists weren't as confident. Derrick Dickey, Perdue's former top aide, couldn't understand the strategy of keeping the candidate away from the spotlight. Dickey had helped the Republican through about seventeen debates and forums during the 2014 cycle—some good, some less so—but at least he had shown up to defend his stances and punch back at his rivals.

"I knew that by showing up and participating and holding his own, that simply doing that sends a message to people," said Dickey. "If you can't stand up and handle the press and deliver a message that connects with people, then how are people going to trust you to do the right things when no one is paying attention?"

======

When Loeffler arrived to the debate stage, she was trailed by a small entourage that included her husband and several top aides, joining the tech staffers and panelists in the otherwise empty multi-level studio. Warnock appeared shortly after, somewhat lightening the tense mood by quipping that he needed no hairdresser for his bald pate. Beyond that joke, though, there was no small talk or pleasantries between the two before the cameras lit up, only a mention of the cute beagle featured in Warnock's ads.

Ahead of the showdown, Warnock's aides had nervously planned out all potentially challenging questions. The Democrat's campaign had brought in Sarah Riggs Amico, the quick-thinking logistics executive and veteran of campaigns for lieutenant governor and US Senate, to play Loeffler in mock debates. Amico had been a skilled debater in high school and college, and her mission to prepare the reverend for a bout with Loeffler was simple: "throw the low blows." After Amico's first skirmish with Warnock, conducted virtually from her suburban Atlanta home, her husband pulled her aside after overhearing her line of attack, his face etched with concern. "You need to call him right now. Because I wouldn't talk to you again if you had said that to me."

One reason he was worried was that Amico had brought up Warnock's acrimonious divorce proceedings and his wife's claims that he ran over her foot with his car. "You tell us to trust women, but you don't even trust your own wife," she said in the mock attack. "I didn't just hit him below the belt," Amico said later. "I hit him there and I stomped on him." Afterward, she took her husband's advice and called Warnock to make sure he was OK; he laughed and said he was fine. It was strange for Amico, too, to spout "crazy right-wing talking points" at someone she considered a friend.

As uncomfortable as it was for Warnock, the series of four mock debates was precisely what he needed to prepare for the rough-and-tumble of a televised showdown. By the last of the sessions, Warnock had more than held his own—and managed to keep a smile on his face no matter what Amico flung his way. He had gone through the gamut, facing topics that ranged from the price of a gallon of milk to probing questions about the nuances of his policy

stances. As they wrapped up, Amico was confident there wasn't anything that
Loeffler or the panelists could do or say that Warnock hadn't already encountered. The last thing Warnock said to Amico before the debate was a hard-
earned note of gratitude: "If I can handle you, I can get by her."

For all their preparations, the faceoff would be remembered as much for
what was not answered as for what was. Loeffler went into the debate with a
mission to cling to her message like spots on dice, even if it meant getting
mocked as a robot mechanically repeating buzzwords. Time and again she
refused to acknowledge Trump's defeat or disparage the president for attacking Kemp, her most important political ally.

Asked five times about Trump's false claims of election fraud, Loeffler
insisted that the president has "every right to every legal recourse" and indicated support for even his most incendiary conspiracy theories, arguing,
"We've got to get to the bottom of what's going on in this state." Warnock
tried to get her to stake out a definitive stance on November's outcome, asking her directly: "Yes or no, Senator Loeffler: Did Donald Trump lose the
presidential election?" Still, she dodged, repeating that Trump had the right
to challenge the outcome in court if he wanted to.

Warnock, too, attempted to avoid thorny questions, including one about
how much the new coronavirus relief package in Congress should cost, saying only that the needs of workers had to be put "at the center" of the aid. He
also refused to say whether he backed expanding the number of Supreme
Court justices to offset Trump's recent conservative appointments to the
bench. "People aren't asking me about the courts and whether we should
expand the courts. I know that's an interesting question for people inside the
Beltway to discuss," he answered. Pressed again, he insisted that he was
"really not focused on it."

By far the most common theme of Loeffler's attacks was the accusation,
leveled thirteen times throughout the hourlong affair, that Warnock was a
"radical liberal" bent on steering Georgia and the nation toward socialism.
She hurled the claims as she endeavored to connect Warnock with the Reverend Jeremiah Wright, Barack Obama's controversial pastor, whom she twice
accused of promoting an antiwhite message. "I'm not going to be lectured by
someone who uses the Bible to justify division," she said.

To Loeffler's supporters, her ferocity displayed an unwavering ability to stay on message. Stephen Lawson, her deputy campaign manager, praised her for sticking to the script despite a "four on one" debate, in a jab at the media panelists. To her detractors she was little more than an automaton who had mechanically repeated memorized talking points. "She sounded like my alarm system when it tells me my door is ajar," quipped Ana Navarro, a cohost of *The View* talk show the next day. "All she did was repeat on a loop 'leftist radical' or 'defund the police' or 'socialism.'"

A false rumor even spread that Loeffler was wearing an earpiece routed to an aide reading her lines; many photos proved that to be untrue. Still, the pace and frequency of Loeffler's attacks caught even Warnock off guard, and some of his supporters opined that he should have responded more forcefully. After the debate ended, Warnock called advisers Adam Magnus, Lauren Passalacqua, and Christie Roberts for a debrief to talk over his strategy. They reassured him he had taken the right approach. "The reverend wouldn't have got into a food fight," Magnus told him. "And you remained the reverend."

That had been his goal. During his closing remarks, Warnock used optimistic imagery to lighten a moment in history darkened by racial turmoil, economic uncertainty, and a raging pandemic. "I think about my dad in a moment like this, God bless his memory. He used to wake me up every morning at dawn and say, 'Get ready, get dressed, put your shoes on.' It was dawn, so it was morning, but it was still dark. It's dark right now, but morning is on the way."

Chapter 22

"THE ZOOM WHERE
IT HAPPENED"

Hours before Jon Ossoff and Raphael Warnock made a pit stop in the Atlanta suburb of Duluth to woo Latino voters, curious onlookers started massing on the lonely patch of pavement outside the Santa Fe Mall. Parked in tidy rows before an outdoor stage, some danced to music pumping from outdoor speakers or wandered inside to grab warm tortillas from taquerias scattered among boutique fashion stores and souvenir shops. They gathered to hear from the two Democratic candidates—but also to catch a glimpse of the candidates' star supporters.

By the time the actress Eva Longoria strode across the platform to a cavalcade of honking car horns, dozens of cars and hundreds of people had crammed into the parking lot wedged between a Sam's Club and a busy interstate highway, attracted by advertisements promoting a "Hollywood in Duluth" event. Joined by America Ferrera, another Latina celebrity, Longoria told the crowd why they had ventured to the diverse bedroom community. "We're not from Georgia but we're Americans. And Georgia, all eyes are on you again," she said. "Let me tell you: you guys saved the soul of this nation in November, and you're gonna do it again!"

The two women were just part of the deluge of out-of-state money and attention that crushed Georgia during the runoff cycle. The cast of the Broadway smash *Hamilton* riffed off their hit song with a "History Is Happening in Georgia" online holiday fundraiser for the Democratic Senate candidates dubbed by political wags "the Zoom where it happened."

On the very same day, state Democratic Party donors received a link to a virtual cast reunion of the holiday movie *Elf* in which many of the film's stars performed a live reading of the script. During the intermission, actor Ed Helms confided that the cast couldn't get the legal permission to sing a show-stopping Christmas tune at the end of the reading because, he quipped with a smile, "perhaps Republicans own the rights."

Stacey Abrams, a proud Trekker, delighted in an online discussion called "Star Trek: The Next Election" that featured her chatting with veterans of the show about the future of the state's politics. Peter Yarrow, the cofounding member of the famed folk trio Peter, Paul and Mary, joined a nine-hour post-Christmas livestream aimed at ginning up turnout, a moment he said reminded him of his activism in 1963 when he performed during Martin Luther King Jr.'s March on Washington. "We let people know it matters like hell to vote—and that it matters like hell to get five others to vote," Yarrow said after the online concert. "I cannot tell you how effective it was, but I can say I know it doesn't matter. We had to do something."

Georgia Republicans railed against the celebrity influence, with Vice President Mike Pence urging conservatives to send "Democrats in Washington and liberals in Hollywood" a message about Georgia's Christian values. But the GOP campaigns were also eagerly fostering their own star culture.

A few hundred people gathered on a drizzly weekend afternoon to watch Lee Greenwood croon fan favorites near a brewery in Canton, in the outer reaches of metro Atlanta, though the worsening weather forced some to leave before he could belt out his famed rendition of "God Bless the U.S.A." Country singer Travis Tritt joined Senator Kelly Loeffler outside a firearms store in the northwest Atlanta suburbs for a performance that combined a political rally with a concert with a gun giveaway. "If you don't get out and vote as a Republican, or if you don't get out and vote as a Trump supporter in this senatorial election," Tritt told the crowd, "you are the biggest RINO I have ever seen!"

The runoff campaign also produced new celebrities.

Blaire Erskine grew up off a dirt road in the Georgia hamlet of Ellaville knowing only a single Democrat—her high school English teacher, who also happened to be former President Jimmy Carter's niece. Trying to make a name for herself in Atlanta, the budding comedian booked stand-up gigs across the city until the pandemic hit. When she found herself hopelessly doom-scrolling on Twitter after Trump's election, Erskine started producing snappy, satirical videos on social media for her friends. She became a viral sensation after she posted one video pretending to be the wife of a Costco character who exploded in outrage after being asked to wear a mask inside the retail store.

Some of her takedowns involved mocking believers of the dangerous QAnon conspiracy farce and Trump supporters, including one satirical send-up in which she pretended to be a robotic version of Loeffler. "Once I went to a palm reader who told me I didn't have any lines on my palms and said she was calling the police," she said in a monotone voice. "I said, 'Good, I love the police.'" Her videos caught the eye of Abrams, who asked her to make a clip explaining the runoff election to confused Georgia voters. Within a few months, Erskine amassed hundreds of thousands of social media followers and a huge audience. "People look to comedians to take in all the news, make it digestible and OK," she later said. "But this wasn't an escape. I wanted to light a bit of a fire and make a difference—to help people come together when it mattered the most."

Ossoff emerged as a superstar to many in the Generation Z crowd with TikTok videos that began airing in early December and quickly collected millions of likes. The clips of him petting puppies and playing into viral memes popular with teens and twentysomethings were the biggest hit yet for any candidate on the still-new social media platform.

The irony, though, was that Ossoff didn't even have TikTok on his phone and was mostly oblivious to the online trends garnering so much attention with younger voters. Just as Congressman Hank Johnson had empowered him as a young staffer to post blogs and use Facebook to further his cam-paign, Ossoff allowed his aides to take the reins on TikTok. When asked later about his alleged prowess on TikTok, Ossoff laughed before revealing the secret. "Good staff work."

Hollywood celebrities weren't the only big names drawn to the runoffs. As Trump continued to falsely insist he was still president, the dual contests became a staging ground for the fight for the 2024 presidential nomination.

In quick succession, senators Marco Rubio and Rick Scott made the trip from Florida to hold separate "Save Our Majority" rallies in metro Atlanta. Senator Tom Cotton of Arkansas told voters in an aging building at the state's fairgrounds in Perry that it was something of a religious calling for Georgians to "hold the line" and ensure that Loeffler and Perdue won another term. Governor Kristi Noem of South Dakota held court in the fluorescent-lit lobby of the Georgia Public Broadcasting studios to try to spin press coverage of the sole runoff debate. Former UN ambassador Nikki Haley tag-teamed with Loeffler at events across northeast Georgia, closer to her native South Carolina. Pence made a range of stops in Georgia's midsized cities. Ralph Reed, the former head of the Georgia GOP and leader of the conservative Faith and Freedom Coalition, declared that the parade of presidential hopefuls might as well be the "opening bell of 2024."

Democrats, for their part, were no longer fearful of tying themselves to national figures they had once carefully avoided. When Ossoff was running to flip a conservative-leaning suburban congressional seat in 2017, he unfailingly sidestepped questions about liberal party leaders by saying he was focused on Georgia-centric issues. But his response to a CNN anchor who asked in November 2020 whether he'd accept Senator Bernie Sanders's endorsement crystallized a political shift. "I welcome his support," he said of the self-described democratic socialist. "His advocacy for ensuring that health care is a human right in this country, for putting the interests of working families over corporate interests, is welcome, is necessary, is appreciated. And so is his support."

Legions of everyday civilians mustered behind the Democratic effort. Nina Rubin fashioned herself part of an army of empty nesters who mobilized to "do what we could to make it happen." Because she couldn't afford to write big checks, she took to Twitter to offer free room and board in her in-town Atlanta apartment to a campaign worker. The writer Ayelet Waldman saw the post and connected her to a Howard University college student named Akeima Young. The sixtysomething Jewish Atlantan and the Black daughter of a minister about four decades her junior forged a fast friendship while living together for more than a month. One night, while Rubin jumped on a Facetime call with her children and grandson to light the Hanukkah candles, she beckoned Young to celebrate the holiday with her. Long days were capped by intense discussions about race and religion, and Rubin felt her connection with Young helped rekindle in a small way the Black-Jewish coalition that had once been so strong in Atlanta.

Some of the most important work played out in quiet subdivisions and apartment complexes as eager volunteers and staffers navigated coronavirus protocols that made in-person appeals a safety hazard. The Republican National Committee rerouted to Georgia six hundred staffers who had been stationed in other battleground states. Combined with the National Republican Senatorial Committee and the two Senate campaigns, the overall GOP effort dispatched one thousand paid staffers across twenty-one regions around Georgia—a staggering effort that rivaled the type of resources devoted to a presidential race. The state GOP said it trained nearly fourteen thousand volunteers during the election cycle, who contributed to a joint effort that led to more than 7 million door knocks in the runoff and placed another 7 million calls.

That doesn't include the contributions from outside groups, like Reed's Faith and Freedom Coalition, which assigned 1,280 paid staff and volunteers to canvass in person or by phone, some of whom spent their Christmas vacations going from door to door in Atlanta suburbs in search of wavering Republicans. "So much hangs in the balance, and I wanted to join in any way I could," explained Caroline Harris, part of a team of Texans that reached hundreds of households a day in the northern outskirts of the city.

The outreach from Democrats and their allies was equally astounding. The Fair Fight voting group founded by Abrams distributed a million large refrigerator magnets urging likely Democrats to vote and raised $24 million in direct contributions to the two runoff candidates, along with making

$20 million in grants for get-out-the-vote initiatives largely designed to turn out voters of color.

Some of the most memorable overtures, though, came in unusual places. Friends Greg Nasif and Curran Ford pulled together a PAC focusing on the "barely touched" voters in Savannah—many of whom didn't have doors in subdivisions to knock on or local area codes to reach—contacting them while they were enjoying the coastal city's nightlife or working in gas stations or convenience stores. Like other dedicated volunteers, Nasif and Ford both temporarily set aside their regular lives in pursuit of a goal to flip the Senate. They found people were much more open to discussing the issues when they were out and about. On New Year's Eve, the two donned pirate costumes and asked young people a surefire conversation starter that helped them connect with dozens of potential Democratic supporters: "Arrrrr you going to vote?"

The overall Democratic effort boasted some forty thousand staffers and volunteers who accounted for 25 million attempts to reach voters. That amounted to ten different contacts for each of Joe Biden's 2.5 million voters in Georgia, with a particular focus on Georgians of color, who were more likely to abstain from overtime contests. "We built the largest ground organization the state has ever seen," said Jonae Wartel, the Democratic runoff director.

The canvassers from both tickets weren't blindly knocking on doors. Vast troves of data turned the average smartphone into a compass pointing toward potential voters, thanks to a stockpile of metrics that included voting records, online consumer history, and even survey details. The data ran through algorithms that accounted for demographics, past participation in elections, and even such intricate details as credit history or buying habits to score voters on how likely they were to back one ticket—and how intensely any given undecided voter needed to be courted. Well-trained staffers came to each welcome mat armed with preprepared scripts, answers to the most asked questions, and thick skin to deal with slammed doors and brusque "leave me alone" demands.

But the bulk of the spending was devoted to the airwaves. Roughly half a billion dollars was spent on TV and radio ads, and tens of millions more devoted to digital spots, smashing state records for political spending. Most of the TV spots were jarringly negative. Ad watchers calculated that about 80 percent of the Republican ads and three fifths of the Democratic ones included attacks on their opponents.

Republicans took great satisfaction in linking the Democrats to their "radical" national counterparts—taking a page from a Republican playbook that had worked in Georgia so well and so often before. "If you vote for Jon Ossoff and Raphael Warnock, who are you really putting into power? Nancy Pelosi, AOC, and Bernie Sanders—the far left with complete, unchecked power," warned one TV ad from the National Republican Senatorial Committee. Most were aimed at Warnock, part of a strategy to motivate white conservatives by tying the pastor to the party's most liberal ideas. In the first three weeks of the runoff, virtually all the GOP attack ads focused on him. Loeffler's were particularly scathing, accusing Warnock of harboring a secret hatred of America and plotting to bring a wave of socialism to the country.

Democratic-aligned groups didn't hold back either, labeling Republican incumbents as gutless cronies who willfully backed a morally bereft Trump regime. They pointed to their opponents' vast bank accounts, with ads depicting iconic images of wealth like yachts and mansions that contrasted with the struggles of regular Georgians during the pandemic. "She's the richest member of Congress," said one Warnock ad of Loeffler. "He grew up in public housing."

More than $930 million would be spent by the parties, the campaigns, and outside groups when all was said and done, making them the two most expensive congressional races in US history by a long shot, according to the Center for Responsive Politics. The four candidates raised more than $500 million combined, with national stars like veteran GOP strategist Karl Rove and Senate minority leader Chuck Schumer directly involved in winning big checks. New groups with names like "Georgia Honor" and "Peachtree PAC" sprang up to funnel cash toward the races. So did the Georgia United Victory Fund, a free-spending group partly financed by Loeffler's husband that spent more than $20 million throughout the cycle, mostly on TV ads and digital media.

TV stations quickly adapted to battleground-level spending on political advertising. In 2017, during the record-breaking US House special election between Ossoff and Republican Karen Handel, the local NBC affiliate leveraged the attention by adding an extra newscast on a sister station for more time to cover the race—and more slots for ad space. With the pandemic keeping many confined to their couches, advertising became an even more crucial outlet to reach voters in the 2021 runoffs.

Some local TV stations cashed in by running more than five hours of political advertising a day. Ads for competing candidates often appeared back-to-back-to-back-to-back in a single commercial break, and shorter five- and fifteen-second spots were tailored for viewers of streaming services. Even out-of-state media outlets benefited. Roughly $35 million worth of ads aired or were reserved in four markets surrounding Georgia, even though only a small slice of the bulk of their audiences could vote in the contest. Ossoff's campaign spent more than $360,000 to air ads in a Dothan, Alabama, market that reached a single sparsely populated rural county in southwest Georgia. Super PACs paid $7,000 for a thirty-second ad on the 6:00 p.m. broadcast for WRCB, *The New York Times* reported, a station in Chattanooga whose viewers almost all lived across the Tennessee line. Democratic ad strategist Rick Dent had simply called the glut of commercials "overkill"—and it was hard to find any voter who would disagree.

Indeed, for Georgians, it began to feel as if there was nowhere to hide. As the holiday season arrived, the carpet-bombing campaign ads became increasingly intrusive, appearing on popular HGTV shows like *House Hunters*, Hallmark Christmas movies, and Food Network specials. Warnock played into the holiday spirit with a TV ad showing him checking off his Christmas list—and struggling with the holiday lights—to remind people to plan to vote. A barrage of ads ran on AMC during a Christmas movie marathon, subjecting kids watching Rudolph and Frosty to warnings about "radical liberal Raphael Warnock." Even those who turned off the screen weren't safe. Glossy GOP mailers pictured a photo of St. Nick weeping into his white gloves with the tag line "Not even Santa will be safe if Warnock and Ossoff win in Georgia."

When my two daughters, both elementary school students, asked Loeffler at a campaign stop in west Georgia if she was tired of the onslaught, she repeated one of the same attacks she had been regularly leveling at Warnock and told the kids it was important to "understand who these candidates are and what we're up against."

As she spoke in the back of a crowded restaurant, the girls' eyes flickered to the flat-screen TV behind the senator, which was airing the very ad Loeffler had been talking about.

Chapter 23

A SHADOW SLATE

On a Monday morning in December, the state's top Democrats took a respite from the campaign trail and filed into the heavily guarded state capitol complex. The sixteen Democratic electors entered through side doors, passing by a phalanx of armed security officers vigilant for any sign of demonstration or disruption, and slowly made their way up to the third-floor Senate chambers. Their mission was ceremonial but crucial: they would soon formally cast their Electoral College ballots to certify Joe Biden's victory in Georgia, no small accomplishment given President Donald Trump's efforts to overturn the results.

The group included some of the party's biggest names: Stacey Abrams was there, of course, as was Nikema Williams, the Democratic Party chair and newly minted congresswoman. So were Savannah mayor Van Johnson and several legislative leaders, along with behind-the-scenes operators like Sachin Varghese, the party's chief attorney and one of its sharpest legal minds.

The process to formally cast the state's Electoral College ballots was typically an overlooked routine. Four years earlier, it played out in speedy fashion, with only two or three reporters squeezed along the back wall of the state Senate to observe the formality. The most noteworthy development during the 2016 vote had taken place well before the vote, when GOP elector Baoky Vu resigned rather than cast a ballot for Trump. But now the proceeding was under extraordinary scrutiny, beaming nationally on cable news stations. Before the vote, Bob Trammell, a rural Democratic legislator who was one of the state's sixteen electors, called it the moment "that says Joe Biden is without question the president." Anyone who took issue with that after it was finalized, he added, "is taking issue with the democratic process."

As she gaveled the December 14 proceedings to order, the party chair made note of its history. "Georgians elected a Democratic president for the first time in twenty-eight years. Twenty-eight years, y'all," said Williams, who was fourteen when Bill Clinton carried the state. Each elector quickly cast two separate paper ballots—one for Biden and one for his running mate, Kamala Harris—before they were counted and verified. Varghese, an immigrant from India, grew emotional as he filled out the latter ballot, certifying the first vice president of Indian descent. Six separate certificates were drafted listing the results, then shipped out to state and federal officials for safekeeping.

Though there was no drama accompanying the outcome, the moment was still dramatic. In one of the back rows, Calvin Smyre leaned back in his chair in appreciation. The seventy-three-year-old retired banking executive was the dean of the Georgia legislature, and since his first election in 1974 he'd earned a reputation more as a relationship builder than a policy wonk. When Democrats were in power, he'd served as connective tissue between rural conservatives and urban Black lawmakers.

With Republicans in command, Smyre had adopted an entirely different role, this one as a crucial bridge between the GOP hierarchy and the Democratic caucus. As Abrams put it that day, "You cannot make a decision in the capitol without consulting the dean of the House." She was right, and neither could most senior Democrats have done so over the previous three decades. In fact, Smyre was the only Democrat in the exclusive group on the Senate floor who was also an elector when Georgia had last turned blue in 1992. "Time flies," he said with a chuckle.

While Democrats on the third floor of the Gold Dome celebrated the formal flipping of the state, a clandestine meeting was taking place one level below. A group of Republicans had assembled behind the heavy wooden doors of Room 216, guarded by a party functionary who falsely claimed to me that an "education meeting" was taking place inside.

GOP chair David Shafer and most of the party's prospective electors had in fact gathered before noon to anoint themselves President Trump's slate in an illegitimate vote. It was part of a nationwide movement to discredit Biden's victory—and, Shafer said, to give Republicans some wiggle room in case any of the last-gasp pro-Trump legal challenges somehow succeeded in court. Among those locked in the room were party activists, donors, attorneys, and two state senators. When Shafer emerged, he was asked whether their action set a precedent that would lead others—Democrats or Republicans—to challenge election results in the future if they didn't like them. "The precedent is that the election contest has not been resolved," Shafer insisted.

What was less clear at the time was that Shafer's action was part of a broader legal strategy to help Trump retain power despite his election defeat. The approach was promoted by John Eastman, a conservative lawyer who put forth a series of steps that Vice President Mike Pence could take to ensure that Trump stayed in office. The six-step plan, outlined in a two-page memo first reported in the book *Peril* by Bob Woodward and Robert Costa, alleged that the results in Georgia and six other states that had "multiple slates of electors" could be thrown out. It ignored the fact that Georgia and the other states never formally approved a competing slate of electors. Shafer and the other Republicans holed up with him inside the second-floor capitol room were simply Trump allies who unilaterally declared themselves electors with no legal basis.

The Eastman memo was just one tangent of the legal escapades by pro-Trump forces. One of the most ridiculed was a federal lawsuit brought by Sydney Powell, an outlandish former member of Trump's legal team who promised to "release the kraken"—a reference to a mythical Scandinavian beast—on Georgia and other swing states. She told Newsmax that Georgia is "probably going to be the first state I'm going to blow up" though her error-ridden legal claims barely merited a fizzle. Powell quietly withdrew the lawsuit in mid-January.

Trump and Shafer sued state elections officials and the election directors of fifteen Georgia counties in December, alleging that the defendants failed to adequately match signatures on absentee ballots, resulting in tens of thousands of ineligible votes. State experts said these claims of conspiracy theories demonstrated a fundamental lack of understanding of election laws. Trump's attorneys scuttled the lawsuit on the eve of a scheduled January hearing.

Perhaps the most shocking lawsuit, though, was filed in December when the Texas attorney general asked the US Supreme Court to toss out election results in Georgia and three other competitive states. The complaint largely recycled discredited claims against Georgia that had already surfaced in other complaints. Still, senators Loeffler and Perdue both endorsed the legal challenge to invalidate the votes of millions of Georgians, along with more than two dozen state legislators and seven Republican members of Georgia's US House delegation. Lining up against it was a broad cross section of bipartisan officials including Chris Carr, Georgia's Republican attorney general. It was soundly rejected by the High Court days later, with the justices concluding that Texas didn't have the right to challenge elections run by other states.

———

The day after the Electoral College vote, Biden staged a rally for Jon Ossoff and Raphael Warnock at a decaying former rail yard in east Atlanta that had become a popular site for movie productions, having hosted scenes from *The Hunger Games*, *The Fast and the Furious*, and *Divergent*. Attendance was strictly limited because of the pandemic, so a long line of vehicles stretched for a mile outside the venue as curious onlookers and invited guests tried to access Biden's first campaign event since his presidential victory.

Against the backdrop of the deteriorating railroad depot, Biden thanked Georgians for voting "as if your life depended on it."

"Guess what?" he added. "Now you're going to have to do it again."

Though Biden didn't have particularly long coattails to drag in Georgia candidates behind him—he outpolled Ossoff by roughly one hundred thousand votes, and many down-ticket Democrats struggled—he was a useful ally for the Senate runoff candidates, as his centrist political brand and popularity made him a more difficult target for Republicans. He could also appeal to an emerging coalition of people of color, white liberals, and suburban swing voters who had helped him tally roughly 2.5 million votes in Georgia.

Biden urged Georgians to remember that the two incumbent Republicans had backed the half-baked Texas lawsuit that challenged the state's election results. "Maybe your senators were just confused. Maybe they think they represent Texas," Biden said. "Well, if they want to do the bidding of Texas, they should be running there instead of here in Georgia."

Biden's most compelling arguments concerned his own agenda, starting with the fate of his proposed new relief package to contain the spread of the coronavirus. Even as health officials readied to distribute doses of newly developed vaccines, many parts of the nation struggled with a deadly new wave of coronavirus infections, which was straining some fragile health-care systems to the verge of collapse.

Biden framed Republicans as "roadblocks" to progress toward a more ambitious aid plan that would send tens of billions of dollars to schools, local governments, and the public health system to combat the pandemic and prepare for future outbreaks. He warned that Democratic defeats in the runoffs would imperil his administration's ability to confront the health-care crisis and other national challenges, leaving him to grapple with the sort of paralyzing gridlock that had dogged the final years of Barack Obama's presidency. "We can get so much done. So much that can make the lives of the people of Georgia and the whole country so much better," he said. "We need senators who are willing to do it, for God's sake."

Biden was happy to highlight a growing headache for the Republicans. Both Loeffler and Perdue had initially backed a relief package that included $600 direct stimulus checks for most Americans. But then came an eleventh-hour pivot from Trump, who suddenly demanded that Congress increase the "ridiculously low" payouts to $2,000. Any fellow Republicans who didn't follow his lead, he added, must have a political "death wish."

It was yet another major complication for Republicans that left the two senators with unpalatable options: Do they side with Trump and liberal Democrats—including their runoff rivals—who pushed for more lucrative subsidies? Or stick with Republican congressional leaders and back a more limited measure?

As the Republicans hesitated, their Democratic challengers tightened the political vise. Both echoed Trump's demand that Congress should immediately include more generous direct checks along with incentives to cash-strapped local governments. Ossoff called the $600 payouts in the GOP aid package a "joke" and "an insult" at campaign stops around the state.

"Here's how to solve this problem: President Trump needs to sign the bill immediately," said Ossoff at a volunteer event in the heart of Atlanta's funky Little Five Points neighborhood in late December. "And then within forty-eight hours, the House and the Senate should pass the additional stimulus to add to the bill so that Americans get $2,000 per person."

A few days later, both Republicans had changed their tune, buckling to pressure to increase the size of the stimulus checks in yet another attempt to stay on Trump's good side. To explain her flip-flop, Loeffler told supporters the more robust checks were needed to "provide relief to Americans because Democrats have locked our country down." Perdue, on Fox News, simply said it was the "right thing to do" for Georgians. When Trump caved to bipartisan pleas to sign the bill, the two senators ignored the contortions he had put them through and released a joint statement praising the president's "relentless pursuit to keep America great." As a Perdue aide put it, "it was another attempt to stay on Trump's good side—even if it meant betraying the senator's own views."

By now, though, an even more odious debate had emerged. Trump and his allies were exerting tremendous pressure on Republican lawmakers to challenge Biden's victory when Congress convened on January 6—a day after the runoffs. The two Republicans, along with other key members of the US Senate, had refused to acknowledge Biden's victory throughout the nine-week runoff period.

But they also both sidestepped a question that was quickly becoming one of the most important in Congress: whether they would accede to the president's demands to block Biden's victory at the US Capitol when lawmakers were to formally finalize the results of the presidential election. "We've got a Senate race to run here in Georgia. We've got to win—the future of the country is on the line," Loeffler said on a rainy December morning after casting her early vote ballot in Atlanta. "I haven't looked at it. January 6 is a long way out, and there's a lot to play out between now and then."

The highwire act got even shakier when a handful of Republican House members, and then a group of GOP senators, decided to support an objection to the Electoral College tally despite there being no credible evidence of any fraud in the election.

Because of a quirk in the law, Perdue wouldn't have a say in the matter even if he won another election. His Senate term was set to end on January 3, two days before the runoff, meaning that Georgia would go without one senator until the runoff votes were certified. Still, he upped the pressure on Loeffler by leading crowds at events to believe he would object to the count. At one stop, he told a young liberal activist named Lauren Windsor who masqueraded as a die-hard Republican that he would "keep fighting for Donald Trump and challenge the Electoral College" on January 6. Her tongue-in-cheek tweet mocking the senator's remarks was amplified by both Trump and Perdue's staffers, who mistakenly thought she was a supporter.

Perdue's campaign was pressed to acknowledge that he couldn't cast a vote even had he wanted to do so, but his operatives remained silent on the issue. It came as no surprise to close watchers of his campaign. By this point in the runoff, Perdue studiously avoided most state and national media, save for a brief appearance at a northeast Atlanta airport hangar, where he delivered a hasty stump speech before disappearing into a group of supporters.

Instead, he embarked on an ongoing statewide bus tour attended at each stop by a small group of devotees that garnered him a bit of local media attention, while favoring frequent interviews on Fox News to announce policy positions and push for donations. Even fellow Republicans were relegated to finding clues on staffers' social media pages for Perdue's travel itinerary. At a Christmas party, one GOP operative pointedly asked a Perdue staffer what the point of a bus tour was when the media wasn't invited. All she got was a blank stare in return. Within his campaign the strategy was clear-cut: The problem Perdue faced wasn't trying to win over suburban voters who had already made up their minds. His bigger challenge was wooing rural Republicans who should have been the most devoted bloc of the GOP electorate but had questions about his loyalty to the president. And his message, as one senior strategist put it, was "Donald Trump. Go vote. Donald Trump. Go vote. Donald Trump. Go vote."

Perdue's approach also left Loeffler in the uncomfortable position of having to constantly answer for both him and Trump to the dozens of reporters now covering the campaigns. During one December campaign stop at a gussied-up "party barn" in the exurb of Cumming, a wealthy conservative area about an hour north of Atlanta, aides promised what would have been the first joint question-and-answer session with Loeffler and Perdue in weeks. A line of TV cameras stood on pine straw beside a scenic pond as the two Senate incumbents wrapped up their campaign stump speeches. But when the press conference began, Perdue immediately melted into the crowd, taking selfies with supporters, while Loeffler was left to respond to the latest questions about Trump's demands that Georgia's election be overturned.

Perdue's no-shows at debates and press conferences belied his campaign's insistence to be involved in broad aspects of the GOP senatorial contests—press releases, announcements, public statements. Tensions between Loeffler's and Perdue's staff members, if not between the candidates themselves, bubbled up, with some Perdue staffers envious of her easier path into office, not to mention the far bigger trove of attacks she could level against Warnock than he had for Ossoff. Loeffler's camp, meanwhile, bristled that they felt as if they were being pushed around by the senior senator's aides. "We felt like we were the junior partner, and they tried to make sure we knew that," said Chris Allen, one of Loeffler's operatives.

On the ground, the Trump-driven split was only growing. A GOP event meant to energize local Republicans in southwest Georgia turned into a two-hour Q&A session at which volunteers aired gripes about Kemp and other officials for not doing more to prevent supposed election fraud from being replicated in the runoff. Carlton Huffman, a Wisconsin Republican strategist who temporarily moved to Georgia to help the senators, watched in disbelief as the pep rally went off the rails.

"That's when I realized the base's mindset was more focused on 'stopping the steal' than keeping the Senate seats," he said. "We had lost our sense of urgency because of our message. Why do you need to save America and run around with your hair on fire to save America if there's a shot that Donald Trump could be president on January 21?"

Chapter 24

THE FINAL CALL

It should have been a joyous occasion. In late December 2020, Governor Kemp stood beside the state's public health commissioner, Dr. Kathleen Toomey, as she received one of the first doses of the coronavirus vaccine that would eventually be distributed to millions of Georgians. Witnessing the launch of vaccinations after nine months of coordinating the state's response to the pandemic, the governor confided, was "almost overwhelming."

Less than an hour later, Kemp glumly stood in the Georgia capitol discussing conspiracy theories, some aimed directly at Kemp's family, from Trump supporters who believed the president had been victimized by a rigged election. It had become a running joke in Kemp's office that the governor must have said the word "distraction" one hundred times a day—as in, talking about reversing the election results was only a costly distraction for Republicans who should be focused on the runoffs.

For Kemp, it was also becoming increasingly personal: he singled out the vicious lies targeting his grieving daughter, Lucy, who had received hate-filled messages about the auto accident earlier that month that had killed her boyfriend.

"We have the 'no crying in politics rule' in the Kemp house. But this is stuff that, if I said it, I would be taken to the woodshed and would never see the light of day," he said. "I can assure you I can handle myself. And if they're brave enough to come out from underneath that keyboard or behind it, we can have a little conversation if they would like to."

Georgia Republican leaders were now beyond hoping that Trump would tire of his obsession with Georgia. "This is the first time Trump has gone for more than a few days on message. We thought he'd change the subject, but he didn't," said a Kemp confidant. As they watched the GOP civil war intensify, the Democratic campaigns couldn't deny a wash of optimism that the stars were aligning in their favor. "I'm nervous. I'm feeling almost too good about our chances. Which means something must be off," one Warnock aide texted fellow Democratic strategists. Loeffler's advisers were growing increasingly pessimistic about her chances. In a December 29 text, one wrote: "It's going to be real close. Real close. And if we lose, we know who to blame."

The Trump effect on the GOP electorate was so profound that Republicans had drafted an entire data set titled "GOP NOT VOTING" detailing seemingly reliable conservative voters who were deemed unlikely to cast ballots in the runoff. "It haunted us. I wanted to hit my head against the wall," said Chris Allen, one of Loeffler's deputies.

While the senator was dreaming up new ways to prove her loyalty to Trump to keep his voters on board, she was beset by distractions from the president and his allies.

A week before the runoff, former New York mayor Rudy Giuliani called a meeting with the Georgia Senate Republicans and their top operatives to level the latest in a string of phony claims. He had just weeks earlier starred in the second of two legislative hearings in the state to air false charges of fraud on Trump's behalf, at one point insisting that "every single vote should be taken away from Biden."

At this private conference call, Giuliani told the senators that they didn't even need a special session—they could unilaterally overturn the election. As he droned on, Loeffler invented a reason to duck out after twenty minutes, citing a nonexistent media interview. A few minutes later, Perdue also got off the line. "Every day we were putting out fires," said one of Loeffler's advisers. "We were a hostage with every limb taped, a gun to our head, and a hairpin trigger."

Trump, meanwhile, had spent the previous month applying pressure to key Georgia officials.

Chris Carr, the Republican attorney general, caught the president's notice when he panned the Texas lawsuit challenging Georgia's election outcome as "constitutionally, legally, and factually wrong." Trump called Loeffler and Perdue on December 8 to vent about Carr's stance.

Carr arrived at his home in suburban Dunwoody that evening around six thirty with a rotisserie chicken from Publix and sides for his wife, Joan, and his sixteen-year-old daughter. Just after he set the meal on the counter, his phone rang with an urgent call from Perdue. The president was angry with Carr, the senator said, because Trump had heard he was calling other Republican attorneys general to warn them not to endorse the doomed Texas challenge. Carr assured Perdue that he was just answering questions from other AGs about the lawsuit and not pushing them to reject it.

"Would you be willing to tell Trump that?" Perdue asked him.

He shrugged. "All right, if this is helpful to you and Kelly, I'll do it."

Carr was given the number for Trump's secretary, dialed it, and was told he was next in line. While his wife and daughter turned on *Elf* in the living room, Carr paced the house waiting for the conversation with Trump. He didn't want to touch his food until the conversation was done. His wife, who was Loeffler's chief of staff, checked in for updates while he waited.

About ninety minutes later, Trump finally got on the line. By then, Carr's daughter had realized what was making her father so anxious and politely left for the privacy of her bedroom. Carr, meanwhile, calmly repeated to Trump precisely what he had told Perdue. "Mr. President, I'm not telling my fellow AGs to get on this lawsuit or not. I'm just answering their questions."

The conversation meandered for about fifteen minutes, with Carr reminding Trump of his support for the president's economic agenda and appointments to the judiciary.

"Yeah, I've done great on both of those, haven't I?" Trump asked.

As soon as the call ended, Carr immediately called Perdue back.

"Well, I think it went well," he told the senator.

Perdue chuckled. "I've had calls with the president where I thought it went well and it didn't, and I've had calls with the president where I thought it didn't go well and it did."

A few minutes later, Loeffler called to check in. "I think we're OK," the AG said.

Carr finally got a plate of food and watched the ending of *Elf*. It was later that evening when the two senators issued a joint statement announcing that they "fully support" the legal challenge seeking to invalidate Georgia's vote. "No one should ever have to question the integrity of our elections system and the credibility of its outcomes," they wrote.

Lower-profile officials also faced demands to tip the scales. Trump's top aide, White House chief of staff Mark Meadows, made a surprise visit to Cobb County on December 22 to watch Georgia's audit of absentee ballot envelope signatures and ask officials questions about the process. A day later, Trump called the chief investigator in Raffensperger's office overseeing the review, an examination of fifteen thousand mail-in ballot envelopes.

"Something bad happened," Trump said to the investigator, Frances Watson, telling her during the six-minute call she had the "most important job in the country right now," then asked if she would be working through Christmas. "When the right answer comes out, you'll be praised," he said, adding: "People will say 'great,' because that's what it's about, the ability to check and to make it right, because everyone knows it's wrong."

A shocked Watson was gracious with the president, asking about his holiday plans and thanking him for the unexpected call. But she responded to his concerns the best way she knew how: "I appreciate your comments, and I can assure you that our team and the GBI, that we're only interested in the truth and finding the information that's based on the facts."

When the audit of Cobb County was finished on December 29, it uncovered only a single case of signature mismatch when a woman signed both her and her husband's ballots. The report was unsparing in its findings: "no fraudulent absentee ballots were identified during the audit."

What became the most notorious incident in Trump's campaign to overturn Georgia's election started with a conference call that crackled to life on January 2. Waiting on the line from Georgia were Secretary of State Brad Raffensperger; his top aide, Jordan Fuchs; and Raffensperger's attorney, Ryan Germany. After a brief pause, an operator chimed in. "I'm just here to conference you in with Secretary Raffensperger and Mr. Germany," the operator said. "We're going to conference you through to POTUS shortly."

"Hello?" Trump opened after a brief pause, before letting his chief of staff Mark Meadows, who had arranged the call, conduct a brief round of introductions. The White House had made eighteen previous attempts to connect Trump with Raffensperger, the *Daily Beast* later reported, each ignored by staffers who thought they were pranks. Now that he had him on the line, Trump took little time to get to his point. "We appreciate the time and the call. So, we've spent a lot of time on this. And if we could just go over some of the numbers, I think it's pretty clear that we won. We won very substantially, Georgia."

He spent the next minutes revisiting false and debunked conspiracy theories alleging fraudulent votes: an accounting of legitimate mail-in ballots tabulated in the hours after the election; a sham claim about ballot-stuffing in Fulton County; lies about thousands of dead people voting. When Trump finished, Raffensperger replied, politely but firmly: "Well, I listened to what the president has just said. President Trump, we've had several lawsuits, and we've had to respond in court to the lawsuits and the contentions. We don't agree that you have won."

Trump wasn't having it. His rallies, he observed to Raffensperger, were bigger than ever. Republicans assured him that it was "impossible" to have lost the state. And, he added, "the people of Georgia were angry." "There's nothing wrong with saying that, you know, that you've recalculated," he told the secretary.

After Trump wound down, Raffensperger kept firm: "Well, Mr. President, the challenge that you have is the data you have is wrong." Again, the president would not relent. "Look, all I want to do is this: I just want to find 11,780 votes, which is one more than we have, because we won the state. And flipping the state is a great testament to our country because, you know, this is—it's a testament that they can admit to a mistake or whatever you want to call it."

He hardly paused with his torrent of falsehoods to pose a question to Raffensperger, who was sitting at his kitchen table with his wife during the call. "So, what are we going to do here, folks?" he asked. "I only need eleven thousand votes. Fellas, I need eleven thousand votes. Give me a break. You know, we have that in spades already. Or we can keep it going, but that's not fair to the voters of Georgia, because they're going to see what happened." He pleaded with them to "find" the votes before the runoffs, saying it would "have a big impact on Tuesday if you guys don't get this thing straightened out fast." If the secretary of state didn't act, Trump warned, it posed a "big risk to you and to Ryan, your lawyer."

Time and again Raffensperger and Germany pushed back, respectful but unwavering. "That's not accurate, Mr. President," the attorney said to one false claim. "That's not the case, sir," he responded to another. Raffensperger suspected that Trump was buying into falsehoods that had gone viral on Twitter. "Mr. President, the problem you have with social media, is that people can say anything." Trump shot back: "Oh, this isn't social media. This is Trump media."

Raffensperger's office taped the recording but hadn't planning on releasing the audio—that is, until the secretary of state saw a tweet from Trump the following morning recounting his version of their conversation. Trump claimed he had spoken to Raffensperger, who was "unwilling, or unable, to answer questions" about his nonsensical fraud claims. "He has no clue!" In a response, Raffensperger wrote: "Respectfully, President Trump: What you're saying is not true. The truth will come out."

Raffensperger's office soon authorized the recording to be released, leaking the full audio to *The Washington Post* and then the *Journal-Constitution* and, later, to dozens of other media outlets. It dominated the already suffocating news coverage of the runoffs, drowning out just about every other local or national story.

Former House Speaker Paul Ryan, a Republican who had mostly avoided criticizing Trump's bid to sabotage the results, called on GOP congress-members to abandon the "anti-democratic and anti-conservative act" of challenging the election outcome. Legal experts lined up to assert that the president's menacing effort to badger and bully elected officials to overturn the results could be prosecuted under Georgia law. On the campaign trail for Jon Ossoff and Raphael Warnock outside Savannah, Vice President–elect Kamala Harris said the recording showcased "the voice of desperation" of a president lurching from one conspiracy theory to another. "It was a bald, bald-faced, bold abuse of power by the president of the United States," she thundered.

Far from being hailed as a hero, Raffensperger faced fresh criticism from fellow Republicans who slammed him for embarrassing Trump so close to the runoff. The Georgia GOP chair said the leak was "mind boggling"; others called it treachery. As for Raffensperger, he said later he was purposely being careful about his remarks—but not because he thought his office might find it necessary to leak the recording. "I realized that what was said was going to become part of the public record of the trial. I was very measured in what I said. I didn't know who [else] was on the call. But I was very cautious."

<hr>

A few hours after the call between Trump and Raffensperger was made public, the president met with Justice Department officials in the White House to entertain the possibility of replacing Jeffrey Rosen, the acting US attorney general, with a more pliable leader willing to sabotage Georgia's election results. These were not idle fears: Raffensperger and other key staffers had hired their own personal attorneys in the final days before the runoff—just in case of political retaliation.

One possible replacement for Rosen was Jeffrey Clark, the acting head of the agency's civil division who had recently drafted a letter that sought to pave the way for lawmakers to invalidate Trump's defeat. The letter, later released by congressional investigators, asserted that it was the Justice Department's view that lawmakers had the "implied authority" under the US Constitution to call themselves into special session to appoint presidential electors even if Kemp continued to object to the idea. The Justice Department wouldn't let him send the letter, with Rosen's top deputy, Rich Donoghue, writing that his legal argument was "not even within the realm of possibility." US Attorney BJay Pak told investigators that Donoghue used a harsher phrase in private: he called it "bat-shit crazy."

Trump ultimately decided against promoting Clark, though he spent part of that January 3 Oval Office meeting complaining about the Justice Department's finding that there was no rampant election fraud in Georgia, a congressional report later detailed. He was particularly fixated on Pak, a former Republican state legislator whom Trump had tapped as Atlanta's top federal prosecutor. Pak had investigated—and did not substantiate—various claims advanced by Trump and his allies, including the false conspiracy theory that a videotape showed suitcases full of illegal ballots being tabulated at State Farm Arena in Atlanta. On the call the previous day with Raffensperger, Trump had disparaged Pak as a "Never Trumper US attorney" and made it known he was unhappy with his leadership.

At the Oval office meeting, Trump told Donoghue and Rosen he wanted to fire Pak and replace him with a friendlier prosecutor. Donoghue convinced Trump not to pull the trigger, as Pak was already planning to step down. Soon after the testy Sunday evening meeting in the White House ended, Donoghue emailed Pak with the subject line: "Please call ASAP." During that call, Donoghue told Pak that the president was obsessed with the claim that he "won" Georgia—and furious with Pak for not going along with the lie, according to people familiar with the conversation. At 7:41 the next morning, Pak sent Donoghue two resignation letters announcing that he would step down from his post.

As for Pak's replacement, Trump insisted on sidestepping a veteran prosecutor next in line of succession and appointing Bobby Christine because, as the congressional report detailed, he thought "maybe something will actually get done." Christine had been the US attorney in Savannah and was a donor to Trump's campaign, but he wouldn't blindly go along with Trump's wishes. He told staffers in a conference call shortly after he took the post that he dismissed two election fraud cases on his first day. "I can tell you I closed the two most—I don't know, I guess you'd call them high profile or the two most pressing election issues this office has," Christine said in a recording obtained by the *Journal-Constitution*. "I said I believe, as many of the people around the table believed, there's just nothing to them."

———

The same day Raffensperger's tape was made public, Kelly Loeffler roamed Georgia barbecue joints and city squares with the latest in the rotating cast of surrogates. Earlier in the week, Senator Lindsey Graham of South Carolina helped her open a New Year's Eve concert, and Senator Ted Cruz of Texas campaigned in the exurbs. Today it was Governor Kristi Noem of South Dakota urging Republicans to make up and unite.

"Reasons I woke up mad," one Loeffler staffer texted. "Thanks to the president, two days before the election we're campaigning with the governor of a state smaller than Gwinnett County rather than our own." Indeed, Governor Brian Kemp had been largely absent from the campaign trail as Trump's explosions escalated. After attending more than eighty events ahead of the November election, for candidates for county commissions to the Senate contenders, he was now relegated to hosting closed-door fundraisers and out-of-the-spotlight events for fear of weighing down the candidates.

He wasn't the only reason Republicans were shorthanded in the final days. David Perdue announced on New Year's Eve that he had been exposed to the coronavirus and went into self-quarantine for the rest of the campaign. Though he never tested positive for the disease, he was in close contact with an adviser who had contracted the virus, forcing him to bunker in an Atlanta townhouse outfitted with a makeshift TV studio for interviews with conservative media.

It was agonizing for Perdue, who talked with Trump by phone every day but itched to get back to campaigning—and to join the president at his final rally, a last dash for GOP voters before the runoff.

———

For the Democrats, the fallout surrounding the Raffensperger tape and Trump's other brazen attempts to subvert the election would not dominate their election-eve messaging. Instead, the Senate challengers and their allies steered voters toward a vision of what a Democratic-controlled Washington could accomplish. Stark black billboards around metro Atlanta promised $2,000 checks if Ossoff and Warnock prevailed, and Biden returned for a final appearance a day before the runoff to make the same argument.

"Their election will put an end to the block in Washington on the $2,000 stimulus check," Biden said. "If you send senators Perdue and Loeffler back to Washington, those checks will never get there. It's just that simple. The power is literally in your hands."

The event was directed at metro Atlanta voters, with a drive-in rally on the outskirts of downtown, not far from where Atlanta had held its Olympic ceremonies. Biden again tied the fate of his legislative agenda to a Democratic sweep. If Ossoff and Warnock fell short, his plans to contain the coronavirus and expand health-care access fell with them. "One state can chart the course—not just for the next four years, but for the next generation." Their wins, he told the crowd, would restore "hope and decency and honor for so many people who are struggling right now." This election was more than about simply adding two Democrats to the Senate, he added. "You'll break the gridlock that's gripped Washington and this nation."

It was a final push from Democrats whose main path to victory relied upon extraordinary turnout from Black voters. And the president-elect's visit was just the most visible in a series of mobilization efforts. Black Voters Matter, an outside group, passed out hundreds of thousands of door hangers to households of color, highlighting issues like voting rights and social justice to inspire voters. Ossoff's grassroots effort kicked into a higher gear, with tens of thousands of unlikely voters on the receiving end of personal calls and texts from his organizers. On the most granular level, local groups came up with creative ways to encourage turnout. In predominantly Black Clayton County, the bluest territory in Georgia, the Black Women's Roundtable handed out food baskets to local families for the holidays—while making last-ditch appeals for votes.

The degree of enthusiasm was astounding, with turnout approaching presidential levels. A record 3 million people voted before Election Day, smashing the previous record for total turnout in a Georgia runoff set in 2008, when 2.1 million cast ballots in the overtime matchup between Republican senator Saxby Chambliss and Jim Martin. This period was crucial for Democrats, who had to build a huge buffer of votes during early voting; Perdue had won about 60 percent of the in-person votes cast on Election Day just weeks earlier. About one third of the early voters in the runoff were Black, according to state data, up from roughly 27 percent during the general election. It was a solid sign for Democrats, since Black voters made up about 30 percent of the state's registered voters. What's more, nearly seventy-six thousand new voters had signed up between October 5 and the December 5 deadline to vote in the runoff.

At his rally, Biden pointed to the early voting surge as another sign of Democratic strength in Georgia. "Thank you for electing me and Kamala. We won—three times here," he laughed, referring to the state's first vote count, its hand recount and its machine recount. "These recounts, you know what I mean? We should count them as three states. We won three times."

———

Biden wasn't alone in putting his capital on the line to test the power of his coalition. As the president-elect spoke in Atlanta, crowds of Republicans swelled outside the airport gates in the northwest Georgia manufacturing town of Dalton, lauded as the "Carpet Capital of the World."

A ninety-mile hop north of Atlanta, Dalton was just a blip on the railroad in the early 1900s when a local woman pioneered a groundbreaking tufting technique to begin making bedspreads and, later, carpets. The industry took off after World War II, and by the 1990s nearly 90 percent of the carpet produced worldwide was made within a twenty-five-mile radius of the city's borders, bringing a tremendous number of jobs to the growing city. Dalton's leaders promised solid middle-class wages and a good quality of life to those with little education, and that prospect of opportunity attracted thousands of immigrants to work grueling shifts at the carpet factories and the chicken-processing plants that sprouted across the region.

Politically, the area became one of the surest sources of Republican votes in the state; Trump won Dalton's Whitfield County by 70 percent of the vote and tallied even higher in the surrounding region. Drivers headed north on I-75 toward the city saw a billboard with red-and-white letters announcing EVERY TONGUE WILL CONFESS JESUS IS LORD. EVEN THE DEMOCRATS.

Trump's popularity was one of the reasons the Senate candidates implored him to campaign in the area. After months of his denigrating Georgia's election, polls pointed to a consistent belief among many Republicans that the election had been sabotaged, stolen, rigged, or otherwise subjected to fraud. Just how deeply those beliefs were held was hard to determine, but a SurveyUSA poll in December indicated that just one in five Republican voters thought Biden had won the contest fairly. "I'm going to vote in the runoffs, but I'm beginning to wonder if it's going to be credible," one Dalton Republican voter, Mitchell Hasty, told the *Journal-Constitution*. While the early vote turnout dipped only a few percentage points in densely populated metro Atlanta, the gap increased to double digits in northwest Georgia and other areas that were supposed to be more reliably conservative—which meant that the GOP candidates would have to vastly overperform on runoff day to make up the deficit.

Given Trump's previous visit to Georgia a month earlier, when his attacks on fellow Republicans had overshadowed his push for the Senate incumbents, no one could be certain what the president would say or do. And Republicans grew even more concerned when the weekend before the rally he launched fresh salvos against his own party. On his Twitter account, the president promoted a poll showing that Kemp lagged former congressman Doug Collins in a potential primary challenge. And he falsely claimed that the runoffs were "illegal and invalid"—effectively undercutting the entire reason for his last-minute appearance.

It was hard to escape the conclusion that people were talking more about Trump than about the incumbents. During a visit to Carrollton, a small town near the Alabama state line, the loudest ovation Loeffler received came when she solemnly said, "God bless America and God bless Donald J. Trump." Perdue was among the loudest voices imploring Trump to focus on the fight for Senate control, and his aides worried that if they stopped appealing to him for help they'd be left with a scorned president who would "really go off the rails" and encourage a boycott of the voting.

The base's mood, it seemed, was already shifting. At a rally in Peachtree City, a wealthy south Atlanta suburb known for its network of golf-cart paths that spiderwebs across the municipality, State Senator Marty Harbin begged local Republicans to contact Vice President Pence and tell him to "please, please, please not recognize Georgia's election" during the vote to certify the Electoral College results in Congress. He was among a group of sixteen Georgia Senate Republicans who signed a letter urging Pence to delay congressional certification of the Electoral College votes for twelve days to allow "for further investigation of fraud, irregularities, and misconduct" in Georgia.

That was only a taste of what Pence faced. The day before the runoff, Pence was imploring Republicans to vote in the two runoff elections at a megachurch in the tiny town of Milner when he was interrupted by Trump supporters shouting at the vice president to "do the right thing" and "stop the steal" on January 6. "It feels like I'm inside a tornado with all kinds of facts and falsehoods swirling around me," said Cade Parian, a west Georgia Republican. "I don't know where the tornado is going to spit me out, but I hope like hell it's with a majority in the US Senate."

Trump's trip to Dalton gave voters like Parian little relief. For weeks, just about every time Loeffler took questions from the media, she was asked whether she would join the GOP movement to block Biden's victory in Congress by challenging Electoral College certification. As she waffled on the issue, her aides privately warned allies that a pledge by the senator to contest the Electoral College results should be taken as a signal that her campaign had hit a new level of desperation.

As Trump traveled to Georgia, and Loeffler's internal polling showed she continued to struggle with the party's base, that moment came in a six-sentence statement issued around 6:00 p.m. on the eve of the runoff. Saying she had "real concerns" about the way the November election was conducted, Loeffler promised to vote to give "President Trump and the American people the fair hearing they deserve." Taking the stage a few minutes later, Loeffler announced the decision to an overjoyed audience. "That's right," she said, her voice straining to cut through the clamor. "We're going to get this done."

Once again, and to no one's surprise, the Trump rally was more focused on the phony claims of election fraud than control of the US Senate. On giant TV screens draped by a towering American flag, the thousands bundled up at the Dalton airport were treated to videos touting more unsubstantiated claims of fraud.

Even the password for the balky Wi-Fi signaled the true purpose of Trump's mission: "SeeYouJan6!" it read.

As Trump flew to Georgia, Perdue was still in quarantine at his Atlanta townhouse, watching anxiously from afar. He was given a chance to edit the president's prepared remarks as Trump's jet neared, but he still couldn't look the president in the eye and tell him, point-blank, that he had to call on his supporters to set aside their misgivings about the November election and show up in force on Tuesday.

Trump triumphantly descended from the Marine One helicopter, which touched down behind a row of yellow school buses along the tarmac. Taking the stage with a smile, he warmed the crowd up with a lie. "Hello, Georgia. By the way, there is no way we lost Georgia. There's no way," he said immediately. "That was a rigged election. But we are still fighting it."

When he stuck to the teleprompter, his words brimmed with praise for the two senators, both staunch supporters of his agenda, and grave warnings that "if you don't show up, the radical Democrats will win." But when he veered off script, he repeated the same grievances he'd aired on social media or in cable TV interviews.

"Those of you that know how badly screwed we got, I want to be clear that we can't let that happen again. We can't let that happen again. We're going to come back, and I really believe we're going to take what they did to us on November third. We're going to take it back," he said.

When he did mention Loeffler and Perdue, it got the crowd roaring in unison: "Fight for Trump!" He assured his supporters that both senators had his back—"Kelly fights for me; David fights for me. That I can tell you."— before turning his focus to those he accused of betrayal.

Senator Mike Lee of Utah was in the crowd to offer his support to the two imperiled incumbents, though the president made clear they were at odds because he wouldn't back the Electoral College challenge, remarking, "I'm a little angry at him." And no rally could be complete without a dig at his favorite Georgia target. "I'll be here in about a year and a half campaigning against your governor, I guarantee you," he said of Kemp, who wisely decided not to attend.

At one point, Trump even gave voice to his insistence on promoting himself over the vulnerable Senate incumbents he was ostensibly there to support. "I don't do rallies for other people. I do them for me." By the time he wound down the meandering remarks, clusters of attendees had already headed home, taking to the darkened roads surrounding the airport in search of their cars.

Democrats watched the Trump implosion with a mix of glee and trepidation. Jonae Wartel, the head of the party's coordinated runoff campaign, couldn't avert her eyes from the political train wreck. "He's literally delegitimizing the entire election a day before the vote," she said once she got over her disbelief. An Ossoff adviser reminded colleagues not to get complacent, warning that Trump's remarks could also make people "want to fight back."

Republicans, for their part, were forlorn. "If you win, is it even worth it? The Washington guys get to go home. We have to pick up the pieces," a Kemp adviser confided.

The *Journal-Constitution*'s top story for the following day's edition wasn't a report on the president's visit. Instead, its headline asked: WAS TRUMP'S PHONE CALL ILLEGAL?

Many of Loeffler's organizers hadn't even bothered to stay for the president's speech but departed the airport not long after the senator spoke, putting signs up along nearby streets in the cold.

"That's all she wrote," Chris Allen, a Loeffler aide, said as long lines of people waited for buses to ferry them back to far-off parking lots. "Hopefully those four minutes of this eighty-four-minute rally are enough."

Chapter 25

"IT'S UP TO GEORGIA"

Jon Ossoff was all of thirty-three years old on January 5, but by the day of the runoff he was already a veteran of four nationally watched votes and had a well-worn plan to cope with the pressure. He started the day with a blitz of media interviews, visited a precinct to thank poll workers, and was back at his east Atlanta home by mid-afternoon.

Election Day is always a strange time for seasoned candidates and campaign staffers, who can't do much more but hope their carefully laid turnout plans spring successfully into action. But in a runoff so close, the four Senate candidates couldn't help but feel that every small decision, even in the waning hours of voting, could be momentous. With three hours until the polls closed, Ossoff sat in his living room and called one mobilizer after another to try to keep them all motivated. While his wife worked an overnight shift at the hospital, Ossoff remained at home in lieu of attending a campaign party during the pandemic, stoking a blaze in his fireplace while calmly waiting for the results. He refused to watch returns, mixing in some meditation sessions between checking in with his aides every ninety minutes or so.

Raphael Warnock's aides weren't quite as placid during the final hours of the chaotic election. Adam Magnus, Warnock's adsmith, rode his bike to as many polling places as possible in Atlanta and neighboring DeKalb

County—and convinced himself not to fall into a downward worry spiral when he saw only a handful of people in those left-leaning areas waiting to vote. The pastor's staffers nervously watched reports on MSNBC of epic lines in Forsyth County, a Republican-friendly area about an hour north of Atlanta, where a queue stretched as far as the camera could pan. Terrence Clark, Warnock's communications specialist, spent the day spinning the media. Privately, as he watched coverage of the Republican energy, he suffered from pangs of self-doubt. *This might be the end of the road for us.*

Kelly Loeffler's camp was equally on edge. Her advisers fretted about reports of low turnout in northwest Georgia, the very same area where Trump had made his last stand the night before. Not far from the Dalton airport, where workers were still clearing the remnants of the rally, Susan Head arrived at Dug Gap Baptist Church to cast her ballot for the Republicans even as she struggled to reconcile their false allegations of irregularities in November. "It may not be for me to say that it was fraudulent," she told a *Journal-Constitution* reporter. "But you kind of worry about that."

Republicans knew there were many voters like Head who harbored doubts about election integrity but, rather than hold their noses and cast a ballot, stayed home instead. But they also didn't know what more they could have done to change those minds. At a final campaign stop at the inner suburb of Sandy Springs, I asked Loeffler if she had any regrets about her campaign. "I know Georgians are tired. We've been called to stay in this race a lot longer than the rest of the country. I know we're going to get it done. But we've left it all on the field. And now it's up to Georgia."

The only candidate not in the public eye, at least not in person, was David Perdue. Still in quarantine, he was relegated to remote campaigning, like his call in to Vice President Mike Pence's speech at a rural megachurch over the weekend when he made a bold prediction that the runoff result would set the course for America for "at least fifty to one hundred years."

In the north Atlanta townhouse they had rented, Perdue and Bonnie had set up a workspace and a studio area, where he conducted about two dozen media interviews a day. Some of his aides quipped that he was now reaching more people in a single day than he would have through a week of barnstorming through rural Georgia. On runoff night, Perdue invited two friends who were also quarantining to his place. When he called an adviser around 9:45 p.m. to ask for his analysis, the senator's TV was off. Perdue was narrowly leading at that point, but the aide girded him for a change of fortune. "We could slip under."

That evening, hundreds of Republicans had gathered at the Grand Hyatt Atlanta to watch the results play out on giant screens tuned to Fox News. Dozens of TV cameras stood vigil in the middle of the room, perched on a four-foot-high platform, while a roped-off section made room for die-hard GOP supporters in front of a small stage. Three bars scattered around the room sold expensive imported beers and mixed drinks as the crowd, some wearing masks but many others barefaced, ebbed and flowed. Trays filled with shrimp skewers, spicy chicken empanadas, and pimento mac and cheese lined the hallway.

A long list of Republican dignitaries was slated to take the ballroom's stage, but Brian Kemp wanted to be one of the first. There were no boos and jeers from this crowd of loyalists and establishment types, many of whom thought Trump's feud with the Georgia GOP had gone too far. Warm applause greeted the governor as he took the microphone wearing a red-and-white "Hold It for Harrison" cap in honor of Harrison Deal, the Loeffler aide whose tragic death had so shaken Kemp and his family.

To his right and left stood his wife, Marty, and their three daughters. By the time he finished his remarks, all four were in tears. Kemp, whose face showed the strains of the runoff, thanked his allies for the "sacrifices that we all have made for nine long weeks." Yes, there was the pandemic and racial strife, both of which he acknowledged. But also wearing on him was the anguish over Deal's death.

"The tragic loss of a young life way too soon, that was a love of our family and a love of Lucy's. I just can't tell you how much we appreciate every single day, people calling and texting me, letting us know that they're praying for us. We feel that. I just want to thank you." He ended with a prayer that doubled as a coda to the runoff: "He left it, like we did, on the field. We will miss him and we know that we will never forget him."

The governor and his allies wouldn't have to wait long for the results, which came in far more quickly than expected. Scarred by the days-long drama following the general election, state officials braced for a doomsday scenario of tedious recounts, drawn-out legal battles, more misinformation poisoning the social discourse, and more threats of violence. Instead, the fastidious work that had gone into preparing the state's counties for a glut of absentee ballots had paid off, and ballots—both in-person and mail-in—were counted more efficiently than many predicted.

A few hours after the polls closed, the trend lines came into view. Though Republicans had built a cushion with early returns in smaller, rural areas, there were too many outstanding ballots from DeKalb County—the biggest trove of Democratic votes—and too few left in the exurbs of Atlanta or the agricultural heartland to make up the deficit. As the first of the outstanding DeKalb votes were added to the tally late in the evening, Democrats began to prepare for victory.

Down the highway from the GOP party, Warnock sat in his campaign office on Edgewood Avenue with six of his closest strategists, each wearing a mask and sitting socially distanced from one another. The reverend seemed unnaturally calm as his narrow lead slowly grew. "If everything we're seeing is reality, you're going to be a US senator," a deputy whispered to him.

Two of his aides, Adam Magnus and Lauren Passalacqua, hadn't helped finalize anything for him to say in advance, in part because they were superstitious, and in part because they didn't think the results would be clear so early. Warnock directed the two to lead the speech with the stories of his mother and father, his way of showing how improbable his rise to the US Senate really was.

With victory in sight, the campaign headquarters started filling up with Warnock's relatives. Two of his sisters, a few cousins, and other kin crowded into the room. Decision Desk HQ called the race for Warnock at 11:13 p.m., and many national outlets followed soon after. When the first of the projections flashed on TV screens, Warnock's family broke out in deafening cheers. His oldest sister dialed up Warnock's eighty-two-year-old mother, Verlene. His boisterous relatives quickly fell quiet.

"Mom, can you hear me?" he shouted into the phone. "This is your son, Reverend *Senator* Warnock."

His family erupted again, before Warnock hushed them so he could listen to her response. A smile slowly crept across his face.

"She says she's still Mamma."

———

Ossoff's race was closer, but he maintained enough of a lead by early Wednesday that a special morning edition of the *Journal-Constitution* greeted worn-out Georgians as they awoke with an all-caps headline: WAR-NOCK ELECTED; OSSOFF LEADS PERDUE.

Republicans weren't ready to concede the high-stakes races immediately, nor did Democrats expect them to. Perdue's campaign announced in a statement at around two o'clock Wednesday morning that it would "mobilize every available resource and exhaust every legal recourse." And Loeffler told a thinning crowd shortly after midnight that she still had a "path to victory." "This is a game of inches," she said.

But the two Republicans knew they had lost. Just as on the night of the general election, some of Perdue's supporters circled the war room earlier in the evening with a round of high fives, mistakenly believing the Republican was going to win by thirty-five thousand votes. And once again, a senior Perdue adviser halted the premature celebration and told them the cold truth: it was Ossoff who was on pace to win by that margin. Loeffler, meanwhile, was in an even worse position than her Republican colleague, lagging Warnock by a larger margin than Perdue trailed Ossoff.

The data that emerged over the next days and weeks showed how it happened. Exit polls revealed that the Democratic candidates had neared a vaunted 30-30 target that had long eluded them: capturing 30 percent of Georgia's white vote while achieving a Black participation rate of 30 percent of the overall turnout. The five core metro Atlanta counties provided roughly half the statewide vote total, but the Democratic turnout in rural counties was staggering as well.

Voting records later showed that more than seven hundred fifty-two thousand Georgia voters who cast ballots in the presidential election didn't vote again in the runoffs. More than half of those no-shows were white voters, and many lived in Republican-dominated rural counties. The two regions with the sharpest turnout drop-offs surrounded the two cities where Trump had staged his pre-runoff rallies: Dalton and Valdosta.

Just after midnight on January 6, Warnock filmed the hastily written victory speech that acknowledged the historic nature of his election. He traced a line from his mother's humble upbringing as a woman who used to "pick someone else's cotton" during her childhood in a speck of a town called Waycross to his new title as Georgia's first Black US senator. "We were told that we couldn't win this election. But tonight we proved that with hope, hard work, and the people by our side, anything is possible," Warnock said. "May my story be an inspiration to some young person who is trying to grasp and grab hold to the American dream."

At 8:00 a.m. on Wednesday, Ossoff also declared victory, promising that he would "give everything I've got to ensuring that Georgia's interests are represented in the US Senate." The vote-tallying was far from complete, but just as in the June primary and the November election, the bulk of the uncounted ballots came from Democratic-leaning metro Atlanta. And as more troves of ballots were added to the final count, Ossoff crept steadily over the 50 percent mark.

The networks called the race for Ossoff shortly after 4:00 p.m. on Wednesday, January 6, making formal the transformation of Georgia into a purple state and cementing Democratic control of the US Senate.

But there were no fireworks or surge to the streets in Atlanta, like the joyful parade at Piedmont Park that had erupted weeks earlier when Biden had been formally declared the presidential victor. The results of runoff elections that had transfixed the nation for more than two months didn't register much more than a footnote on the TV networks and even ran below the fold in the hometown *Journal-Constitution* the next day.

Just as Ossoff was declared the race's winner, completing an unprecedented flip, thousands of hell-bent insurrectionists, inflamed by the same Trump lies that had loomed over the runoffs, stormed through police barriers, scaled the US Capitol's walls, and were stampeding through its halls in a full-scale attack on the nation's seat of democracy.

Chapter 26

A GLIMPSE OF WHAT'S POSSIBLE

A bleary-eyed Senator Kelly Loeffler arrived at the US Capitol the morning after her election defeat determined to make good on her last-minute promise, revealed to thousands of jubilant Donald Trump supporters two nights earlier, and vote to invalidate Joe Biden's election victory. Holed up in a heavily guarded basement under the US Capitol complex, she began to have second thoughts.

As the first rioters surged into the building, overwhelming unprepared security officers, a Loeffler aide sent a series of increasingly alarmed texts to her staffers back in Georgia.

"I think they're in the Capitol."

"They just rushed me into the Senate chamber."

"Officers just pulled out their guns."

"They're taking us to the basement."

Sheltering in a makeshift bunker along with most of the rest of the US Senate members, Loeffler and her colleagues scoured their smartphones for updates; a staffer's speedy phone charger became one of the most sought-after amenities, drawing a long line of aides waiting to juice up their main connection to the outside world.

Above them, chaos reigned as members of the mob, some bedecked in Trump paraphernalia, ransacked offices and scoured the building for lawmakers. "Hey, what's the Senate side? Where's the Senate? Can somebody Google it?" asked a rioter clad in camouflage.

A violent attack on the chamber itself was only narrowly averted before Loeffler's group was rushed to safety when a quick-thinking US Capitol Police officer, Eugene Goodman, lured the mob away from an unguarded entrance to the chamber and then sprinted toward Senator Mitt Romney to warn of the oncoming insurrectionists.

Down in the bunker, staffers raided vending machines for drinks and snacks, and picked over trays of hot beef and potatoes for heartier sustenance. Small clusters of senators huddled in different parts of the room, ruminating on what to do. Some wanted to continue the Senate proceedings from the basement; others talked of speedily returning to their chambers once the mob was expelled. But a consensus emerged: the Senate had to get back to work, quickly, to confirm Biden's victory and send a message to Americans that the rule of law still mattered after the attack.

Many in the anxious room erupted into applause when, on TVs tuned to CNN, President-elect Joe Biden pleaded with Trump to condemn the violence that had put the democracy under "unprecedented assault." Hearts sank when the cable channel aired a prerecorded speech from Trump in the Rose Garden in which he empathized with the insurrectionists, starting his message with the same lies that had ignited the attacks. "We had an election stolen from us, a landslide election," he said. Trump tepidly nudged his supporters to "go home," before ending with a tacit endorsement as they ransacked the US Capitol. "We love you. You're very special." Under siege from these "special" people in the building's basement, aides and senators groaned in disgust.

Back in Atlanta, a heavily armed security detail rushed Secretary of State Brad Raffensperger and his deputies to safety after protesters linked to a local militia gathered outside the state capitol. As officers cordoned off the Gold Dome, Governor Kemp held a press conference to condemn the pro-Trump mob and to announce an extension of an executive order that allowed him to deploy Georgia National Guard troops to protect the building. Before he left the podium, he fumed at fellow Republicans who demanded he subvert the election to favor Trump: "For those of you that have been calling for a special session, you can now see what that would look like."

Democrats had gone to sleep the night before overjoyed that the state had broken twice from its long GOP history in a nine-week stretch, flipping the state for Biden in November and then sweeping the Senate runoffs in January to elect the first Black and first Jewish US senator in state history. Now they were forced to grieve an assault on democracy with the rest of the nation.

Stacey Abrams had planned to relish the victories, a culmination of her efforts over the past decade in laying the groundwork for Democratic successes. The Fair Fight voting rights group had become a towering force in state politics. Two years earlier, in the throes of defeat, she had reminded her supporters that "revenge can be very cathartic." Now it was hers to enjoy. "Across our state, we roared," she tweeted shortly before midnight on runoff night. "A few miles to go . . . but well done!"

But as the mob descended on the US Capitol, a sense of gloom emerged instead. Zoom meetings among Democratic staffers and thank-you calls to star volunteers turned into grieving sessions. Many staffers of color, who had worked so hard to secure Warnock's historic victory, were traumatized by the images of Confederate flags being carried through the halls of Congress. Some wondered aloud how the rioters would have been treated had they been Black.

From the pulpit of his church a few days later, Warnock put into words the mixed emotions of Georgia Democrats: "Just as we were trying to put on our celebration shoes, the ugly side of our story, our great and grand American story, began to emerge. We saw the crude and the angry and the disrespectful and the violent break their way into the people's house."

━━━

As security officers restored order at the US Capitol, Loeffler faced a decision. By then a few die-hard Trump loyalists had changed their minds about blocking Biden's Electoral College victory, though others still insisted on going forward with their objections even though they were doomed to fail. Nor did she have any backup, since Perdue's term had ended on January 3, leaving her the sole US senator in Georgia. Loeffler didn't want to be branded a flip-flopper so quickly after announcing her decision just two days earlier. But the riot forced her to reconsider. To Loeffler, objecting to the outcome would only prolong a foregone conclusion—and guarantee more media coverage that she felt was bad for both Republicans and the nation.

"When I arrived in Washington this morning, I fully intended to object to the certification of the electoral votes. However, the events that have transpired today have forced me to reconsider, and I cannot now in good conscience object to the certification of these electors," she said from the Senate floor. "The violence, the lawlessness and siege of the halls of Congress are abhorrent and stand as a direct attack on what my objection was intended to protect, the sanctity of the American democratic process."

When the joint congressional session reconvened, four of Georgia's GOP House members introduced the challenge. The petition was promptly rejected by Vice President Mike Pence because no US senator from the state had endorsed it. Back home in Georgia, one of Loeffler's deputies glanced down at a torrent of incoming text messages.

"Your boss is a Benedict Arnold," read one.

═══

As he watched the carnage at the US Capitol, Trump told his aides he was happy that the two Senate incumbents lost, according to a person familiar with the conversation. They deserved their defeat, he added, because they didn't do enough to defend him. Of course, the two Republicans had seemingly done everything they could imagine to placate the president, but that proved impossible.

Some leading Georgia Republicans cast blame on Trump for what they saw as a betrayal of the party's ideals. Lieutenant Governor Geoff Duncan, already one of the president's most vocal Republican critics, didn't hold back after the GOP defeats. "Absolutely it's his fault. He's the tip of the spear," Duncan said. "If the president wasn't talking about misinformation and farfetched conspiracy theories up until the day of the vote, then millions and millions of other Americans wouldn't have been talking about it. Republicans didn't show up because they were told to believe the elections were rigged," he said to me.

The Trump effect was an important factor in the GOP defeats but far from the only one. Jon Ossoff and Raphael Warnock overcame historic challenges by generating off-the-chart turnout: the nearly 4.5 million people who voted in the runoffs were more than double the number who cast ballots in the 2008 US Senate overtime contest, and easily exceeded the 2016 presidential election turnout. And in many parts of the state, particularly in predominantly Black areas where Democrats needed to run up the tally, the two challengers improved on Biden's margin of victory.

In DeKalb County, the most important Democratic stronghold in the state, about 95 percent of voters from the November election to the runoff returned to the polls, in part because of a highly organized "vote tripling" strategy that asked voters to text three friends to remind them to cast their ballots. The DeKalb Democratic Party paid ninety field staffers and mobilized dozens of volunteers to execute the strategy at every early voting location in the county for the three-week period, and Ted Terry, the former US Senate candidate who had recently been elected a DeKalb commissioner, credited the process with "exponential returns" in the vote total.

But it took more than high turnout in densely populated areas. Biden captured 1,671 votes in tiny Randolph County—enough for a 54 percent share of the majority-Black county in southwest Georgia, a short hop from the Alabama state line. Headed into the runoffs, Randolph County's Democrats set a goal to outdo Biden's performance, and with all the cash and volunteers flooding Georgia, they now had the resources and volunteers to make good on the promise. Bobby Jenkins, the local Democratic Party chair, put together the type of campaign operation never seen before in a county of fewer than seven thousand souls.

Local volunteers banded together with Democrats from Alabama and Florida to canvass door-to-door. An enthusiastic New Yorker served as the field organizer. An Alabama software guru helped analyze voter registration data. Other veteran operatives helped train local partisans on strategic communications and fundraising. "We'd never seen anything like it," Jenkins said. "If I were a betting man, I wouldn't have bet we would have pulled it off. But we did." Warnock outdid Biden's total by seven ballots; Ossoff had just one to spare.

Ossoff's innovative field operation paid off, too. Over the course of the nine-week race, the three thousand organizers hired by his campaign had connected with hundreds of thousands of voters. By runoff day, some two hundred thousand voters were contacted directly by one of those young staffers. "That program won the race," he told his aides after the campaign.

"We did everything right. We had to," said Sarah Riggs Amico, the former Senate candidate turned party activist. "We had to pitch a perfect game, and we did."

—————

Loeffler ended her campaign two days after the runoff, followed a day later by a scathing concession from Perdue that didn't mention Ossoff's name and, in a parting shot to his hated rival, falsely claimed that he himself had "won the general election." He told friends that he would still be a US senator if not for a quirk in the law that required runoffs, though he also had no stomach to contest his defeat in court. During a round of golf at the Mar-a-Lago club in Florida a few weeks later, Trump bristled at him for ending the race and declining to fight on.

Though neither Democrat had demanded a concession, it allowed them to each take the oath of office without the specter of the legal challenges or fresh calls for recounts that had plagued the aftermath of the general election. When Raffensperger formally certified the outcome of the Senate contests on January 19, Loeffler was in the middle of her farewell address from the US Senate floor, a speech that boasted of her conservative record in her single year in the chamber and attacked the "mainstream media" for critical coverage.

Earlier that day, a much quieter process took place to clear the way for Ossoff and Warnock to be sworn into office by Vice President Kamala Harris shortly after her inauguration: a matter of routine paperwork that had grown far more complicated after the insurrection. Washington officials needed copies of state documents confirming their wins. And they had to be hand-delivered—no simple task, considering the tight timeline and the heavy security after the pro-Trump riots that effectively turned the US Capitol into an armed camp.

Rhonda Wilson, a longtime key aide in the Georgia governor's office, was selected to carry out the task. As state elections officials prepared to finalize the certification, Wilson caught an 8:30 a.m. flight from Atlanta to Washington's Reagan National Airport.

Inside her oversized purse were two pre-drafted documents that would ensure the two Democrats could take their oaths of office and, by extension, guarantee the peaceful transition of power in the US Senate. Both were signed and dated by Kemp and carefully enclosed in a manila envelope wrapped in a folder and a plastic sheath. Wilson didn't want to leave anything to chance. *They are not going to get messed up because of me*, she thought.

When she stepped off the Delta Air Lines flight, a security official immediately escorted her to a private waiting room not far from the gate. Just after the secretary of state's office certified the results, Wilson called US Senate officials to deliver the news. A Capitol Police officer raced to the airport to pick up the paperwork and deliver it to the chamber's officials. Wilson never left the airport and caught a flight back to Atlanta, landing around 4:30 p.m. and honored to play a "very small part in the peaceful transition."

———

Georgia's enduring paradox came into full display on Wednesday, January 20, when the heart of the Confederacy and the cradle of the civil rights movement sent a Black preacher and a young Jewish man to the US Senate. Hours after Joe Biden and Kamala Harris were sworn into office outside the Capitol, the vice president administered the oaths to Ossoff and Warnock to formally give Democrats control of the US Senate.

Tucked into Ossoff's coat pocket was a century-old ship's manifest that documented the journey to Ellis Island of his great-grandfather, Israel, and his great-grandmother, Annie, more than a century earlier. "A century later, their great-grandson was elected to the US Senate," he said.

The Hebrew Bible that he solemnly held as he took the oath belonged to Rabbi Jacob Rothschild, the leader of Atlanta's historic synagogue The Temple and a key ally of Martin Luther King Jr., who had encouraged the city's Jewish community to fight for equality and oppose racism. Rothschild's congregation had been bombed in 1958 by white supremacists angered by the rabbi's civil rights stances, a turning point in city politics that bound together civic leaders and Jewish Atlantans who committed to being more engaged in progressive local politics.

The new senator's swearing-in selection symbolized the longstanding relationship between Jewish and Black communities and the "necessity of re-animating the spirit of the civil rights movement and building alliances to pass landmark civil rights legislation," explained Ossoff, who had celebrated his bar mitzvah at The Temple about twenty years earlier. "Fighting for the people of Georgia means fighting for equal justice. And the alliance between Blacks and Jews in the civil rights movement is a model for what we can achieve when we continue to build the multiracial and multigenerational coalition we're building now."

The last time Warnock had come to the US Capitol complex, in 2017, he had been arrested for leading a protest of Trump administration budget cuts in the rotunda of the Russell Senate Office Building as he knelt in a prayer circle with four others. Now, he noted with a smile, Capitol Police "just had to show me to my office."

A few days earlier, the pastor had delivered his first sermon at Ebenezer Baptist Church since his election, speaking to rows of empty pews in livestreamed remarks. "You must know that this is a glimpse of God's vision of a more inclusive humanity that embraces all of God's children. I'm just grateful to be a part of this," he said, telling his flock that "violence does not have the last word." "God is still up to something in this world. So don't give in to cynicism, don't give in to fear. Don't give in to hatred, don't give in to bigotry, don't give in to the xenophobia."

But the true scope of his victory, he recounted to *The Daily* podcast, might not have hit him until a few days later. He was taking a walk around his Atlanta neighborhood when a little boy, about nine years old, who lived around the corner recognized him.

A few minutes later, Warnock's doorbell rang. He opened the door to find the boy and his brother, clutching a poster from the campaign with his picture on it. The kids wanted to know if Warnock would sign it.

"This nine-year-old boy looked up, saw somebody who looked like him, and got a glimpse of what's possible for his own future."

Epilogue

"ALL CARTER SEES"

On a crisp April day with a gentle breeze blowing from the west, Democrats gathered in a parking lot in Atlanta's suburbs, surrounded by a tight cordon of security officers. Food trucks sold tacos and slushies on the edges of the blacktop, and giant banners that read GETTING BACK ON TRACK marked President Joe Biden's goal of administering as many lifesaving doses of the coronavirus vaccine as quickly as possible.

Many of the attendees had already received at least one dose, but safety precautions were in full effect as Biden arrived to commemorate a milestone in his young administration: his one-hundredth day in office. His beeline to suburbia was a thank-you for delivering him to the White House and enabling his agenda—and a sales pitch for his next priorities.

The victories by Jon Ossoff and Raphael Warnock had narrowly sealed Democratic control of Congress, and Biden was in a good mood. Most of his cabinet appointees had sailed through the US Senate. He had surpassed his aim to put 100 million vaccines into the arms of Americans within his first one hundred days in office, though too many people still refused to get inoculated. And Congress had moved forward with an unprecedented second impeachment trial against Donald Trump, this time over the violent mob he helped foment. The charges against Trump referred to his attempt to bully

Georgia Secretary of State Brad Raffensperger, though the former president was ultimately acquitted after too few Republicans joined Democrats in voting to convict him on "incitement of insurrection" charges.

Biden's signature accomplishment in his first hundred days was the $1.9 trillion American Rescue Plan he had recently signed into law, a massive package of aid that delivered $1,400 direct payments to millions of Americans and included hundreds of billions of dollars in relief for school systems, local governments, and state agencies.

It was the election of Ossoff and Warnock, he told the crowd that day, that "made the difference." "It passed by a single vote. That means we owe a special thanks to the people of Georgia. Because thanks to you, the rest of the American people were able to get the help they need."

Their victories, too, meant he had a path—an exceedingly slim one, but still a path—to pursue a legislative agenda that also included plans to strengthen voting rights protections, reform policing procedures, combat climate change, expand the nation's social safety net, and bolster the crumbling infrastructure network. Just ahead of his visit, he had proposed an additional $4 trillion in spending that wouldn't have been conceivable without Georgia's flip. "Folks, it's only been one hundred days," Biden said. "We're working again. We're dreaming again."

The nation's tilt to the left generated a sharp Republican backlash in Georgia, where Trump's popularity among conservatives remained high. Governor Brian Kemp opened the year in the worst of straits. Internal polling showed his favorability numbers deep underwater, with nearly 60 percent of Republicans disapproving of his performance. He was even struggling among "soft" Republicans—those who didn't live and breathe conservative politics—so much so that there was internal discussion that he might not run for another term. "He did his duty even though he knew it could mean he won't be governor again," said one Kemp deputy forlornly as Biden prepared to take office.

The governor never played up that prospect, stating early and often that he would run for a second term. His poll numbers had soared and dipped before, and each time there was a major fluctuation he had reminded himself of the old adage that if you want a friend in politics, get a dog. Nor did he swipe back at Trump, instead consistently framing himself as a loyalist of the former president who was only upholding his constitutional duty.

Yet it was also clear to Kemp that the Trump-driven antipathy toward him wasn't going away. Even as the governor was outlining his reelection strategy in an interview with me, a scathing mass email from the former president attacking Kemp landed in inboxes. The governor groaned at the message. "I can only control what I can control. I learned that a long time ago in politics. And you've got to pick the right battles to be successful."

Early in 2021, more than a dozen county GOP organizations passed "censure" resolutions rebuking Kemp, and he was getting used to getting booed at party gatherings.

Privately, he told friends that the Republican civil war had already cost the GOP two US Senate seats. If the party wasn't careful, he added, it would cost Republicans the governor's race, too.

Kemp attempted to rebound during a legislative session dominated by Republican efforts to rewrite Georgia's election law. The GOP-controlled legislature narrowly passed an overhaul of voting rules that included new ID requirements, which made it harder to cast an absentee ballot, limited the number of ballot drop boxes, banned volunteers from handing out food or water to voters in line, shifted early voting days, and gave lawmakers more oversight of local elections.

It also ensured that a marathon runoff like the one Georgians had just experienced could never happen again. Instead of a nine-week race, runoffs would now be a four-week sprint to the finish. Almost as soon as he could, Kemp signed the changes into law, flanked by senior Republican leaders in a closed-door ceremony briefly interrupted by the arrest of a Democratic state legislator who had been knocking on the heavy wooden door outside his private office to gain access to the event.

The voting changes electrified both sides of the partisan divide, with Democrats comparing the changes to Jim Crow–era tactics. But it was the corporate protests that soon followed that inflamed tensions. After Coca-Cola and Delta Air Lines—two of Georgia's most iconic companies—opposed the new restrictions, Major League Baseball outraged conservatives by yanking the All-Star Game from Truist Park in metro Atlanta.

Kemp became the public face of the legislation, and a tear of media appearances helped shore up his poll numbers. By late April, former congressman Doug Collins ruled out a run for governor. But Kemp's troubles were far from over. Trump frequently predicted the governor would lose his race for reelection, even saying at a September 2021 rally in central Georgia that he would have preferred that Stacey Abrams had won.

Other Republicans on the wrong side of Trump's wrath faced their own reckonings. Lieutenant Governor Geoff Duncan opted against seeking another term, explaining that he'd rather focus his energy to "get this party back on track" with a vision for a post-Trump GOP 2.0 than fight with the former president's allies on the campaign trail. And Raffensperger became the underdog in his quest for a second term, with Trump backing a loyalist congressman who promoted his lies about election fraud and had labeled the insurrection attempt a "1776 moment" on social media hours before the mob descended on Congress.

Trump faced his own problems in Georgia, too, in the form of a criminal probe by the Fulton County district attorney's office into whether the former president and his allies committed election fraud in their attempts to overturn the election. Some who vouched for the former president's lies about election fraud, meanwhile, were rewarded with praise from Trump and adulation from his fans. Newly elected Congresswoman Marjorie Taylor Greene was exiled from her US House committees for spreading dangerous misinformation, but she was received by fawning crowds at GOP rallies in Georgia and, by the year's end, around the nation.

There was hardly any time for either side to regroup, not with looming 2022 elections that featured Warnock and every statewide constitutional office from the governor down to the agriculture commissioner on the ballot. The state Republican Party produced an "after-action report" that didn't acknowledge its defeats, instead perpetuating Trump's claims and scapegoating Raffensperger.

Still, senior Republicans ticked through all the what-ifs themselves. What if Kelly Loeffler hadn't had such a tough primary opponent? What if Republicans had attacked Warnock sooner, rather than let him advance to November with a free pass? And most of all, what if Trump had focused his energy on helping Republicans keep the Senate—or at least toned down his talk of a "rigged" election?

Kemp would lament the first point, insisting that he had worked to impress upon the "powers that be" that Loeffler could have reached more voters in metro Atlanta as an outsider, a woman, and a business executive if she hadn't had to burst to the right to keep Collins at bay. Raffensperger dwelled on the latter question, in particular, and chided the two Senate Republicans for not standing up to Trump. "It's all about unity. And elections are won when the party is unified," he said. "They should have navigated through and told the president, 'I support you, but we have to run our races.' And they didn't do that."

The two defeated Republican senators didn't fade away. Loeffler started a voter mobilization group aimed at Republicans to counter Abrams's decade-long efforts to rev up left-leaning voters. She called it "Greater Georgia," and she used it to keep her political platform in the state in case she sought higher office again.

Former senator David Perdue ruled out his own comeback bid against Warnock in February 2021 but by the end of the year was being urged instead to challenge Kemp. Trump, meanwhile, had publicly encouraged Herschel Walker, a former Georgia football legend who had lived for the last few decades in Texas, to return to his home state and run for the US Senate against Warnock. After Walker entered the race, Trump said Walker was a "great football player and will be an even better US senator—if that is even possible."

Could Democrats replicate their success in 2022 and beyond? A Democratic analysis credited the wins to a spike in absentee voting and a surge in Black turnout—both factors that could not be counted on without a global pandemic and the polarizing presence of Trump on the ballot in 2022.

No one could be certain, either, whether the suburban shift that had turned Republican bastions into Democratic territory was firm or a fluke. Stuart Stevens, a senior Republican strategist, said the Democratic upsets relied on a string of amazing developments that was akin to "winning the World Series—by pitching four perfect games."

On the March evening when Congress passed the coronavirus stimulus plan, Jonae Wartel checked her phone and saw a blitz of contributions to her Venmo account, some only a few dollars, with messages suggesting she spend it on wine and booze. She had just returned to Washington from a short vacation in Mexico, recuperating from her sprint as the Democratic runoff director, and asked her friends why she was the sudden recipient of small-dollar donations.

"You know what you did," wrote one of her happy patrons.

Months later, even a mention of the runoff drama made her emotional. Georgia was where she was born, where her mother and sisters and cousins live. Her family is in Cobb County, in a district once represented by Newt Gingrich and Tom Price. Now, she pointed out, it was held by Democrat Lucy McBath and two new senators. "That's why it's hard to imagine doing another campaign again," she said. "It doesn't get better than that."

Scott Hogan, the executive director of the state Democratic Party, felt similarly transformed. "That we were successful in defeating a sitting president trying to overthrow the government, with Georgia as his vehicle, will forever stay with me," he said. "It's not lost on me that this will likely be the most important thing, professionally, I will ever do." And if that ends up being the case after his political career is over, Hogan added, he won't mind at all.

At Biden's hundredth-day celebration, Ossoff and Warnock joined the president and the First Lady onstage, holding their hands aloft as a rendition of "Higher and Higher" thumped from the loudspeakers. Away from the stage, Congresswoman Nikema Williams quietly watched her young son, Carter, dance and race on the pavement, grinning from ear to ear. "That's all he sees," she mouthed to herself, shaking her head.

After the president set off on Air Force One, the food trucks departed, the stage was disassembled, and the crowd melted away, the congresswoman shared what she meant during that private moment.

"I grew up in a home with no indoor plumbing and no running water. And now I'm with a president who wants to lift people up from poverty," she said. "And that is all Carter sees."

ACKNOWLEDGMENTS

Whew. I'm the type of journalist who lives by the deadline. Working for a week on a story can seem like a ridiculously long time. I love the thrill of breaking news and steady shoe-leather beat reporting. That's why this book was such an exciting challenge. And that's why my first debt of gratitude goes to the hundreds of people I interviewed over the last year who helped shape this book. I'm so grateful for all your help.

I wanted to write a book at various points in my career, but it was the talented Justin Brouckaert who helped bring this to life in late November 2020. Brouckaert patiently worked with me to draft the proposal that became *Flipped* and helped me navigate the publishing world. I haven't stopped singing his praises since.

He also helped get this project in the hands of Rick Kot and the stellar folks at Viking. I'm thankful for Kot's guidance and confidence, Camille Leblanc for her devotion to this project, and Susan VanHecke for her eagle-eyed edits.

I wouldn't have started the book without the backing of the brass at the *Journal-Constitution*. Kevin Riley, Leroy Chapman, Susan Abramson Potter, and the inimitable James Salzer (who will be upset that I used so fancy a word to describe him) have all championed my career, as have former *AJC* editors

Charlie Gay, Monica Richardson, and Bert Roughton. Jim Galloway, the original Political Insider, provided a daily example of how to handle thorny situations at the statehouse with grace and aplomb. It has been a constant pleasure to work with the talented *AJC* politics team, including Jim Denery, Maya T. Prabhu, Isaac Sabetai, and David Wickert. Mark Niesse, the premier voting rights reporter in the South, offered precision edits and suggestions. I couldn't be prouder to collaborate daily with the indefatigable Jolt duo of Tia Mitchell and Patricia Murphy, who also gets credit for the book title. Special thanks to former and current colleagues Amy Glennon, Ben Gray, Ryon Horne, Katie Leslie, Aaron Gould Sheinin, Jeremy Redmon, Kelly Audette, Matt Kempner, Jay Black, Alyssa Pointer, Curtis Compton, Bria Felicien, Bill Rankin, Chris Joyner, Tamar Hallerman, Daniel Malloy, Bill Torpy, and the brilliant AJC Society—Jennifer Brett, Ligaya Figueras, Shannon McCaffrey, and Scott Trubey.

I'm so lucky to have these lasting friendships: Ari and Rachel Weitz; Michael and Blair Kruger; Brad and Stephanie Friedman; Jon and Tova Javetz; Ryan and Jaime Schwartz; Dori and Ryan Mendel; Ben and Rachel Miller; Tal and Jenna Nudelman; Rebecca and Andy Siegel; Dan and Carly Cooper; Josh and Joanna Rothstein; and many others. Thanks, too, to my lawyer, Adam Struletz, and his sidekick Greg Swartzberg for their invaluable advice and agreeing to waive all legal fees for eternity.

Our beloved neighborhood has become our family. Our QuaranTeam cheered this book every step: Nick and Sarah Friend; David and Diana Margolis; and Josh and Spring Taylor. The AC Guys Group kept me laughing, the firepits and lake trips filled weekends with warmth, and the AC Cyclists gave me daily exercise options. The Dunwoody Burger Club helped negate all those workouts. I cherish the memory of my late friend, Jarrod Mendel, who inspired me with his enthusiasm for Georgia politics and the law. Each day, I also hold dear the legacy of Tom Crawford and Dick Pettys, esteemed statehouse journalists who illuminated the way for so many.

The UGA squad truly proves we never bark alone, particularly professors Charles Bullock, Charles Davis, Audrey Haynes, Janice Hume, and Lori Johnston. Fellow Bulldog Lauren Patrick channeled our Old Pal with her stellar advice. The Red & Black will always be my journalism bedrock, though Crema and Alon's became my new office.

I'll forever appreciate the late, great Conrad Fink for instilling in me WWFD—a sense of duty I refer to as "What Would Fink Do?" I'm fortunate to call other legends my friends and colleagues: Mark Arum, Richard Elliot, Lori Geary, Bill Nigut, Keith Pepper, Rose Scott, Scott Slade, and Shelley Wynter. Each has honored me with a broader platform to share my work in Georgia, including Nigut, who has been one of my greatest cheerleaders. I'm grateful that Barry Bedlan, Susan Fields, Michael Giarrusso, Bobby Macris, I. J. Rosenberg, and Jim Schiffman helped get me into this career and the WCPJ crew—Adam Ashton, Andy Netzel, Kelly Patrick, and Lisa Rossi— helped me stay here. Jonathan Allen, Mara Davis, Edward-Isaac Dovere, and Adam Lazarus each offered timely encouragement that I could actually pull this book off.

My brothers, Lenny and Max Bluestein, lovingly trash-talked me at just the right time. Their wives, Sara and Valerie, are the sisters I never had. My in-laws, Paul and Audrey Mande, offered unflinching support. My mom, Lisa Karesh, sparked a love for writing and debate, along with care and compassion for the people behind the headlines. And my late dad, Barry, was an icon of strong work ethic whose memory motivated me to work the crazy hours to finish this project.

Our puppy, Charlie Marbles, kept me on my toes, literally, as I wrote this book, nipping at my feet if I sat still too long. My daughters, Brooke and Nicole, amazed me with how they thrived through the pandemic with two parents who were busier than ever. I am so proud of their curiosity, creativity, and their Bluestein Blog videos.

None of this would have been possible without my soulmate, Sheryl, who somehow makes it look easy balancing a demanding career, a fulfilling family life, an always-packed schedule, and a husband who loves her more than she'll ever know but also insists on riling up the kids right before bedtime.

I love you forever, Sheryl, and am so proud of the life we have built.

INDEX